FAVORITE RIFLES AND CARTRIDGES

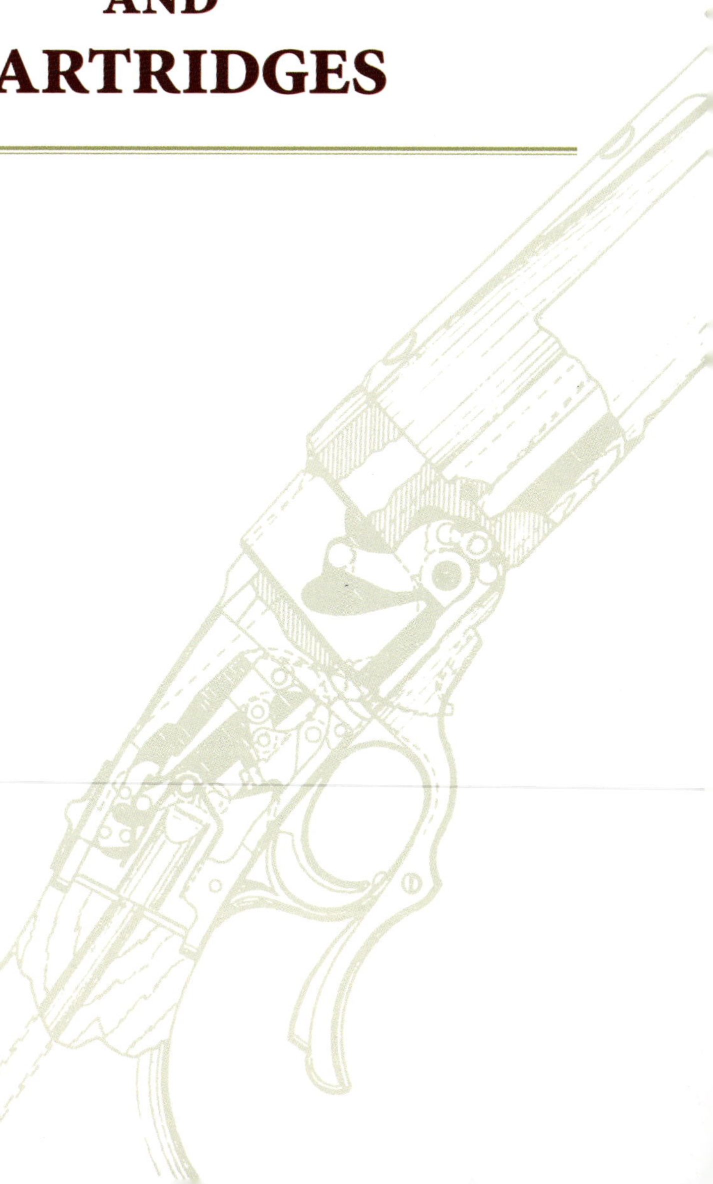

FAVORITE RIFLES AND CARTRIDGES

CRAIG BODDINGTON

Essex, Connecticut

An imprint of The Globe Pequot Publishing Group, Inc.
64 South Main Street
Essex, CT 06426
www.globepequot.com

Distributed by NATIONAL BOOK NETWORK

Library of Congress Catalog Card Number: 2021942053

ISBN 978-1-57157-509-8

First edition

Printed in India

To My Old Friend and Longtime Publisher
Ludo J. Wurfbain
Native of Holland, American Patriot, Passionate Hunter

Forty years, a lot of good books.
Admittedly, some better than others,
but Safari Press has never sacrificed quality.
Maybe we've got a couple more left in us!

Table of Contents

FOREWORD

Craig Boddington and I met in June 1982 at the annual convention of the Outdoor Writers Association of America, held that year in Spokane. At the time I was a Montana freelance writer who occasionally took other, short-term jobs to fill in the blanks. That ended the next year, partly thanks to Craig, who then worked for Petersen Publishing as the editor of *Guns & Ammo* Specialty Publications and associate editor of *Petersen's HUNTING*. During our conversation we discovered we'd been born about two weeks apart (he's older), and had two common interests: hunting big game and a lifelong fascination with hunting rifles. By the end of the conversation, he assigned me an article involving both subjects for a *Guns & Ammo* annual.

The next year he became editor of *HUNTING*, and started assigning me a few articles. In 1991 he hired me to write the magazine's new hunting optics column, and I also started writing more features. You get to know somebody well when working for them, and I'd have to pick Craig as perhaps the best magazine editor I've worked with, among several dozen candidates, partly because he made very quick, firm decisions about proposed columns and features—a great help to writers, who often have little clue of what's inside the disorganized minds of some editors.

This was long before e-mail became the rule. A couple of times a year, I'd print out a list of ideas for him and snail-mail it to Petersen's headquarters in Los Angeles. Three days later I'd receive my letter back, with very brief notes handwritten next to each idea, usually "yes" or "no," but sometimes "hell no" or "yes, but include mule deer." Eventually I realized this was partly because Craig is highly disciplined, something honed during his career as a Marine officer.

But there's another reason for his swift and decisive editing, as well as his highly successful writing career. While Craig claims he's not as skilled a wordsmith as some other gun and hunting writers, he has something quite a few of those writers don't—an apparently almost innate sense of what hunters and shooters want to read. This is partly due to Craig being an avid reader, one source of his definite dreams for his hunting life.

Eventually Craig grew weary of working as an editor in a huge city and decided to live as a writer in less urban places. In the meantime I'd also edited a couple of magazines, and pretty successfully, thanks largely to lessons learned from Craig's example. When Petersen Publishing started searching for a new editor for *HUNTING*, my name came up, and Craig even called one day to semi-jokingly suggest we "switch jobs." But by then technology had progressed enough that my editing was done from Montana, and there's no way Petersen's would allow that—and there was also no way I would live in Los Angeles.

We've always kept track of each other, and occasionally even hunted together—although as Craig sometimes points out, not often enough. Part of the reason was that Craig traveled far more, while I spent more time hunting in my native Montana. While I've traveled to hunt widely enough to wade, at least briefly, in four of Planet Earth's five oceans (I did wear insulated hip boots in the Arctic Ocean), Craig *really* traveled, to a total of 65 countries—one reason he won the Weatherby Award. Even if I added up all the countries, states, and provinces I've hunted from Alaska to Africa, it wouldn't come close to 65 different destinations.

He wrote about those hunts, of course, and the rifles he used. His experience has helped other hunters (including me) who don't travel as much. When heading to some distant destination I've never hunted before, I know that Craig has already been there, often multiple times. So I search my Boddington library and reread his experiences, and he also sometimes offers personal advice.

I went to Botswana in 2003, after rereading Craig's hunting stories and rifle advice about the Okavango Delta, but he also personally suggested buying two pairs of high-top, canvas basketball shoes, one to wear while wading in the Okavango's abundant lakes and streams, and another to wear when hunting the next day, while the first pair dried. High-tops are desirable because they won't get pulled off when lifting your feet from soft mud, and canvas dries quickly.

So I went to a local sporting-goods store and bought two pairs of black Converse Chuck Taylor All Star High Tops, and Craig was exactly right. However, neither pair ever dried on their own. After the first day's hunting I put the wet pair next to the door of my tent, which faced the sun. But when I returned from hunting the next evening, they weren't there. Instead they sat next to the cleaned and pressed clothes on my cot. The camp staff evidently decided they were part of my daily laundry (after all, they were cloth) and not only washed and dried the shoes, but the laces—and even pressed the laces with their fire-heated irons before reinserting them in the clean shoes.

Craig's rifle, cartridge, and ammo preferences have been similarly helpful—one reason I eventually settled on a CZ .416 Rigby as my primary buffalo rifle. This wasn't a purely practical decision, but like many of Craig's choices, it was partly due to tradition. We're both part of the generation of hunters who grew up when wood was *the* material for rifle stocks. While a few "plastic" stocked rifles had already appeared—my first such memory is of Remington's Nylon 66 .22 rimfire—high-quality walnut was the ideal.

While we both own enough synthetic-stocked rifles to hunt anything on earth, some chambered in cutting-edge twenty-first-century cartridges, we tend to own more "classics," because we still find more pleasure in hunting with such rifles. Both Winston Churchill and Spanish philosopher George Santayana penned comments on how those who forget the past are doomed to repeat it. But there's a gunwriter variation for hunters of a certain age: "Those who remember the past are doomed to happily repeat it."

In this book Craig happily picks the .270 Winchester, a traditional hunting cartridge for almost a century now, as his favorite long-range round for medium big game, instead of one of the many other .270 Winchester approximations that have appeared since 1925, including .270 "magnums," the .280 Remington (both standard and "improved"), and the recent 6.5 PRC. I have owned and hunted quite a bit with two .270 magnums and both kinds of .280s, and now own a synthetic/stainless 6.5 PRC made by custom gunsmith Charlie Sisk, which so far has worked fine on one buck mule deer. But I also own two .270 Winchesters, both wood-stocked. One is a Jack O'Connor Commemorative Winchester Model 70 Featherweight, with a stock made of spectacular American black walnut, and its very first group at 100 yards measured under half an inch with factory ammo. The second is a Ruger No. 1B, custom-stocked in fine European walnut by some unknown artist. The No. 1 was recently purchased, very lightly used, at a local gun store, and is also very accurate, so it will go hunting sometime soon, probably before the 6.5 PRC.

I knew Craig liked the .270 long before reading *Favorite Rifles and Cartridges*, but I did not know that his favorite all-round prairie-dog cartridge is the .204 Ruger. It's also mine—and for exactly the same reasons Craig lists. In fact, he has remarked on the similarity of our tastes in hunting rifles—as has well-known Alaska brown-bear outfitter and guide Phil Shoemaker, who grew up in the same era. If all three of us ever get together, we'll probably end up in a semi-geezer discussion of classic rifles that might seriously annoy younger hunters who believe "practical" hunting rifles weren't developed until the twenty-first century.

Hunters and rifle addicts who read much about the subject tend to pick their favorite authors who mostly agree with their own choices. Even professional writers often react the same way, and that's admittedly one reason I really enjoyed reading *Favorite Rifles and Cartridges*. I am certain many other readers will too, especially those of a certain generation—and they're probably still the majority of hunters who actually read books. Thanks again, Craig!

John Barsness
Townsend, Montana
May 10, 2021

Part One
Introduction

CHAPTER 1

THE RIFLE, THE GAME, OR THE HUNT?

"Beware the one-gun man" is an old saying, and it contains much truth. Some experienced hunters spend most of their careers relying on just one hunting rifle. For any given game animal, hunted under any possible conditions, there must be dozens of appropriate rifles and cartridges. Winnowing the field down to just one may be done by circumstance or preference. If the former, then we wish for suitability and some degree of versatility; if the latter, both are probably present in some measure.

Either way, the advantage is obvious: Having just the one tool, the hunter becomes totally familiar with its capabilities. Limitations are also accepted. Having never been a "one-gun man," I imagine that, at least to some degree, one would tailor hunting methods and techniques to best ensure optimum suitability for that single rifle.

Clearly the concept works, and there are many examples. Grancel Fitz developed much of the Boone and Crockett trophy scoring methodology currently in use. Back in the 1950s, Fitz was the first known hunter to take all recognized varieties of North American big game, all with a Griffin & Howe Springfield .30-06. A generation later, my friend J. Y. Jones used a battered Remington .30-06 to accomplish the same feat. In both cases, the choice was by preference; Fitz and Jones achieved success in life (as well as hunting), and could have purchased other rifles as needed.

The mysterious old desert rat, Charlie Ren—who guided Fitz, Jack O'Connor, and my uncle, Art Popham to desert sheep in pre-World War II Sonora, may well have made his choice by circumstance. Ren seems to have carried only an iron-sighted 1899 Savage, and

O'Connor quoted him as commenting that he needed "nothing more than his .25-35." During his lawless days in Mexico, Ren accounted for a lot of desert rams, and, for sure, many Coues whitetails and desert mule deer as well. One could perhaps raise concerns about both the versatility and suitability of the .25-35, but Ren made it work, which is what a one-gun man does.

Collectively, there is no group of hunters with more widespread worldwide experience than the winners of the Weatherby Hunting and Conservation Award, presented annually since 1956. By the nature of the award and requirements to win it, the rifle choices of

J. Y. Jones and I are here with my very good tahr from Nepal, 2010. J. Y. took all his North American species with a .30-06; when he went on to hunt in Eurasia, he chose a 7mm Remington Ultra Mag. I am not *a one-gun man, and here I'm holding my Blaser R8 with a .300 Blaser Magnum barrel.*

Weatherby winners are not restricted by circumstance. However, it's amazing how many of them do most of their hunting with just one primary rifle. From the beginning with Herb Klein, it's telling how many of them chose a fast .30-caliber. Early on, the .300 Weatherby Magnum was a common choice, but not universal. Mahlon "Butch" White, a wonderful guy as well as great hunter, has a worn-silver pre-'64 Model 70 in .300 H&H that he's used since he was sixteen. By his reckoning, this rifle has taken fifty wild rams and all of the Big Five except elephant. Butch is a "one-gun" man. In recent years, some Weatherby winners have reported relying on .300 Jarrett rifles, a couple on .300 Remington Ultra Magnums, and one used a .300 Winchester Short Magnum.

However, the point isn't their preferences, but the fact that, without restrictions or limitations, many of my fellow winners *chose* to rely on one trusted rifle/cartridge combination for most of their hunting. Again, there are advantages, especially when that choice is very versatile and suitable for a wide range of game.

What this really tells me is that, for Grancel Fitz, J.Y. Jones, and the globe-trotting Weatherby winners who choose just one rifle/cartridge, it was the *hunt* that was most important. The *rifle* was just a tool, albeit an essential and much-loved one, and, whenever possible, they chose to use the most familiar and trusted tool.

There is certainly nothing wrong with this, and much right with it. However, this has certainly not been my course. I *like* rifles, and I enjoy shooting and tinkering with them. Also, as a gunwriter (which is what I consider myself), it's been part of my job to write about different rifles and cartridges. On the one hand, this has been an advantage; trying different rifles under field conditions has given me more to write about. I would never describe myself as a brilliant writer, but you've got to admit that I've been prolific! If asked to describe what I write about, I'd say that about 25 percent is pure hunting, another 25 percent pure firearms and shooting, another 25 percent the two put together (as in "guns and loads for gazorks"); and the final 25 percent conservation topics and equipment other than rifles.

Grancel Fitz, creator of the Boone and Crockett scoring system, with his first ram, a Dall sheep he took in 1935 with his classic Griffin & Howe Springfield .30-06. Fitz would be the first person to take all North American big-game species . . . all with the .30-06 Springfield. (Photo courtesy of Robert Anderson)

Interestingly, that third topic is probably my favorite: I love hunting, and shooting, and sporting firearms. So, now forty-some years into this weird career, the most fun is trying to put them all together. Whether lasting value exists or not, imagine how much thinner my body of work would be if I focused more on pure hunting, or just on firearms, or only on shooting!

There are drawbacks. I have my favorites, both in rifles and cartridges, and this book is specifically about those favorites. However, as a gunwriter, with editors to answer to (who have advertisers to answer to), there have been many times when, departing for a distant hunt, I've paused at the gun safe and made apologies to good friends

Herb Klein took this Ovis ammon darwini *(Gobi argali) in Mongolia in 1966 with a custom Weatherby Mark V in .300 Weatherby Magnum. Klein was an early investor with Roy Weatherby and the first recipient of the Weatherby Award. Like many early Weatherby winners, he did much of his hunting with a .300 Weatherby.* (Photo courtesy of Robert Anderson)

Weatherby Award winner Bruce Keller getting a tune-up at the SAAM shooting course in Texas with Doug Pritchard. Keller is a serious and experienced mountain hunter, and his favorite for sheep and goats is the wildcat .300 Jarrett.

for leaving them behind. Hey, it's part of the job. As I will say again and again, there are lots of good choices. There have been many hunts where I wished I could have taken Old Betsy out of the safe for another romp, but the New Girl on the Block needed an exercise run. It goes with the territory, no regrets. If I've ever felt hampered on a hunt by choice of equipment, it's usually because of a choice I made, not something forced on me.

Now, one might think that all gunwriters or, perish the thought, today's outdoor "celebrities" (I hate that word!) are equally knowledgeable with both firearms and their uses (i.e., guns *and* hunting). This seemed true in the 1970s. Certainly Jack O'Connor, Warren Page, Elmer Keith, and Charlie Askins were equally adept and experienced in both hunting and shooting, and all could talk with experience about competitive shooting. The same is true of the "stars" that followed: Jim Carmichel, Bob Milek, John Wootters. Today, print media have given much ground to video and television, and will undoubtedly yield more ground to digital. Also, we are in an age of specialization, and sadly, *hunting* is no longer as important a purpose for firearms as it once was.

But, among colleagues of my generation, I have long been surprised at how few write effectively about *both* guns and hunting. Really, it's a matter of mind-set and interest. I'm fascinated by hunting, and equally fascinated by sporting arms (especially rifles). Good news for me: It's a strength that has stood me well through a long career. In this age of specialization, not everyone needs to be diversified, but I'm happy that it's worked so well for me.

I'll name names, because these guys are friends as well as colleagues, and we've had this discussion in person. Jim Shockey has been wildly successful; he is a hardcore and driven hunter. Jim Zumbo, a bit older

Being a gunwriter, I get the opportunity to test a variety of rifles, and many have right-hand actions. In November 2020 I used the new Springfield Waypoint in the also-new 6.5mm PRC to take this excellent Georgia whitetail.

While I am hardly a one-gun man, I sometimes feel that using a certain rifle is an important part of a hunt. This left-hand-converted Sedgley Springfield .30-06 with aperture sight was a rifle I badly wanted to use to take an elk. I got my chance with this Colorado bull.

than me, has had an amazing career. Both are primarily hunters and neither, by their own admission, are "gun guys." The *hunt* is what matters to them. Shockey made his bones with modern muzzleloaders (the archetypical one-gun man). Zumbo, the original elk guru, was first a .30-06 guy, later moving to a .300.

To both Shockey and Zumbo, it has always been the *hunt* that mattered; the *rifle* was an essential tool, not intrinsically or aesthetically more interesting or attractive than a shovel. This is pretty much the approach taken by many dedicated and successful hunters, including the Weatherby winners who could afford almost anything but commonly retreated to a favorite choice when the time came to pack the gun case.

There is an opposite approach, seen almost daily in social media posts and questions, and at least every few minutes at a convention or trade show. There are many people (who are also hunters) in search of the ideal, perfect rifle (and, to be complete, cartridge, bullet, and optic combo) for a certain hunt for a specific animal. Yes, of course, the hunt matters. The experience is desired. Success is preferred, but defeat can be accepted. Most important, though, is to enjoy the experience with the rifle that is their concept of the exact, precise, *perfect* combination. In fact, the hunt (win, lose, or draw) almost serves as a graduation exercise for that ideally suited rifle, which in some cases was conceived and built for that particular experience.

This is the opposite approach from that taken by the one-gun hunter. The search for the *perfect* rifle can become esoteric. But, after all, it's fun. Beauty and suitability are in the eyes of the beholder. I know smart guys who have gone back through the annals of cartridge history, resurrecting at great cost modern rifles in near-obsolete cartridges such as .256 Newton, .276 Pedersen, .318 Westley Richards, and .350 Rigby Rimless Magnum. This was simply their preference, since there is no situation where these, or any other single cartridge, can be considered the only viable choice.

Tony Lombardo on his range with a gorgeous 1930s Griffin & Howe Springfield with a G&H side mount. I greatly admire classic rifles like this, but virtually all of my personal rifles have either left-hand or ambidextrous actions.

I have long conceded that a scoped rifle is a more effective choice than an open-sighted double for buffalo hunting. But hunting with a double is fun *and a critical aspect of the hunt. I took this Tanzanian buffalo with a C.W. Andrews .470 in 1988.*

Speaking of cartridges, there are many hundreds with much redundancy. Not to be insensitive, but a whitetail buck doesn't care much if he was struck in the right place with a 7x61 Sharpe & Hart, a .275 H&H Magnum, a 7mm Page Super-Pooper, a .280 Ackley Improved, a .280 Remington, or 7mm Remington Magnum. I think that buck does care, a lot, if he was struck in the wrong place. Always and forever, within a fairly wide window of velocity and energy requirements, *where* the bullet strikes, meaning how skillfully it was directed, is much more important than case dimensions.

So far, I've talked mostly about the rifle and the hunt, but the game also matters—at least to some of us, in some circumstances. From George Orwell's *Animal Farm*: "All animals are equal, but some are more equal than others." Most hunters have a "totem animal" that we place on a taller pedestal: Cape buffalo, elk, greater kudu, wild sheep and goats. This is totally personal and possibly meaningless but, the more special the animal (or hunt), the more special the choice of rifle and cartridge.

I make no apologies, but although I appreciate modern advances, I have a "thing" for tradition (and it's OK if you don't). As a boy, I read my Hemingway, song and verse (and I could recite it). I worshipped his Griffin & Howe Springfield—with its aperture sight that he blew through to clear water droplets.

I have never owned a Griffin & Howe rifle, but like most of my generation, my first centerfire rifle was a 1903 Springfield, and I had an R. F. Sedgley (the blue-collar contemporary of Griffin & Howe) Springfield .30-06 with aperture sight (there was absolutely no way to mount a scope). In those days, not so long ago, I could still resolve apertures very well, and that rifle produced some very fancy groups in good light.

I shot an OK (*not* spectacular) Colorado 6x6 elk with it, and took it to Africa the next year. At last light, I shot a mature (but definitely *not* huge) kudu bull with it. I felt just like Papa Hemingway! These were situations where the *rifle* was more important than the hunt.

You may have a "totem" animal that you simply must hunt with a certain rifle and/or cartridge. This is totally valid. I have some cool old lever-actions, mostly Savage and Winchester, that I fantasize about taking on certain hunts. Probably won't happen; I'm past the point of spending money on various hunts I've done and enjoyed. However, whether the box is someday checked or not, there are some rifle/animal/hunt situations still on the bucket list.

I came into the hunting world in a much different time, even though it wasn't so long ago. I have absolutely no need (and, really, no desire) to take another lion; I had my chances in that different time, when there were more lions and they were commonly on license. I've taken my share. But I always wanted to take a lion with a double rifle. That would be one of those situations where the *rifle* would be more

Here I am sitting over a bait in Idaho with a 1937 Winchester M71 in .348. When the bear came out, it was too dark to resolve in the aperture sight, so I switched rifles for a scope-sighted 9.3x62mm. This is a clear example that I consider the hunt to be what matters most!

important than the hunt. In 1988 I took a lovely lion with an open-sighted .416. That was back when I could *see* iron sights; they were only a minimal handicap. As was common then, a lion was on license, but we weren't really hunting a lion, we just bumped into him while tracking a buffalo herd. The .416 Rigby was a wonderful choice, and the lion rug hangs on the wall as I write. But it was not the *experience* I dream of, to do it with a good double rifle.

Things changed fast; the African lion was in trouble long before the hunting community properly responded to the crisis. But, in certain areas, lions are still overpopulated and are problematic. PH Dirk de Bod, Donna, Brittany, and I were at a campfire in Namibia, celebrating Donna's leopard, when one of the landowners rolled up with *two* "problem lion" permits. This area, private land on the edge of

Etosha, had a problem with too many lions, and we'd seen the tracks. We struck a deal, and it was a lot of money to me. But times were changing fast, and the cost was nothing compared to what a free-range lion hunt would be worth in just a few years. Therefore, it was my last lion, and I knew it. All I had, and what I used, was a .300 RUM loaded with a 200-grain Swift A-Frame. It was plenty of gun, an awesome bullet, and a wonderful old lion . . . but I do wish I could have taken him with a more traditional rifle. With an unexpected opportunity, the *hunt* immediately took priority; the *rifle* defaulted to the best choice available.

If you are a hunter first, there are many times when the *rifle* must defer to the *hunt*. As we shall see later, one of my fetishes is the Winchester 1886/Model 71 action. My problem, now that I am in my late sixties, is that I can no longer resolve iron sights as well as I once could. So, I love the gun, but must accept the judgment of Father Time.

In the spring of 2019, I was sitting behind a pine tree in Idaho, watching a bait and hoping a black bear might come in. On previous evenings I'd seen—and passed—several bears on this bait. Most were small, but one was a gorgeous and large bear the color of Hershey-bar chocolate. Tempting and legal, but outfitter Michael ("Sparky") Sparks had this bear on trail camera, and we were dead-certain she was a sow. So, I passed.

I was hoping to use an early ("first year of manufacture") Winchester Model 71 in .348 Winchester, with the aperture on the bolt. It was a lovely rifle, and very accurate with Hornady's new LeveRevolution load. Years back, I did a lot of black bear hunting with other M71s in .348, but this one was a new (old) friend, and I really wanted to take a bear with it. But, after all, I didn't really *need* another black bear, so this was a situation where the *rifle* was more important than the hunt.

We got down to sunset on my last evening. Small bears I'd seen before had come and gone, but conditions were perfect, calm and slightly cool. To our knowledge no monster bears were frequenting this bait, but in addition to the chocolate sow, there was an average-size boar.

He came in five minutes after sunset. The bait barrel was deeply shadowed. Despite several tries, I simply couldn't resolve the front sight against the bear. Well, the light clearly wasn't going to get better. I leaned the .348 against a tree just to my left, exchanging it for a Montana Rifles 9.3x62mm with scope.

I am not proud of this. During archery seasons, bow hunters don't get to exchange bows for rifles when the light is too dim or the shot a few yards too far. But my only commitment to the iron-sighted lever-action was moral, not legal. I switched it out for the scope-sighted rifle and flattened the bear. So, in case there were any questions, in the final analysis, it really is the *hunt* that matters most to me. The *rifle* is secondary—but it's an important second. I spend a lot of time trying to figure out the ideal choice for an upcoming hunt and, for sure, I use my favorites when I can . . . but I am not a "one-gun man."

Chapter 2

I Should Have Kept That One!

I am not a collector of any type of firearm. Instead, you could call me an accumulator. It's not entirely random; my tastes and preferences run to sporting rifles, with a strong bias toward ambidextrous and left-hand actions. In my job as a gunwriter, a lot of firearms come through my hands, but I don't keep many of them.

In hunting-camp conversations I'm amazed at how many people assume that guys like me get to keep all the guns we write about. Uh, no! Once in a while, sure, but the norm is that test firearms must be returned within a certain time frame, or purchased. If the latter, a "good guy" wholesale price is the norm. I have colleagues who are notorious for not returning test firearms, but everyone knows who they are, and I don't want to be painted with that brush. I also have colleagues who, as a matter of long habit, purchase every firearm that comes their way. Toward the tail end of their careers they will have amassed quite an accumulation (if not a collection), and probably a valuable estate.

The problem with that course of action, at least for me, is space and safe storage . . . and, after all, how many firearms can you enjoy, shoot, and take care of? Without question, I have too many firearms, including shotguns and handguns as well as rifles. I have some that I couldn't part with, including some well-loved old friends that I suddenly realize I haven't shot for years. Then comes the reality of space limitations.

Back in the 1980s, when I was living in Los Angeles and working for Petersen Publishing, I was burglarized three times. The first time, I wasn't yet thirty. I didn't have any "good" guns, but I lost almost all

I took this big black bear in British Columbia in May 1974 with a .375 H&H on a right-hand Mauser action. It had a nice stock in Bishop walnut, and it was just one of several rifles that I lost to burglaries in Los Angeles in the early 1980s.

the guns I'd grown up with, including some handguns I'd inherited. The only survivors were a couple of guns in the trunk of my car. The last gun from my youth that I still have is a Winchester Model 12 factory skeet 12-gauge. By the second break-in, I'd started to rebuild, and I lost some pretty good stuff. There wasn't much left for the third cleanup crew, but they got a Savage 110 in 7mm Remington Magnum. Somehow, that Model 12 shotgun survived.

I didn't want to go through that again, so I made a vow that I would never have firearms stored in closets or hidden under beds. Ever since, I've kept firearms in secure safes. A vault room (with

Claymore mines!) would be better but, after all, I'm a gunwriter; that's not a luxury I've been able to afford. So, I've gone the gun safe route. Actually, gun safes, plural. Which leads to the next restriction: How many gun safes is there space for?

So, for quite some years now, I've tried to maintain a strict rule: When the safes are full, it's time to cull the herd. This is a brutal rule, and it's led to tough decisions, and not always good ones. Probably as a legacy from those long-ago burglaries, I try not to get too attached. Lightning can always strike again, and there's always the randomness of fire, flood, or tornado. Mind you, I like rifles that shoot straight, and I like rifles that look good, and I like rifles that handle well. So, I do get attached. But, when the gun safes are full, I have decisions to make. Inevitably, I've let some great rifles slip through my fingers.

Also, trading up and down is fun, so I do that, though not always consciously. Also, the firearm industry changes constantly; companies fold, new companies start, old friends retire or move

When hunting with Finn Aagaard in 1979, I used a Valmet over/under with .30-06 barrels to take my first aoudad. Unfortunately, this rifle, along with multiple sets of barrels, was also stolen in a burglary.

I took this nice bull from Northwest Territory's Courageous Lake caribou herd in 1980. It was NWT's first nonresident caribou hunt, and the rain was nearly constant. The wood stock on this Savage 110 in 7mm Remington Magnum warped badly, so the rifle became my first synthetic-stocked rifle . . . and then it was stolen.

on. When these things happen, it may no longer seem likely that I'm going to write any more about a certain rifle. So, not being a collector, these things influence my decisions when I'm in a trading mood, or culling the herd.

I lost some nice guns in those burglaries. Remember the Finnish-made Valmet over/under system? With the rifle barrels, the bottom barrel could be adjusted so you could sort of "regulate" the barrels to shoot together. I had a set of .30-06 barrels that I hunted with quite a bit. Accuracy wasn't spectacular, but I fiddled with it and it would hold better than two minutes of angle (MOA). I also had 12-gauge shotgun barrels. When it was stolen, I'd just gotten a set of 9.3x74R barrels, so recently that I didn't yet have ammo.

Jack Pohl, owner of the old E. C. Bishop gunstock firm in Warsaw, Missouri, was a friend of my dad's. I lost three rifles stocked in Bishop's best walnut, truly a shame. But one rifle I especially wish I could get back was a plain and simple factory Savage 99 in .358 Winchester. It had come in as a test gun maybe a year earlier. I bought it, added a Williams receiver sight, and I'd done some hog hunting with it before it went away. It shot well, but I didn't have it long enough to consider it a favorite. However, the Savage 99 is always a cool rifle, and the .358 Winchester is a neat little cartridge. Had it not been stolen, I'd probably still have it. At the time, Payton Miller and I worked together at Petersen Publishing, and we did a lot of weekend hog hunting. Now, forty years later, whenever I run into Payton at a SHOT Show or other event, he's almost certain to say, "Man, I wish you still had that 99 .358." So do I!

The .358 was never a big seller, and it's not a common chambering in the Savage 99. Still, they're out there, and used 99s aren't expensive. Actually, I just checked the web, and saw two or three for sale. So that's a long-lost rifle I could replace. But a home invasion leaves deep-seated

This well-worn Model 12 "factory skeet" shotgun is one of few firearms I still have from my school days. Luckily, it was in the trunk of my car the first time I was burgled. I still have it, and I used it to win the Grand National Quail Hunt in Enid, Oklahoma, in 2007.

bitterness, and I've never replaced in kind any of the guns that were taken. I had both a Luger P-08 and a Walther P-38, World War II prizes from a relative. I enjoyed shooting them, but I've never owned another of either pistol. One of these days, though, I'll see a Savage 99 .358 I can't pass. I still have dies, bullets, cases, and some ammo, so that's an excuse, isn't it?

There was one unexpected benefit to getting cleaned out: the chance to rebuild my battery with left-hand actions. I've always been incurably left-handed. When I was young, left-hand actions were

I shot this California hog with a Savage Model 99 with aperture sight. This rifle is in .300 Savage, and my long-lost 99 in .358 was almost identical (and even better for hogs), but I've never replaced it.

rare so, like most lefties, I grew up shooting right-hand bolt-actions, operating them by reaching over the top of the receiver (and scope) with my left paw. The proper way to operate a bolt-action is to keep the rifle shouldered, eyes on target, working the bolt with the shooting hand. This is impossible with a wrong-handed action but, with practice, a lefty can reach over the top pretty fast. Most of the bolt-actions I had, including those with that beautiful Bishop walnut, were right-hand actions with left-hand stocks.

In fact, in that period, I had exactly one left-hand bolt-action, a Savage 110 in 7mm Remington Magnum, purchased between burglaries. That rifle was also the first rifle I ever had that wore a synthetic stock. The factory walnut stock warped so badly on a rainy 1980 caribou hunt that I replaced it with an early Lee Six fiberglass stock. Of course, that rifle went away with everything else.

Although availability was nothing like today, by then left-hand bolt-actions were fairly common. Since I had no choice but to start over, I made another vow: Henceforth, my personal rifles would have left-hand or ambidextrous actions. Business is business, of course. So, I still use and write about right-handed rifles. I'm still pretty fast at reaching over the top when I have to and, if the truth must be known, I can shoot a rifle fairly well off my right shoulder (although shotgunning is hopeless).

It seemed silly to have a mixture of right- and left-hand actions, so, as I rebuilt, I went lefty. Convenience and speed aside, there is a real, though remote, safety issue. In the event of a catastrophic failure, such as a case head rupture, firearms that eject to the right are designed to vent hot gases and shrapnel to the right, away from a right-handed shooter's face. For a lefty using a right-hand action, the effect is just the opposite: All the bad stuff is directed straight into the right side of your face. The problem is the same with actions that are ambidextrous in operation, but still eject to the right. This includes lever-actions that I love: Marlin, Savage, Winchester Model 88.

Do I lay awake nights worrying about this? No. You have to work at it (and usually do something really stupid) to blow up a modern

I took this very wide Zambezi Valley buffalo with Russ Broom in 1992. I'm using my C. W. Andrews in .470; Russ is holding a continental double in .500 3-inch. I definitely should have kept the Andrews rifle, but circumstances required its sale.

firearm. Still, there is sound rationale for lefties to use southpaw actions. I sometimes mention this to fellow left-handers, and I make a point of it with right-handed friends who have left-handed kids.

I've never regretted the decision to go lefty. However, I must admit that I regret being left-handed! Many of the rifles I admire, like classic Mausers and pre-1964 Model 70s, are totally right-hand and do me little good; I have to worship them from afar. At least I can enjoy my lever-actions and falling-block single-shots. At some point in the not-too-distant future, our kids will regret even more that Donna and I are both left-handed. Have you ever tried to sell a left-hand rifle? The kids are all right-handed. The jury is out on the grandkids, so hope remains!

I have a problem passing up left-hand guns, whether I need them or not. But when the gun safes are full, it's decision time. These are hard choices. I suppose I've bought, sold, and traded hundreds of firearms. This book is a good exercise because I had to give serious thought to which of those were and are my genuine, lasting favorites.

On the one hand, I suppose I'd like to have back *all* the firearms I've let go of. On the other hand, I'm sure glad I don't have to worry about where I'd put them! In the end, of all the rifles I've voluntarily sold or traded, there are just two that I *seriously* wish I'd kept.

In the days when mirror-image left-hand bolt-actions were scarce, it was relatively common to convert the bolt handle from right side to left. The job is complex gunsmithing but, in effect, it reverses bolt rotation from counter-clockwise to clockwise, usually possible with Mauser dual opposing locking lugs.

Col. Charles Askins and I went on a muskox hunt in the Northwest Territories in 1990. Askins was also left-handed, but in his day mirror-image actions were less common. He had a collection of left-hand conversions, which require complex gunsmithing that is rarely done today.

WINCHESTER
SUPREME
Birchwood Casey

Col. Charles Askins was also a left-handed gunwriter. The first time I saw his gun room at his house off Blanco Road in San Antonio, my eyes nearly popped out. The room was a long rectangle with stand-up gun racks along both walls. One entire wall was nearly filled with left-handed rifles. We looked at a few, and almost all were conversions.

Mind you, a conversion is just that: bolt operation is switched, but ejection remains to the right, so that distant safety issue remains. With today's availability of left-hand bolt-actions, there's really no reason to convert. It's a difficult and expensive job, and I don't know any current riflesmiths who would even consider it. I have owned exactly *two* left-hand conversions. Interestingly, those are the two rifles I most wish I'd kept.

R. F. Sedgley converted this Springfield .30-06 (above and left) to a left-hand action in the 1930s. This complex work was spectacularly executed. Although aperture-sight only, its accuracy was amazing. This is one really nice vintage rifle that I definitely should have kept.

Although I did some North American hunting with the Sedgley Springfield, it went to Africa just once. One afternoon in South Africa it accounted for a kudu, not a huge bull, but it was a memorable event, and for just a few seconds, I felt like Papa Hemingway.

The first was a Springfield .30-06 made by Reginald Sedgley, a great riflesmith who operated R. F. Sedgley Inc. in Philadelphia from 1916 until his death in 1938. He was a contemporary of Griffin & Howe, and his rifles are often described as "blue-collar" Griffin & Howes. I'd always wanted a Griffin & Howe Springfield, a rifle that speaks of Ernest Hemingway and Grancel Fitz. Most Sedgley rifles are "plainer" than most G&H Springfields. However, *this* left-hand conversion was done with amazing skill. At first glance you could see that it was a Springfield action because of the knurled cocking piece. But you immediately realized there was something wrong with it; the bolt handle obviously wasn't in its proper place.

This Sedgley Springfield was a classic of its day, good but plain straight-grained wood, 26-inch barrel, Lyman receiver aperture sight on the rear bridge. Sedgley cataloged left-hand conversions, but collectors have told me that he may have made no more than five. Former Ventura County Sheriff Larry Carpenter saw the rifle in a gun shop and snagged it for me. This was in the mid-1990s, when I still had 20/10 vision and could really shoot with an aperture sight. That rifle would produce MOA groups all day long, and the action was incredibly smooth. I did some local hog hunting with it, and shot a few deer and one bull elk with it. It went to Africa just once and, as I said in the previous chapter, I shot a kudu bull with it. It was not a huge bull, but it was a wonderful thrill.

Although clean and excellent, it wasn't a valuable rifle; I didn't sell it for financial gain. I let it go because of pure vanity. A few years ago, I developed an astigmatism that, when I was shooting iron sights, made me see *two* front sights. Frustrated with myself, I got rid of two or three iron-sighted rifles. More recently, a good eye doctor has the problem mostly corrected with glasses and I'm back in business. I wish I'd gone to the doctor first, and I wish I'd kept that Sedgley Springfield!

I used this left-hand-converted pre-1964 Winchester Model 70 in .375 for nearly twenty years. The conversion wasn't done well and required work, but the rifle became an old friend, and I should have kept it. On its first outing, in Zambia in 1984, it accounted for my first big buffalo, an assortment of plains game, and my best lion.

The last time I took my left-hand-converted Model 70 in .375 to Africa was in 1996 when I went with Bob Petersen and Ken Elliott to Zambia. By that time, I'd rebarreled the rifle, and, although the stock showed hard use, the barrel was nearly new. I wish I still had it!

The other left-hand conversion came to me in early 1984, shortly after my final round of burglaries, when I was fresh out of rifles. A left-handed guy in the Los Angeles Safari Club had lost vision in his left eye and was converting to right-hand shooting. He had several left-hand rifles for sale, and I bought two: A nicely stocked Remington Model 700 in 7mm Remington Magnum, and this pre-1964 Model 70 .375 H&H converted to left-hand bolt. The stock was factory; the original right-hand cut for the bolt handle was patched, but the woodwork was done much better than the metal.

The conversion was a mess. The bolt release was a plate with a screw; in order to remove the bolt, you had to remove the screw. I was on the range, preparing for an African hunt, when the weld let go and the bolt handle came off in my hand! I think Jack Lott was with me on the range that day, but for sure Jack reattached the bolt handle, and replaced the Mickey Mouse bolt release with a Sako release.

By serial number, the rifle dated to the early 1950s. This gent had bought it used years before and had no idea who had done the conversion, so I never knew. In late October 1984 I took it on an amazing safari in Zambia, taking my best lion, best sable, best Livingstone eland, first big buffalo, and more. I don't know how many times I took that rifle on safari. It went all over southern Africa, a couple of hunts in C.A.R., at least twice to Tanzania. And to Alaska and Zambia, literally A to Z.

It was very accurate, and really liked a handload with Sierra's 300-grain GameKing. It was nicely used when I got it, but over time the stock was nearly black and most of the bluing was gone. Then, suddenly, the groups started to open up. I can't take full credit for shooting the barrel out. That would be quite a feat with a .375, so I assume it had been shot a lot when I got it. It took some digging, but I managed to find a new 25-inch Winchester .375 barrel of the same contour. I continued to use it with the new barrel for several more years. And then I sold it. I have no idea what I was thinking when I let that one go.

Well, I know what I was thinking. The gun safes were full, and it was time to cull. I had three other .375 H&H rifles, which seemed redundant. So, I said goodbye to a dear old friend. I should have kept that one!

Part Two
My Favorite Cartridges

As a gunwriter, I've used many cartridges. It's not quite correct to say that I've never met a cartridge I didn't like, but virtually all perform as the manufacturers say they will. This is especially true today, when most serious shooters have access to chronographs; the days when manufacturers could sprinkle a lot of "blue sky" into their published data are long since over.

Although often used interchangeably, "cartridge" and "caliber" are not synonymous. Properly, caliber is the bullet diameter. A cartridge is the whole ball of wax: case, primer, propellant charge, and projectile. A cartridge designation, such as ".308 Winchester," denotes both the bullet diameter and the unique case dimensions associated with that designation.

Some bullet diameters, including 6.5mm, (.264-inch), 7mm (.284-inch), and .30-caliber (.308-inch) are much more popular than others, with numerous cartridges using the same projectiles. There is also much redundancy in performance, so much that preference becomes kind of a personal choice, based on history, experience, reputation, or perhaps simply good performance in a well-liked rifle.

I am not suggesting, and do not mean to imply, that my favorite cartridges are the best *in their respective calibers. Nor are all useful bullet diameters represented among my favorite cartridges. I freely admit that I had a hard time shortening the list. My personal favorites may not be the "best" cartridges in their respective bullet diameters, but they are cartridges I've used over long periods of time. And, often, they are cartridges that I've used, drifted away from . . . and keep coming back to.*

The .204 Ruger

Chapter 3

Although it didn't make my "favorites" list either as cartridge or rifle, we should start the real meat of this volume with the understanding that a good .22 rimfire is the base of any serious shooter's battery. The odds-on choice is the .22 Long Rifle. Accurate and inexpensive, the .22 LR is almost indispensable and irreplaceable for hunting small game, practice, formal and informal target shooting, and just plain fun shooting.

When bad habits creep in, the best cure I know is to drop back and work on the basics with a good .22. With mild recoil, soft report, low ammunition cost, and amazing accuracy, there's no better way to work on breathing, trigger squeeze, and sight alignment, and lots of shooting with a .22 is just about the only way I know to cure a flinch.

In 1979, recently off active duty with the Marines, I interviewed for a job as junior editor at *Guns & Ammo*. Howard French, *G&A*'s great editor, grilled me. One of his standard questions, I learned, was: "Do you have a .22?" Howard was a tough guy, difficult to work for, but his firearms knowledge was encyclopedic. He figured if you didn't have a decent .22 rimfire you weren't a serious enough shooter to fit in at *G&A*. I think he was right! At the time I had (and still have) my first .22, Ithaca's inexpensive falling-block single-shot. Like millions of other shooters, I had (and still have) a Ruger 10/22. (Both were at my parents' house in Kansas City, far from Los Angeles burglars!)

A few years later I acquired (and still have) a left-hand Kimber Super America bolt-action in .22 LR. Great rifle, great cartridge. In the pandemic fall of 2020, I took it into my Kansas woods and spent some time squirrel hunting, something I should do more often. I

A good .22 is essential to any rifleman's battery, irreplaceable for practice and small game. The backdrop here is my Kansas woods, and I'm holding a mess of squirrels that I took with my left-hand Kimber Super America in .22 LR.

was inspired by a friend from the Boone and Crockett Club, Richard Hale. He sent me a photo of a mess of Missouri squirrels he shot with a Winchester Model 52 .22, and I realized it had been too long since I spent a day in the squirrel woods being patient and focusing on head shots.

The .22 LR is the world's most popular cartridge, sold in billions (with a "b") annually. The .22 WMR or .22 magnum offers more power and range. Likewise, the .17 HMR, which can be shockingly accurate.

However, both are a bit too powerful and destructive for edible small game, and much costlier to shoot. So, for practice, plinking, and small game, an accurate .22 LR is ubiquitous. Almost all of us have at least one, and we should probably spend more time shooting them.

The .22 LR is often used on pests around the farm as well as for small game. At my place, we're infested with armadillos! The .22 LR is certainly adequate, but it's a short-range tool. When I tackle varmints, I want accuracy equal to the .22 LR, but more velocity and range. In other words, I need a "varmint rifle."

The varmint rifle is a uniquely American tool that had its origins among Eastern woodchuck and crow hunters, who wanted both range and accuracy. Our varmint rifle probably descended from the English "rook rifle." A rook is a type of crow; the rook rifle needed to be accurate but moderate in power, as it was used for rooks, foxes, and badgers in the settled English countryside, where having bullets flying long distances was not a good idea.

When you brought the concept of the "pest rifle" into more spacious America, accuracy was still essential, but more velocity and greater range were desirable. Our American "varmint cartridges" may be used for burrowing rodents such as prairie dogs, woodchucks, ground squirrels, and gophers. They may be also used for foxes and coyotes and, sometimes even pressed into service for deer hunting.

Many of the popular varmint cartridges still with us go back to the early days of smokeless powder. Interestingly, the first smokeless-powder .22 centerfire was not envisioned as a varmint rifle. Developed in 1912 by Charles Newton for Arthur Savage, the .22 Savage High-Power used a heavy-for-caliber 70-grain bullet at a fast (for 1912) 2,800 fps. It was highly touted for deer-size game but, with the fledgling expanding bullets of the day, it was damned. It had a short-lived following, but the varmint cartridges that followed, in the 1930s, are still with us.

The .22 Hornet, a lovely little cartridge, was developed in 1930. Based on the .250 Savage case, the .22-250 (a.k.a. .22 Varminter) was also developed in the early 1930s as a wildcat cartridge. It remained a

Rod Herrett (in front of me), Bill Bynum, and Kevin Howard on an Idaho rockchuck shoot with Winchester ammunition. We used numerous cartridges on this hunt, from a .22 LR and .22 WMR on up to a .220 Swift. There are many good varmint cartridges; the biggest difference among them is effective range.

perennially popular non-standard cartridge until finally "legitimized" by Remington in 1965. Introduced in 1934, Winchester's .220 Swift was the first (and remains one of few) factory cartridges to exceed 4,000 feet per second.

The .220 Swift is based on the 6mm Lee Navy semi-rimmed case. Since the .22-250 already existed, one must wonder why Winchester chose this obscure, nearly obsolete case. After a lifetime in this business, I don't pretend to always know what the engineers are thinking. The only semi-rational explanation: In 1935, Savage was serious competition to Winchester, and both companies were lever-action dominated. I suppose it was unthinkable for Winchester to use a *Savage* case! Oddly, they did it again in 1964, intending to replace the

.220 Swift with the rimmed (and almost forgotten) .225 Winchester, which was based on the .219 Zipper case (which, in turn, was based on the rimmed .30-30 case). The .22 Hornet and .220 Swift still have followings, but the .22-250 remains the most popular fast .22 centerfire.

Later developments had different origins. The .222 Remington (1950) was developed as a super-accurate benchrest cartridge by Remington's great engineer (and ardent benchrest competitor), Mike Walker. The mild, accurate .222 was a dominant varmint cartridge into the 1970s. The .222 Remington Magnum (the loser) and .223 Remington (the winner), were developed as military hopefuls. The .17 Remington came out of Australia, developed by hunters there to combat the plague of non-native foxes. The idea was a light, fast, frangible bullet that would enter, but not exit, thus reducing pelt

Bud Boddington took this Texas gobbler with his Kimber in .22 Hornet. My dad loved shooting prairie dogs with his .22 Hornet, and the old Hornet is still a fine short-range varmint cartridge.

Left, a Savage 110 in .22-250; right, a rebarreled Ruger M77 in .25-06. Both rifles are obviously "varmint-accurate." The .22-250 has become the "standard" long-range varmint cartridge; the .25-06 is the largest cartridge commonly used for varminting. Both are effective, but both are a bit too powerful to call shots through the scope.

damage. Recent .22 centerfire developments, such as the .22 Nosler and Federal's .224 Valkyrie, are designed to fit into an AR platform, and provide better performance with the super-heavy .224-inch bullets (up to 80 grains) now in vogue.

The varmint cartridge spectrum doesn't run just from .17 to .22. The 6mms are in there pitching, and, with lighter bullets, some serious varmint shooters prefer .25s and even 6.5mms. Realistically, however, anything above a .22 centerfire burns more powder than is necessary to get the job done. Equally important is the matter of recoil. No, a 6mm (an old .243 Winchester or new 6mm Creedmoor or Hornady's brand-new 6mm ARC) isn't going to beat you to death. However, in classic varminting, such as sniping woodchucks down long valleys or spending a day in a prairie dog town, when you combine distance, size of target, and vagaries of wind, it must be accepted that not every shot will hit. The ideal situation is to call your shots through the scope and correct with the next round.

Unless the rifle is very heavy, even the fastest .22 centerfires, and everything larger, have a bit too much bounce to properly view the strike through the scope. The .17s have merit, but the light .17-caliber bullets are highly susceptible to wind drift. Also, the fastest .17, the .17 Remington (another 4,000-fps merchant), tends to foul barrels quickly, requiring frequent cleaning to maintain accuracy. This is not a problem for woodchuck and coyote hunting, but a bit of a pain for high-volume shooting such as prairie dogs.

Over the years I've done a bit of 'chuck shooting, both woodchucks and rockchucks. We do a lot of ground squirrel shooting in California, and of course I hunt coyotes. However, I've done more prairie dog shooting than all the rest put together. Dad and I were introduced to prairie dogs on our first pronghorn hunt in Wyoming, when I was just barely a teenager. With our pronghorns already hanging

Many current varmint cartridges go back to the early twentieth century. Left to right: .22 Savage High Power (1912); .22 Hornet (1930); .250 Savage (1915); .22-250, based on the .250 Savage and wildcatted before 1920; 6mm Lee Navy (1895); and .220 Swift (1935). The long-obsolete 6mm Lee Navy was the parent case for Winchester's .220 Swift, probably to avoid competition with Savage.

The .220 Swift broke 4,000 fps in 1935. Eighty-five years later this is still the practical velocity limit. Few factory cartridges reach 4,000 fps; among them, left to right are: .17 Remington, .204 Ruger, .22-250, .223 WSSM, .220 Swift, .243 Winchester. Even these can only reach 4,000 fps with light-for-caliber bullets.

in his barn, rancher Lester Wright (of Wright, Wyoming) took us to a prairie dog town and we shot up all the ammo we had. Dad used his .308; I had a .243. Back then, we didn't know about hearing protection; truth is, I haven't heard a watch tick since that first day in a prairie dog town.

Dad had a friend, Dale Brashears, and he knew of (then rare) prairie dog towns in western Kansas. This was still in the 1960s, but by then we had an early Ruger No. 1 in .243, which remained a go-to varmint rifle for many years. Brashears had one of the early *factory* .22-250s. Of course, we were impressed; that was a *real* varmint rifle! But Dad and I did fine with light bullets in our .243s.

In those days, the super-accurate little .222 Remington was a standard choice for medium-range varminting. For work at longer ranges, the .220 Swift was still out there, but I've rarely seen one in the field and have never owned one. After finally being legitimized by Remington in 1965, the .22-250 took over as the dominant long-range varmint cartridge, and remains so today.

The .222 Remington Magnum and .223 Remington are slightly faster than the .222 Remington, designed to meet military specifications. The .223 was introduced in civilian form in 1962, before its adoption by the military as the 5.56mm (later the 5.56x45mm NATO). Although the .223 and 5.56mm cartridges are almost identical, chamber specifications are not exactly the same. It's okay to shoot .223 in the 5.56mm chamber, but 5.56mm ammo should not be fired in a .223 chamber. Either way, the .223/5.56mm became the world's most popular centerfire cartridge, in just a few years blowing the .222 Remington Magnum off the market.

Not necessarily to follow the crowd but because both cartridges made sense, from about 1980 my primary "varmint battery" was comprised of a .223 for medium-range shooting, and a .22-250 for longer ranges, both in various platforms over the years. Purists will always argue that the .222 is more accurate, but that depends more on rifle and ammo, and I'm not a benchrest competitor. In good barrels, I've had great accuracy from both the .223 and .22-250. Both are powerful enough for any "varmint" shooting. And, with heavier bullets and where legal, both can be pressed into service for deer-size game.

However, in the specialized arena of shooting smaller rodents like prairie dogs and ground squirrels, there is a major difference between the .223 and similar cartridges and the .22-250 and anything larger. Here's the deal: Up to about .223 Remington in velocity and power, you can call your shots through the scope, observe the strikes, and make corrections. This is not possible with a .22-250 or anything larger. It's an exaggeration to say there is "too much kick," but there's just enough recoil to take you off the target. Then again, the .22-250 has the advantage of being much faster than the .223 and having greater range. I used them both quite happily for many years.

My primary purpose for a varmint rifle has always been a more-or-less annual prairie dog shoot. I consider shooting prairie dogs in

Here I am practicing field-shooting positions in a prairie dog town with a Rock River AR in .223/5.56mm. The .223 is the world's most popular centerfire and an excellent varmint cartridge. I typically use the .223 out to a couple hundred yards then switch to the .204 Ruger.

the windy West the world's best teacher for learning how to call wind and adjust for deflection. Typically, I'd "warm up" at closer range (sometimes with a .17 HMR, .22 WMR, or .22 Hornet), then switch to a .223, either in bolt-action or AR, for medium-range shots. When shots within 300 yards or so got scarce, I'd go to the "big gun" and take out the .22-250.

The Nesika bolt-action is known for accuracy and popular in benchrest circles. Around the turn of the millennium, Nesika was part of Dakota Arms in Sturgis, South Dakota. I hadn't paid any attention to the growing interest in the .20-caliber (.204-inch bullet diameter), but I went to a prairie dog shoot with the Dakota/Nesika folks where they were showcasing several wildcat/proprietary .20-caliber cartridges. The Nesika rifles were wonderfully accurate, and I was impressed by how well the .20-calibers held up in wind. Maybe not as good as the fastest .22 centerfires, but better than .17s, and you can call your shots through the scope.

As you'll see throughout this book, I have little interest in non-standard wildcats. We have plenty of factory cartridges to choose from. I handload, so ammo problems can be solved, but non-standard cartridges are an extra pain. So, although I was impressed, I initially had limited interest in the .20s. Then, in 2004, in a joint development by Hornady and Ruger, the .204 Ruger was introduced. It is based on the by-then-obscure .222 Remington Magnum, necked down to take a .204-inch bullet. As with most factory cartridges, I would *never* say that the .204 Ruger has the best or most ideal case dimensions for the caliber. However, it is readily available and very fast, pushing light 24- or 32-grain bullets over 4,000 fps, and 40-grain bullets to 3,900. The cartridge was new when I got my hands on a Ruger No. 1 single-shot in stainless steel with a laminate stock.

My buddy, Gordon Marsh, on the bench with his Savage 110 in .22-250. Gordon also uses a Ruger No. 1 in .204 Ruger; the .22-250 is his "big gun," which he employs only for long-range shooting.

We'll discuss the Ruger No. 1 in greater detail later in this volume. Hampered by two-piece stock and the screw through the fore-end into a barrel fixture, not all No. 1s are extremely accurate, but I've had good luck with medium- and heavy-barreled versions. My .243 was very accurate, and a heavy-barrel No. 1 varminter in .22-250 was a real tack-driver. As was this new No. 1 in .204 Ruger. It was a test rifle, which I first used on a Wyoming prairie dog hunt, then quickly purchased when I got home.

Although the 40-grain bullets are slower, they buck wind better than the lighter slugs, and almost as well as the fastest .22 centerfires with varmint-weight bullets. Also, backing off from 4,000 fps probably increases barrel life. As evidence, my .204 has been in use since 2004 and shoots as well as when it was new. Since then, it has remained my "go-to" varmint rifle. Fortunately, I don't shoot prairie dogs as aggressively as I once did; otherwise, I'm sure the barrel would be long gone! Remembering our house rule about not allowing the gun safes to overflow, I no longer own a .22-250; the .204 has replaced it as my long-range varmint rifle.

I still have .223 rifles in both bolt-action and AR form, and their purpose remains the same: I use them for medium-range shooting and to practice field shooting positions. Then, when closer targets become scarce, I break out the .204. For the last few years my prairie dog shooting partner has been Gordon Marsh, proprietor of the Wholesale Hunter and LG Outdoors e-commerce sites. Interestingly, Gordon also uses a Ruger No. 1 in .204 as his primary long-range rifle. He often starts with a .17 HMR, then shifts to a .223 before going to the .204. Unlike me, however, he still uses a .22-250 as his "big gun."

Extreme accuracy is the first criterion for any varmint rifle. For shooting in the West, this is followed by resistance to wind. The .204 delivers, but it also allows the shooter to call shots through the scope. Like the .22 LR, the .223/5.56mm is an essential utility cartridge, but without question the .204 Ruger has become my favorite varmint cartridge.

My Ruger No. 1 in .204 Ruger has been my "go-to" varmint rifle since shortly after the cartridge's introduction in 2004. The accuracy of this rifle is exceptional. I use it gingerly to reduce barrel wear!

Important note: With bullets of 60 grains and heavier intended for the purpose, the .223 is viable for deer-size game; you just have to be careful. The .204 is *not*; its little bullets aren't heavy enough. So the .204 Ruger is not a crossover varmint/deer cartridge, by any stretch or in any context. I will always have reservations about .22 centerfires for deer but, with appropriate bullets, I've taken a lot of deer with various .22 centerfires. The .204, available in bolt-actions and AR platforms as well as my single-shot, is an awesome varmint cartridge, but that's what it is: a *varmint* cartridge.

The .270 Winchester

Chapter 4

Winchester's timeless .270 has not *always* been a favorite cartridge of mine. Believe it or not, it was not always Jack O'Connor's favorite, either. O'Connor had an early Model 54 Winchester in .270 shortly after the cartridge was introduced in 1925, but he didn't keep it. The number of desert rams O'Connor took between 1935 and 1946 isn't precisely known, but only the last one (in 1946) was taken with a .270. He shot several with the 7x57, which remained a favorite cartridge to the end of his life. He also used the .257 Roberts and, although no photo is known to exist, he took one desert ram with a Winchester Model 71 in .348 Winchester.

From the 1940s onward, however, O'Connor became a staunch and outspoken advocate for the .270 Winchester, considering it nearly perfect for the mountain sheep he loved to hunt, and fully adequate for game up to elk. O'Connor also used the .270 to take multiple moose and grizzly bears. I don't think this is necessarily because he thought it was the best choice, but because his moose and grizzlies were mostly incidental to his sheep hunting; as any of us would, he used what he was carrying when a chance came along.

I got my first .270 in about 1970. The action was an Interarms Mark X Mauser, right-hand bolt with 20-inch barrel, stocked with a Mannlicher-style Bishop stock in very nice dark walnut with left-hand cheekpiece. I used it to take a few deer and my first black bear. However, I was a child of the 1960s magnum craze, and in those days I remained unconvinced that the .270 was adequate for anything larger than deer.

That was silly, but it was some years before I appreciated just how silly! Fortunately, I (mostly) kept that opinion to myself. In my early

I took this axis buck in Texas in 1979 with my first .270, a right-hand Interarms Mark X Mauser action. Its full-length Mannlicher-style stock was in an excellent walnut, and it had a 20-inch barrel. This rifle accounted for my first whitetails, first black bear, and this beautiful axis buck.

days as a budding outdoor writer, I just didn't write much about the .270. After that short-barrel .270 went away, several years passed before I got another. Maybe by then I'd grown up a bit.

The .270 Winchester was and is popular. No cartridge is everyone's cup of tea, but whether you like it or not, the .270 Winchester is ubiquitous. As I progressed from an unknown and struggling freelancer to magazine editor, I used quite a few test rifles in .270 Winchester. Good accuracy and mild recoil were almost a given, but since most of the "loaners" were right-hand action, I didn't bite.

In those days, CNC machining was new. Gunmaker Pete Grisel was an early wizard at programming CNC; he was so good that he left the firearms industry and did well in the medical field. Before that happened, he teamed up with Don Allen and they created Dakota Arms. Don was mostly the "wood guy;" his stock duplicating machine remains the standard, and today Dakota is still using some of the great walnut that Don accumulated. Pete Grisel was the "metal guy." When Dakota Arms was formed, the Pete Grisel action, with Don Allen wood, formed the basis for the Dakota Model 76. I can't remember exactly what I was thinking, but when I got a Dakota M76 I ordered it in .270 Winchester. Perhaps it's obvious: I'd mellowed (and matured)!

That rifle became a good friend, and I hunted with it a lot for a dozen years and more. It went to Montana in 1994 when I drew a Montana bighorn tag; to Scotland and Austria for red stag, chamois, and roebuck; and to Zambia and Zimbabwe in 1996, where it accounted for a variety of antelopes (but nothing really large). Along the way, it shared much of the hunting I do the most of: deer, wild hogs, and in those days, pronghorns almost annually.

I think the last time I hunted with it was in February of 2002. My old friend Mike Ballew was director of the NRA Whittington Center near Raton, New Mexico. I was leaving soon to take over a task force in the Persian Gulf. Mike had an opening for a late elk hunt, so Chub Eastman and I both took him up on it, Chub with a 9.3x64mm, me with the Dakota .270. I was using handloaded 150-grain Nosler Partitions, and I drew the longest shot I've made on an elk, just over

I drew my first bighorn tag in Montana in 1994, and I used my Dakota .270 Winchester to take this gorgeous ram. This was the first sheep I took with a .270 . . . but definitely not the last!

400 yards on a snowy hillside. I knew the distance and the drop, and the morning was dead still. I held at the top of the bull's withers, and the bullet penetrated both shoulders, cutting across the top of the heart. By then, I had no reservations about the .270 as an elk rifle. But, if I still had them, this would have dispelled any residual concerns. The bull, a good 6x6, attempted one step and went over backward into deep snow.

I'm still not certain the .270 is *perfect* for elk, but it's adequate. There are lots of great elk cartridges. Chub took a slightly better bull with his 9.3mm, and practically flattened it. Sensible choices for elk probably start with the faster 6.5mms, include the .270s, and run on up to the .33s. Perhaps not all the way to 9.3mm (.366-inch bullet), but the .270 Winchester is far from the bottom.

Well, if a little is good, then a lot must be better. So surely the .270 Weatherby Magnum and .270 Winchester Short Magnum (WSM) must be better than the .270 Winchester, right? Yes, in some ways. The .270 Weatherby was Roy Weatherby's initial factory cartridge in 1946, and is still one of the flattest-shooting of all hunting cartridges. I've dabbled with the .270 Weatherby, and I had quite an affair with the .270 WSM.

The .270 Winchester was *fast* in 1925, and it remains speedy today. The .270 Weatherby and WSM are faster by a couple hundred feet per second. They deliver more energy, and in my experience, you can *see* the additional energy yield on larger game animals. Years ago, in South Africa, Jim Morey shot a waterbuck—a big, robust antelope—frontally with a .270 Weatherby, dropping it flat in its tracks with an impressive impact I will never forget.

I'm not sure a .270 Winchester would have been that dramatic. Who knows? No two shots on game animals are exactly the same, and no two animals react exactly alike upon receiving a bullet. I have no

Through the 1990s I used a Dakota .270 Winchester to do a lot of hunting on several continents. I shot this excellent Austrian red stag, uphill about 250 yards away, and it was literally flattened with a single 140-grain AccuBond bullet.

The Dakota .270 only went to Africa a couple of times, but the cartridge provided good service. I took my only black lechwe in 1996 on the floodplains of Zambia's Bangweulu, using a 150-grain bullet.

issues at all with the .270 Weatherby, a wonderful hunting cartridge with little recoil for its capability. If you study ballistics charts carefully, to this day there are few cartridges that shoot flatter than the .270 Weatherby. It hits hard, and recoil is mild. It is limited primarily by both rifle and ammo availability.

The .300 WSM is the most popular of the many new short magnums introduced at the turn of the millennium. However, we have plenty of, even too many, .30-caliber magnums that are similar in performance. The unbelted short magnum that interested me most was (and is) the .270 WSM, which I think is the second-most-popular of the group. The .270 WSM is almost as fast as the .270 Weatherby, but able to be housed in a short bolt-action. I used it quite a bit in three different rifles, including on a long hunt in Mongolia, and on my second Marco Polo hunt in Tajikistan.

The capability is wonderful. The only problem is, going all the way back to Peter Paul Mauser in the 1890s, most bolt-actions have not been engineered to feed short, fat cartridges shaped like these unbelted short magnums. This became obvious with the Winchester Super Short Magnums (WSSMs), great little fireplug-shaped cartridges that do everything they are supposed to do. Unfortunately, few platforms fed them well, and they quickly passed into cartridge history. The problem is not as extreme with the (more or less) .308 Winchester length of the unbelted short magnums, including the .270 WSM, but it exists, and I ran into occasional feeding problems in the field. That's not a problem if the first shot is always good, but sometimes you *need* another shot.

In early 2002 I hunted with Chub Eastman at the NRA Whittington Center in New Mexico, and I made a long shot on my elk with my Dakota .270. Eastman used a 9.3x64 Brenneke to take the bull pictured above. The range from .270 to 9.3mm probably defines sensible elk cartridges: the .270 is a bit light, a fast 9.3mm is a bit much, but both are perfectly adequate.

Muskoxen are powerful and stocky, so my outfitter in Greenland recommended a .30-caliber minimum. That's probably good advice, but this bull dropped quickly to a single 130-grain Barnes X from a .270 Winchester.

Mongolia is still very much a horse culture. In winter, wolf predation on horse foals is a major problem. While there, I had a rare opportunity to take two wolves running together. I dropped the first one, and of course that was the moment when my .270 WSM failed to feed. I don't think it was a conscious decision, but I haven't used the .270 WSM since.

The .270 Weatherby is still faster, and in a good action, smooth feeding is normal. My friend Zack Aultman has a lot of long-range opportunities for big whitetails on his place in southern Georgia, and he loves the .270 Weatherby, with good reason. It's been many years since I used the .270 Weatherby. Although I've done a fair amount of hunting with the cartridge, I've never actually owned one. My procession of .270 Winchesters, on the other hand, has been long.

Right now, even with our self-imposed restriction on numbers of rifles, we have three .270s. I concede both the .270 WSM and .270 Weatherby are faster, shoot flatter, and deliver more energy. However, I can't envision a hunt, or a game animal, where I might take a .270

WSM or Weatherby but wouldn't consider the .270 Winchester adequate. The other two are faster and more powerful, but not by so much that they take the .277-inch bullet into a different class.

Gunwriter Dave Petzal, long with *Field & Stream*, is a contrary and irascible old curmudgeon, a good friend, and extremely astute rifleman. Some time back he wrote a very good piece bashing the .270 Winchester. In his experience, accuracy was typically pedestrian and, in these days of long-range mania, seriously hampered by bullet selection. I agree with the latter. From the beginning, in 1925, the .270 Winchester was considered a hunting cartridge, never a match cartridge. Most of its bullets have thus been hunting bullets, with little thought to benchrest-level accuracy or extreme-range performance.

Left to right: .270 Winchester, .270 WSM, .270 Weatherby Magnum. Historically, these have been the factory choices in .277-inch hunting cartridges. All three are excellent. Winchester's new 6.8 Western and Nosler's 27 Nosler will increase bullet weight and extend range, but it's unlikely they will erase the .270 Winchester.

I used a left-hand Browning A-Bolt in .270 Winchester to anchor this big bezoar ibex in Turkey. Jack O'Connor had it right all along: The .270 Winchester is a great mountain cartridge!

Driven by today's rage for range, this is changing slowly, with a few aerodynamic, high ballistic coefficient (BC) bullets available from Berger, Hornady, Nosler, and Sierra, but it's nothing like the selection available in 6.5mm, 7mm, and .30-caliber. Because of the lack of bullets, no .270 cartridge has been the darling of the extreme range crowd. Guess what? Shooting game at extreme range isn't my thing, and is unlikely to become my thing. So, for my purposes, the .270 Winchester is just fine (and shoots flat enough) for any shots I'm likely to take.

That said, as I was in the middle of writing this book, Browning/Winchester announced the new 6.8 Western, a .270 cartridge based on the .270 WSM shortened just a bit, and designed around new .277-inch bullets from 160 to 175 grains. With the case shortened, the 6.8 Western can be housed in a short action and, at long last, it brings the heavy-for-caliber, low-drag bullets the .270 craves. I'm very interested in this cartridge and intend to play with it; with a heavy bullet at a bit less than 3,000 fps, it beats most of the 6.5mms, keeps pace with most 7mms, and kicks less than the .30-calibers. The only fly in the ointment: Those extra-heavy bullets need a one-turn-in eight-inches (1:8) rifling twist. The .270s have long been barreled with 1:10 twist. I might consider getting a new barrel for the Blaser, but we're not going to rebarrel our .270 Winchester rifles!

The .270 Winchester is just fine to 400 yards and, under ideal conditions, I've stretched .270s quite a bit farther. Now, if I were a 1,000-yard competitor, or if I seriously wanted to shoot at game beyond 600 yards, the 6.8 Western may prove the ticket. But, while it's fun to ring steel at extreme range, that's not the kind of hunting I do. Always remember, please, this book is about *my* favorites. Mine don't have to be yours.

As for accuracy, I suppose it depends on what you want (and need). I must agree with Petzal: Match-grade accuracy is not the .270's strong suit; benchrest matches are generally not won with hunting bullets. That said, I've never seen the .270 to have an "accuracy problem" or be especially finicky. In part, this is aided by a vast selection of factory

I have used both the .270 WSM and .270 Weatherby Magnum. They deliver more energy and shoot slightly flatter, but they don't do anything the .270 Winchester cannot do. I took this excellent Marco Polo argali with a Winchester M70 Featherweight in .270 WSM.

loads and closing on a century of handload recipes. Over the years I suppose I've had a couple dozen .270 Winchester rifles come through my hands. Some I considered spectacularly accurate. Donna's MGA .270 is; my Joe Balickie .270 is; and the .270 barrel we have for our Blasers is the most accurate of the barrels we have. These are all chambered to .270 Winchester.

All are consistently sub-MOA with a variety of loads (which is saying something). On a good day with good loads, all will print the occasional quarter-inch group. These rifles all wear sporter-weight barrels, as have just about all the .270s I've ever encountered. In fact, I don't think I've ever seen a .270 with a heavy barrel.

Jack O'Connor's famous Biesen No. 2 rifle was based on a pre-1964 Winchester M70 Featherweight with light barrel that happened to be exceptionally accurate. Winchester did a limited edition of semi-production .270 rifles, based on the current M70 Featherweight with a stock styled like O'Connor's Biesen No. 2. I had a chance to do a story on the rifle, and the sample I got printed quarter-inch groups straight out of the box. Darn right, I wanted to buy it, despite my rule about not owning guns with right-hand actions. Fortunately, the small run of these rifles was pretty much sold out. I think this one was promised to someone else, so I couldn't buy it anyway, but I was tempted to try.

That O'Connor commemorative probably wasn't the most accurate .270 I've encountered, but it was exceptional for *any* production rifle. When anyone, including my friend Dave Petzal, suggests the .270 isn't especially accurate, I think of this rifle . . . and my own .270s.

Exactly why the .270 Winchester exists is uncertain. Obviously, the Winchester engineers wanted to use the .30-06 case to create a

Left to right: 6.5-06 (wildcat); .270 Winchester; .280 Remington. Exactly why Winchester chose the .277-inch bullet for its .270 is unclear. By 1925 wildcatters had probably experimented with both the 6.5mm and 7mm on the .30-06 case. Had Winchester chosen either diameter (.264 or .284), the .270 might not exist. The best answer is, probably, in the post-World War I era, Winchester was reluctant to use a "foreign" bullet diameter.

Winchester's O'Connor commemorative edition of the M70 Featherweight was based on O'Connor's Biesen No. 2. The one I took to the range produced spectacular groups, calling into question the old myth that .270s aren't especially accurate.

cartridge of smaller caliber, with lighter bullet, that would be faster, shoot flatter, and, perhaps above all, generate less recoil. The .30-06 is the most powerful cartridge ever adopted by a major military. Although a great elk cartridge, the .30-06 is needlessly powerful for deer-size game, and more velocity/flatter trajectory is useful for mountain hunting. O'Connor loved the .30-06, but his wife, Eleanor, considered it a cannon.

The .270 Winchester fell perfectly into the niche. But why a .277-inch bullet? The .25-06 was wildcatted well before 1925 because the .250 Savage was extremely popular. Likewise, the 6.5-06 and 7mm-06. In 1925 Savage was a serious competitor to Winchester, so the .250 Savage bullet diameter probably wasn't on the table. In post-World War I xenophobic America, "European" bullet diameters probably weren't, either. But why .277-inch? The answer isn't known.

Mauser experimented with a lot of cartridges for various countries. There was an experimental 6.8mm (.277-inch) Mauser cartridge developed for China, but never produced. It is so obscure that even Frank Barnes's *Cartridges of the World* has no photo. Maybe the Winchester folks knew about this cartridge. Surely, they didn't pull the diameter out of a hat, but although close, it doesn't exactly split the difference between any known 1925 bullet diameter and the .30-06's .308-inch bullet. For whatever reason, they settled on .277. The 7mm-06, with a .284-inch bullet, eventually became the .280 Remington, another great cartridge. The 6.5-06 (.264-inch bullet) remains a fairly popular wildcat, as fast as the .270, with the advantage of the 6.5mm's long, heavy-for-caliber bullets. Although never adopted in factory form, the 6.5-06 is a great cartridge. If a European bullet diameter had been chosen—either 6.5mm or 7mm—and *if* there had been better propellants in 1925, it's possible the .270 Winchester might not exist at all.

I took my best-ever mule deer in Alberta in 2012 with a single, 130-grain TTSX from a Kimber Mountain Ascent in .270 Winchester. The .270 is plenty of gun for any and all deer hunting and most mountain hunting.

Donna used her Blaser R8 with a .270 Winchester barrel and a 130-grain SST to take this beautiful ram in Mongolia. The Altai argali is the largest wild sheep in the world, but the .270 Winchester is plenty of gun.

That's speculation. It's a matter of real history that the .270 Winchester was introduced in 1925 and caught on quickly. Its legend continued to grow when O'Connor adopted it as his personal gimmick. It is still popular, a powerful and versatile cartridge that shoots flat, hits hard, and (as intended) produces a lot less recoil than its parent, the .30-06. Loads vary, but you can figure a 130-grain bullet at about 3,100 fps; 140-grain bullet at 3,000; and 150-grain bullet at 2,900.

There are other options, but these are the most common. For elk or the full run of African plains game I've usually used 150-grain bullets; for deer and mountain game I've generally used the faster 130-grain slugs. Or, depending on accuracy in a given rifle, I've often used the 140-grain "compromise" bullet. While there may not be many "low drag" or match-grade .270 bullets, *all* hunting bullets are offered in .277-inch, most in all three common bullet weights.

In effect on game, there isn't much difference between 130 and 150 grains, although bullet construction makes a difference. In recent years I've pretty much stuck with the most common 130-grain bullets: They're fastest, and plenty adequate for the game I hunt with a .270.

When it comes to my favorite cartridges, there's a big jump between the .204 Ruger and .270 Winchester. So, "why" is a fair question. I've explained why, for my purposes, I prefer the .204 to the fast .22 centerfires. But, among popular bullet diameters, I'm skipping 6mm (.243-inch), .25-caliber, (.257-inch), and 6.5mm (.264-inch). All three need a bit of discussion.

Like so many Americans of my generation, I took my first big game with a .243 Winchester, and I've done a lot of varmint hunting with it. The .243 is still a wonderful crossover big-game/varmint cartridge. That said, I like to go lighter for varmints and heavier for big game. Although useful and versatile, I don't own a .243 right now,

Left to right: .243 Winchester, .257 Roberts, .264 Winchester Magnum, .270 Winchester. There are dozens of great cartridges well suited to deer-size game. Approaching the century mark, the .270 Winchester is as good as any—and better than most!

I took this chamois in southern France, and it presented me with one of my most difficult mountain shots. It was a 400-yard shot, not all that far, but the combination of a small target and a stiff wind was a challenge. The rifle is a Kimber Mountain Ascent .270 Winchester and I used Hornady 130-grain American Whitetail ammunition. The hold was 18 inches into the wind and a bit high; the chamois went down with one shot.

and I've never owned a rifle chambered to any other 6mm cartridge. The 6mm Remington is slightly faster and some could say better. The .240 Weatherby is awesome, but uncommon and ammo is scarce. I think the new 6mm Creedmoor is a better cartridge than the .243 because it can handle the longer, heavier bullets now in vogue. But I don't have one and have no real use for one. Undoubtedly, I'll have another .243, but I've been too intermittent with it to consider it a real favorite.

I've hunted at least a little with *all* the factory .25-caliber cartridges from .25-20 to .257 Weatherby Magnum. I have a good Savage 1899 in .250 Savage that belonged to my late friend Joe Bishop, and a gorgeous Dakota in .257 Roberts, wonderful rifle. I love both of them and like the cartridges. Thing is, I'm just not a .25-caliber guy. I do like the faster .25s for medium-range hunting. However, I've noticed there's a break there: .25s don't hold up as well in the wind as 6.5mms and .270s. At one time I theorized that the .25-06 was the ultimate pronghorn cartridge. I was wrong, simply because of wind drift: In that limited application, the faster 6.5mms and the .270 Winchester are better. I'll probably take my next pronghorn with the .257 Roberts, not because it's the best choice, but simply because I like the rifle and want to use it more.

Although I have a 6.5mm Creedmoor (who doesn't?), it certainly isn't a favorite; it's just not fast enough. When I was a kid, I had a .264 Winchester Magnum, and I have a good one now. Even though I still like the .264, I'd be Don Quixote tilting at windmills if I tried to sell it as a favorite cartridge. I also have a 6.5-.300 Weatherby Magnum. Mine is very accurate and the 6.5-.300 is a screamer, although a bit over-bore capacity and finicky about powders. To me, in 6.5mm the formula for success is to get a (roundabout) 140-grain bullet to about 3,000 fps. The .264 will do this, but so will the wildcat 6.5-06, the 6.5-.284 Norma, the 6.5mm PRC, the new 6.5mm Weatherby RPM, and other non-standard cartridges.

Maybe someday one of those will become a favorite, but for now I default to Jack O'Connor. Before 1960, he correctly described the .264 as "not being able to do anything his .270 couldn't do." Without much more recoil, the .270 Winchester is faster, shoots flatter, and is more powerful and more versatile than the 6.5mm Creedmoor. Absent the longer-for-caliber and wonderfully aerodynamic 6.5mm bullets, my .270 is not as good a long-range cartridge as the faster 6.5mms. However, for *my* purposes, there's nothing any 6.5mm will do that I can't do with a .270. And that is why the .270 Winchester is a favorite.

A Tale of Two Sevens

Chapter 5

Bullet diameter .308-inch, what we call ".30-caliber," is America's most common and most popular caliber among big-game rifles and cartridges. Until the recent popularity of the accurate, mild-kicking 6.5mm Creedmoor, the 6.5mm (.264-inch) bullet diameter was primarily a European standard, with limited following in North America. But the 7mm (.284-inch) became popular on both sides of the pond, and is the bullet diameter of numerous excellent and effective cartridges of both European and American origin . . . so many that it's unlikely that anyone has meaningful experience with all of them.

I do not, certainly. I've had at least passing experience with most 7mm cartridges and have completely missed just a couple: I've never squeezed the trigger on a 7-30 Waters (a .30-30 necked down to 7mm developed by gunwriter Ken Waters). And I don't think I've ever laid eyes on a 7x61 Sharpe and Hart rifle. The 7x61 S&H was an excellent 1950s belted cartridge developed in America, but chambered by the Danish firm of Schultz & Larsen. Despite great potential, its thunder was quieted by Winchester's .264 Winchester Magnum in 1958, and then silenced completely by the 7mm Remington Magnum, introduced in 1962.

Other than those two, I've hunted with most 7mm rifle cartridges in all velocity ranges. The .280 Remington is an awesome cartridge, perhaps the most versatile hunting cartridge based on the .30-06 case. As I said in the previous chapter, if Winchester had adopted the 7mm-06 in 1925, the .270 Winchester might not exist, and I'd have less to write about. However, it's impossible to love all cartridges

My old friend and mentor Bert Klineburger took this Mongolian argali probably about 1982. Bert and his brother, Chris Klineburger, pioneered much of the Asian mountain hunting we enjoy today. Both were staunch 7mm fans; the rifle is a standard Remington Model 700 in 7mm Remington Magnum. To reduce baggage weight, Bert and Chris often shared this rifle. Lord knows how many sheep and goats it accounted for! (Photo courtesy of Robert Anderson)

equally. I've owned .280s and hunted with the cartridge quite a lot, but I find it too redundant of the .270, and, for larger game, not equal to the .30-06.

The 7mm Remington Magnum is a wonderfully versatile cartridge. I've hunted with it a great deal, have owned several excellent rifles so chambered, and I still have one. Although he had an awesome gun collection, my buddy Joe Bishop did almost all of his mountain hunting with an out-of-the-box Sako in 7mm Remington Magnum. Likewise, both Bert and Chris Klineburger, who opened up much of the Asian mountain hunting available today, were staunch 7mm magnum fans. In fact, to simplify things, they often traded one long-used and well-battered 7mm Remington Magnum between them.

I've also hunted with the fastest 7mm cartridges, including Layne Simpson's 7mm Shooting Times Westerner (STW), the 7mm Remington Ultra Magnum (RUM), and the speediest of all, John Lazzeroni's 7.21 (.284) Firebird. All are wonderfully effective, with surprisingly mild recoil for the performance. But I have owned none of these, and none of the fastest 7mm cartridges comes even close to being a genuine favorite.

My reasoning is not at all the same as Jack O'Connor's, who steadfastly stuck to his guns in insisting that the 7mm Remington Magnum couldn't do anything his .270 couldn't handle. I disagree. For now, 7mm bullets are available in a much greater weight range than .270 bullets (at least until the new 6.8 Western comes on line). Although there's only .007-inch (seven thousandths of an inch)

There are many 7mm (.284-inch) hunting cartridges at various velocities. I have used all of these and others, but I prefer the milder 7mms, usually stepping up to a .30 if I want more velocity. Left to right: 7mm-08 Remington; 7x57 Mauser; .280 Ackley Improved; 7mm WSM; 7mm Remington Magnum; 7mm RUM.

I took this huge South Texas whitetail in 1991 with a David Miller 7mm Remington Magnum. I used this and other 7mm Remington Magnum rifles a lot, all over the world. Remington's "Big Seven" is a great cartridge, but despite much happy use, I never managed to fall in love with it.

difference between .277 and .284, common 7mm bullets up to 175 grains place the faster 7mms in a slightly different class from the .270, which has traditionally maxed out with a 150-grain bullet.

My rationale for not including any of the fast 7mm cartridges among my short list of favorites is pretty simple: If you need that kind of speed and power, then I don't think the 7mms are as effective as the equally fast .30-calibers, offering more frontal area and greater bullet weight. In part this is because I have done so much African hunting, where size of game varies tremendously. In the more specialized world of mountain hunting, the faster 7mms make sense while, in Africa, a .30-caliber with 180- or 200-grain bullet makes *more* sense.

So, despite long and happy use and much confidence in them, I can't include any of the fast 7mms among my favorite cartridges. There are, however, two 7mm cartridges on my short list. Technically, just one: The 7x57mm (aka 7mm Mauser) is my favorite 7mm cartridge. But it's very difficult to write about the 7x57 logically and overlook the more recent and ballistically identical 7mm-08 Remington. So, in fairness, this must be a tale of *two* sevens.

Developed by Peter Paul Mauser and introduced in 1892, the 7x57 is the original 7mm rifle cartridge. It was among the first cartridges designed for smokeless powder, and is the oldest smokeless powder cartridge still in common use. Spain adopted the 7x57 in 1893; it would eventually be used by the militaries of some twenty countries. These include the two Boer republics in South Africa: Orange Free State and Transvaal. Anticipating hostilities with Great Britain, Transvaal's president, Paul Kruger, purchased 37,000 of the latest Model 1895 Mauser in 7x57 and some 40 million cartridges. Thus, in dual accidents of history, in 1898 U.S. troops faced 7mm Mausers in the Spanish-American War, and British troops faced them in the Second Boer War.

Both we and the Brits came away with healthy respect for the 7x57, and it quickly became a common sporting cartridge on both sides of the pond. In 1897, London gunmaker John Rigby obtained a twelve-year exclusive deal with Mauser for importation of Mauser actions and rifles into the United Kingdom, including Crown colonies. As part of this arrangement, and using the British convention of naming cartridges by land diameter rather than groove or bullet diameter, Rigby renamed the 7mm Mauser ".275 Rigby." There were no changes to the cartridge: 7x57, 7mm Mauser, and .275 Rigby are simply different names for the same cartridge, identical and fully interchangeable.

Rigby did introduce a high-velocity load with a 140-grain spitzer bullet rated at a very impressive 2,900 fps. I'd love to chronograph some of these cartridges! There was a time when American reloading manuals suggested such speed was practical (and safe). Today's manuals are more conservative, but you can still get pretty close. The

My first 7x57 Mauser rifle was this Mark Bansner on a left-hand Remington M700 action. I hunted with it quite a bit, taking various game including this nice Kentucky whitetail that turned out to be a tough crossing shot at a dead run.

fastest load I could find in a recent manual is in the *Nosler Reloading Guide No. 8*, suggesting a maximum load of 51.5 grains of RL19 yielding 2,892 fps for a 140-grain bullet in their 22-inch test barrel.

As .275 Rigby, the 7x57 has a long and rich history. It was the clear favorite of ivory hunter W. D. M. "Karamojo" Bell. Bell used a number of different rifles, and he most definitely *did not* take all of his thousand-plus elephants with the .275 Rigby. He also didn't use Rigby's fast load, writing that the barrel of his .275 was never "polluted by the passage of a soft-nose bullet." Bell used either the original 173-grain solid, or the British 175-grain, both round-nosed bullets. It's known that Bell hunted elephants with early 6.5mms, the .303 British, and .318 Westley Richards as well as the 7x57 and, after World War I, he used a .416 Rigby and a .400 Jeffery double. However, he took a lot of elephants with his .275s and definitely loved the cartridge. Over several decades, Rigby built him half a dozen .275s.

Jim Corbett owned only one, presented to him in 1907 for dispatching the notorious man-eating tigress of Champawat. Corbett used his .275 for the rest of his life, taking both man-eating tigers and leopards with it, although he preferred his .450/.400 double for tigers.

It's a stretch to say that the 7x57 ever became wildly popular in the U.S., but it quickly achieved a small and loyal following. After World War I, when bolt-actions began to slowly overtake the all-American lever-action, the 7mm Mauser was a standard chambering, though never as popular as the .30-06. Although certainly best known for championing the .270, Jack O'Connor was a big 7x57 fan. He used it to take the majority of his desert sheep between 1935 and 1946, and he owned one or another 7x57 rifle for the rest of his life.

My old friend Mike Ballew, longtime director of the NRA Whittington Center, used to manage the big Dye Creek ranch in northern California. In those days the place was overrun with both black-tailed deer and feral hogs. Mike is an astute rifleman, and not ashamed to admit he doesn't like recoil. For hunting blacktails, he always used a .243, .25-caliber, or 6.5mm, all perfect for these small-bodied deer. Wild hogs garnered more respect. Part of his job was

The 7x57 (a.k.a. the .275 Rigby) is perhaps most famous for its use on elephants by W. D. M. "Karamojo" Bell. While I haven't pushed the 7x57 quite that far, I did use my Ramirez 7x57 with 175-grain Barnes Super Solids to brain this big-body Argentinean water buffalo.

guiding pig hunters—lots of them. When guiding for hogs, Ballew would always pack a "big gun." His idea of a big gun was usually either a .270 or 7x57. It was about forty years ago that I borrowed his 7x57 to take a hog, the first animal I took with a 7x57. I decided I had to have one, and haven't been without at least one ever since.

Right now, I have three: A gorgeous Dakota Model 10 single-shot roll-marked .275 Rigby; a Ruger No. 1, and a Todd Ramirez bolt-action that we'll hear more about later. Unlike O'Connor, I have not used the 7x57 for mountain sheep. Unlike Bell, I have also not used the 7x57 for elephants. For really large game, and for situations where long shots might be required, I'm pretty sure there are better tools. That said, I have used the 7x57 a whole bunch, on all the continents, and for a wide variety of game. I have not used it for elk, although you surely could, but I've taken several red stags with it, a few pronghorns, numerous African antelopes of various sizes, a few sounders worth of wild hogs, and a lot of North American deer. It does its work with efficiency, little fuss, and very little recoil. To me, it is one of those cartridges that delivers performance far beyond what its paper ballistics might suggest.

Almost anything that I've said about the 7x57 can be said equally about the 7mm-08 Remington . . . except for the long history. Back in 1980, when the 7mm-08 was introduced, I was a junior editor at *Guns & Ammo*. Colleague Payton Miller and I took on the assignment of wringing out the new cartridge, in the plain-Jane Remington Model 788. Payton and I made several runs up the Central Coast trying hard to take a couple of hogs with the new cartridge. Oddly, we failed, and never managed to "blood" the new cartridge before the deadline.

Like most 788s, the rifle was extremely accurate, but Payton and I were both a bit perplexed as to the purpose and intent of the 7mm-08 cartridge. This was one of (many) times I got it wrong. Had we managed to take game with that rifle we might have thought differently about

The 7x57 has never been wildly popular in America, but it has long had (and still has) a loyal following. In 2019 Dan Guillory used a Winchester M70 to take the best buck of the season at my "Timber Trails" whitetail operation.

In 1988, I used a Steyr-Mannlicher 7x57 with Austrian Hirtenberger bullets to take a variety of game in New Zealand. This big red stag was literally knocked off its feet at 150 yards.

the 7mm-08. Within the year, we were up at Dye Creek with Chub Eastman, then with Nosler. Chub was shooting a 7mm-08 with the very first AccuTip bullets. On the first morning, Mike Ballew got him onto an exceptional boar, huge for the area. The 140-grain AccuTip from the little 7mm-08 (at moderate velocity) broke both shoulders, exited, and flattened the boar. Payton and I kind of looked at each other; maybe we'd misread the little 7mm-08!

Like the 7x57, the 7mm-08 is mild-mannered and effective, and it has advantages. First, it can be housed in a short action. Second, it is loaded to its full potential. The Sporting Arms and Ammunition Manufacturers Institute (SAAMI) has a maximum pressure specification of 61,000 pounds per square inch (psi) for the 7mm-08. The 7x57's SAAMI maximum pressure specification is 51,000 psi. So, even though the 7x57 has greater case capacity, factory loads don't approach full potential, and reloading manuals are increasingly conservative.

So, as currently loaded, the 7mm-08 is at least 100 fps faster than the 7x57; the 7mm-08 is standard with a 140-grain bullet at about 2,800 fps. Out of concern for older actions still in use, current loading manuals hold the 7x57 to lower pressures than the 7mm-08, so even with handloads the 7mm-08 wins the velocity race.

Since I don't consider either of them long-range hunting cartridges, the difference is not significant, and performance on game is pretty much the same. Although it was slow to catch on, the 7mm-08 is now more popular than the 7x57, with a better selection of factory loads.

It was primarily for this last reason that both of my daughters, Brittany and Caroline, have 7mm-08s. Both took their first game, California feral hogs, with a .260 Remington. A decade apart, both quickly switched to 7mm-08. Ammo availability was a factor but, also, perhaps as a matter of random bad luck, I experienced finicky accuracy with several .260 Remington rifles.

Other than tradition and nostalgia, the only real advantage the 7x57 might have over the more modern 7mm-08 is, with greater case capacity and fitted into standard (versus short) actions, that it does slightly better with heavy bullets. Left to right: 7x57 with 175-grain Barnes Super Solid; 7x57; and 7mm-08, the latter two with 140-grain Hornady GMX.

Caroline used New Zealand Chris Bilkey's Tikka 7mm-08 Remington to take this big red stag. A single 140-grain bullet did the trick nicely.

I got Brittany a Kimber 7mm-08, which has remained her "go to" rifle for nearly twenty years. Caroline is shorter than Brittany; when she got interested in hunting, all the potential rifles I had for her were stocked too long. She took her first animal with a "youth model" Ruger Model 77 in .260 Remington borrowed from August Harden. It worked and she liked it, so I got her one with a ridiculously hot-pink laminate stock. Unfortunately, in this particular rifle accuracy wasn't very good, so I rebarreled it to 7mm-08. Good call, and we haven't looked back. Like Brittany, Caroline has taken most of her game with the 7mm-08.

Between the 7mm-08 and 7x57, the 7x57 clearly wins on history and tradition. These are probably poor reasons to choose a cartridge, so whenever someone asks me what cartridge they should get for a new hunter, I consistently recommend the 7mm-08. The fact that it can be housed in a short action means a lighter, handier rifle, and this is important to shooters of smaller stature. It is also my impression that the 7mm-08 is, on average, the more accurate cartridge of the two. Again, this could be bad luck, but I've rarely seen a 7x57 that was spectacularly accurate, while I've encountered a lot of 7mm-08s that were tack-drivers. I'm sure that, in part, ammo for the 7mm-08 has seen much more intensive development than loads for the old 7x57, but the comparison has generally held with handloads as well as factory loads. The 7mm-08 is often more accurate, and certainly its shorter (and thus relatively fatter) case is more efficient.

The accuracy issue has rarely mattered to me. As hunting cartridges, I figure both need to be kept within 300 yards. Thus 1.25

Brittany on the sticks in Namibia with her Kimber 7mm-08. Both of my daughters have done most of their hunting with 7mm-08 rifles, which have light recoil and amazing performance.

Donna used her Dakota 7mm-08 to take this California hog just at sunset. Neither Donna nor I have used the 7mm-08 a great deal; she prefers the .270 and I prefer the 7x57, but we both have great respect for the 7mm-08.

or even 1.5 MOA groups are plenty good enough. Some 7x57s will do much better, and I *expect* better from a 7mm-08, and usually get it.

Aside from history and tradition, there is another area where the 7x57 wins, sort of. Although there are exceptions, most bolt-actions are short (sized for the .308 Winchester family of cartridges); standard (sized for the .30-06); or long (sized for the .375 H&H family). And, there are magnum actions for extra-large cartridges like the .416 Rigby. The 7mm-08 fits into a short action. The 7x57 does not; it requires a standard .30-06-length action. Technically, this action is longer than needed, so action space is wasted and more steel must be used.

However, the 7x57 was designed around a long, heavy-for-caliber 173-grain bullet. The 7x57 uses this bullet very well. And, with plenty of action length, it can also be used with modern long, heavy-for-caliber high BC bullets. The 7mm-08 really cannot; longer, heavier bullets must be seated deeply in order to fit into a short action, intruding into powder space and reducing velocity. Both cartridges work just fine with bullets from 140 to 150 grains, which are the weights I generally use. Only once, I used 175-grain Barnes Super Solids, a very long bullet, in the 7x57 to brain a water buffalo. So, if you have a yen to use extra-heavy bullets, the 7x57 wins.

Between the two cartridges, the 7x57 is definitely my favorite. The short-action advantage has never meant much to me, and while it may seem silly, I place value on nostalgia and tradition. As I said, right now I have three 7x57s, and I've owned and used others. Although I've equipped both my daughters with 7mm-08s (and recommended the cartridge to many), I've never actually owned a 7mm-08 rifle.

At an SCI show a couple of years ago, Duke McCaa at Gulf Breeze Firearms had a lovely Dakota M76 in 7mm-08 on consignment, with a slightly shortened stock that fit Donna perfectly. It took a few months to close the deal, but we bought it. So, it remains technically correct that I have never owned a 7mm-08. Instead, Donna has one, and hopefully she'll let me borrow it now and again. If not, I'm perfectly happy to keep on using my 7x57s.

The .30-06 Springfield

Chapter 6

Most successful military cartridges become popular sporting cartridges in the country (or countries) that used them, especially if an extended run as the service cartridge coincides with a significant local hunting market. The .303 British, for example, served as Great Britain's military cartridge from 1888 to 1957. As a rimmed cartridge, its popularity among hunters was somewhat hampered by its being chambered in few sporting rifles. Even so, the .303 was used by hunters throughout the British Empire, and is still frequently encountered wherever the Union Jack flew. The 7.65mm Argentine Mauser was in service from 1889 into the 1970s, and remains a standby among South American hunters. The 6.5x55 Swedish Mauser was used by the Swedish and Norwegian militaries from 1894 to 1995, and remains a standard choice among hunters in all the Scandinavian countries. The 8x57 Mauser was adopted by Germany in 1888 with a .318-inch bullet (8x57J), changed to .323-inch bullet (8x57S) in 1894. It remained in service through both world wars, and remains popular among German-speaking hunters.

The .30-06 was adopted by the U.S. military in 1906 and remained the primary rifle cartridge for U.S. forces for nearly fifty years. From the 1920s to the present, it has been one of America's most popular hunting cartridges, sometimes at the very top of the heap but always in the top few for sales of ammo, new rifles, and reloading dies. Although probably not the *most* popular sporting cartridge anywhere outside the U.S., the .30-06 is a world standard. It is available almost everywhere, chambered by almost all manufacturers of sporting rifles, and all manufacturers of sporting ammunition load it.

Most early smokeless military cartridges became popular sporting cartridges in and around the countries that used them, but only the .30-06 became a true worldwide standard. Left to right: .303 British (1888); 8x57 Mauser (1888); 6.5x55 Swedish Mauser (1894); .30-06 (1906).

In the U.S., our various deer are the most numerous, widespread, and available big-game animals. So, deer hunting is the most common use for the .30-06. In the 2020 Kansas rifle season, our deer hunter numbers were down a bit due to COVID concerns, but three of our ten hunters brought .30-06 rifles. Considering the tremendous number of suitable choices, that's a strong showing for a cartridge that, at this writing, is 115 years old.

So, the .30-06 is *still* popular, and still a great hunting cartridge. That said, it's needlessly powerful for deer-size game. It gets the job done, but I think it's a better cartridge for elk than for deer.

Like so many American shooters from the 1920s at least through the 1960s, my first centerfire rifle was a surplus 1903 Springfield. I think it cost $40, and in those innocent days it was ordered through the mail. The rifle was in great shape, but its World War II-era barrel had two-groove rifling. Kansas City gunsmith Howard Baucher rebarreled it with a new six-groove surplus military barrel for another ten bucks or so. I put it in a drop-in Bishop replacement stock, and added a Williams receiver sight on the rear bridge.

I didn't actually hunt with that rifle until some forty years later. My initial hunting was done with a .243. However, that old Springfield shot very well. It taught me how to shoot with aperture sights and, although it kicked hell out of teenage me, I loved shooting it.

In the mid-1970s, having been obsessed by Africa for years, I'd saved enough pennies and started seriously planning my first safari. I had a .375 for the big stuff and I certainly had suitable rifles for plains game. However, I decided I had to have a new rifle, and it must be a .30-06. I'd been reading about Africa much too much: Ernest Hemingway used a Griffin & Howe Springfield on his 1933 safari, and Robert Ruark used a Remington in .30-06 on his 1952

Thanks to its popularity, .30-06 loads have evolved over the last 120 years. Hornady's first run of .30-06 Superformance ammo with 165-grain bullet produced 3,016 fps, well into magnum .30 territory!

My first centerfire rifle was this partly sporterized Springfield .30-06 with aperture sight and drop-in Bishop stock. I didn't hunt with the rifle as a kid, but I used it many years later to take this big California boar.

safari that gave us *Horn of the Hunter.* Africa-struck kid that I was, I needed a .30-06.

So, in 1976, I trotted down to the Camp Pendleton PX and bought a Ruger Model 77 .30-06, complete with Ruger's Bicentennial rollmark. I topped it with my very first variable scope, a Redfield 3–9X. Variables weren't new, but at least through the 1960s they were widely distrusted, often showing significant shifts in point of impact as magnification was changed. Up until then, as my gunwriter heroes preached, I used fixed-power scopes, mostly 4X, but I also had a 3X Weaver and a Redfield 2.75X. For varmints, I'd been using a fixed 6X. In 1976 I'd never owned a riflescope with as much magnification as 9X.

On that first safari, I started out with some embarrassing misses. Harry Selby, telling Robert Ruark that everybody misses at first, said, "It's the light." Not true. It's the nerves! I wanted it so bad, and I started off shooting so poorly! Fortunately, I snapped out of it, completing the safari with a remarkable string of one-shot kills. That hunt was in Kenya; our first hunting block was up on Mount Kenya's forested slopes. At that point, most of my hunting experience had been in the American and Canadian West. I was neither familiar with, nor good at, shooting in thick stuff. Our second block was on the dry Tsavo plains south of Voi. This was more familiar habitat and some shots were fairly long.

I was shooting handloaded 180-grain Nosler Partitions, cooking along at 2,800 fps. The Partition was and is a great hunting bullet; at that time, it was just about the only "premium" hunting bullet available. I shot very well in the latter two-thirds of the safari, the Partition bullets performed wonderfully, and I thought the .30-06 was magic. From the perspective of forty years, I now appreciate that part of my success was based on my newfound scope magnification; you shoot better if you can see better! Some of the longer shots in Kenya might have been difficult at 4X, but they seemed quite simple with the 3–9X cranked up all the way.

So, there probably wasn't any magic, but I came off that first safari with tremendous respect for the .30-06, respect that I still have. It is

My first African safari, in Kenya in 1977, made me a lifelong believer in the versatility of the .30-06. This gerenuk probably presented the toughest shot of the safari: It's a small antelope and the distance was something over 300 yards (in pre-rangefinder days). The rifle is a 1976 Bicentennial Edition Ruger M77, which was unfortunately stolen in the early 1980s.

powerful, fairly flat-shooting, and usually accurate. But I think its longest and strongest suit is its wonderful versatility.

I don't carry that to extremes, although some have. In the 1950s, Grancel Fitz was the first person known to take all twenty-nine varieties of North American big game, using his Griffin & Howe Springfield .30-06. A generation later, my friend J.Y. Jones used a Remington .30-06 to accomplish the same feat, well-told in his book *One Man, One Rifle, One Land*. Both Fitz and Jones took all four North American wild sheep, the big bears, and bison, with their .30-06 rifles. Eleanor O'Connor took her one and only elephant, in Zambia, with a .30-06, using 220-grain solids. She also used the .30-06 for tigers in India. And, if you recall your Hemingway, on the *Green Hills* safari, Papa used his .30-06 for buffalo, rhino, and lions.

Sure, you *can*. But there are better tools for highly specialized situations. I haven't used the .30-06 for any of my sheep hunting, nor for big bears, and certainly not for thick-skinned African game. I have used it for a lot of elk hunting, as well as deer, black bears, caribou, pronghorns, and more. But here's the thing about North American hunting: Over here, we typically hunt our animals one at a time. If the one rifle you have happens to be a .30-06, you're in pretty good shape; remember the advantage held by the one-gun man! In North America we can sort of plot and scheme and dream about the perfect, ideal rifle for a given hunt. We are also not restricted in the firearms we can own, and we have perhaps the world's greatest availability of firearm choices.

Africa is a different situation. You may focus on certain key animals, but most African hunting areas have at least a dozen different varieties of antelopes of varying size. When you start out from camp you may know what you're looking for, but you have no idea what you might

The .30-06 probably isn't the perfect choice for caribou, but few cartridges are more versatile. I took this High Arctic Islands caribou on Victoria Island with a Savage .30-06. It was a bitter, subzero morning.

This nice Colorado 6x6 bull was the first elk I took with a .30-06 and using a Remington Custom Shop M700 with 165-grain Core-Lokt bullets. The .270 is probably a better mountain cartridge, but the .30-06 is an awesome elk cartridge.

actually encounter. This places a major premium on versatility. The rifle must be accurate enough, powerful enough, and have adequate range to take most anything you might encounter. Dangerous game is more specialized, but you can always have a cased heavier rifle in the truck "just in case." Your plains game rifle, however, must be capable of handling the full range of antelopes, plus pigs and zebras. Faster 6.5mms and the .270 are fine, various 7mms work, and provided you can handle the recoil, there's nothing wrong with choosing a magnum .30 or .33-caliber, or sticking with a .375.

There are many good choices, but since 1977 I have never found a *better* or more versatile choice for Africa's non-dangerous game than the .30-06. It is also a wonderful choice for hunting leopard. The only place I draw the line: I think the .30-06 is a bit on the light side for eland, Africa's largest antelope, which is much bigger than buffalo. I have seen eland taken cleanly with the .30-06 (and, for that matter, with the 7x57 and 7mm-08). Even so, if eland is on the menu, then I'd prefer to use a more powerful rifle.

The comparison between the .30-06 and .308 Winchester is similar to that between the 7x57 and 7mm-08, but not exactly the same. The .30-06 requires (and defines) a standard-length action. The .308 Winchester was developed as an experimental military cartridge, based on a shortened .30-06 case with the intention of using a shorter action, with lighter and more compact ammo, while giving up as little velocity as possible. In 1952, it was introduced as the .308 Winchester, five years before its adoption by the military as the 7.62x51mm NATO.

With greater case capacity, the .30-06 will always be faster than the .308. With heavier bullets, the difference will increase in short bolt-actions, semi-autos, and lever-actions simply because you run out of action space. That said, newer and more efficient powders have

The .308 Winchester, left, is based on a shortened .30-06 case. With less case capacity, the .308 cannot be as fast as the .30-06. However, despite 20 percent less powder capacity, the more efficient .308 case produces about 93 percent of the .30-06's velocity.

Ron Silverman, Chuck Herbel, and I are all smiles over this nice Timber Trails whitetail. Silverman is a true believer in the .308: He has four .308 rifles, shoots them all a lot, and has total confidence in the cartridge. So far, his numerous Kansas deer have required no tracking.

narrowed the gap. With bullets up to perhaps 180 grains, the velocity gap between the .308 and .30-06 isn't more than about 100 fps. Few game animals are likely to know the difference.

Once again, it's impossible to love all cartridges equally. I am a lifelong, die-hard .30-06 fan. I am *not* a .308 Winchester fan. However, in performance on game, there isn't enough difference to argue about. Again, the .30-06 does better with heavier bullets. In these days of extra-long, heavy, low-drag bullets, we're starting to see more .30-caliber bullets of 200 grains and heavier. With them, the .308 starts to fall behind. However, for most hunting purposes, there isn't much that can't be done with a good .30-caliber 180-grain bullet. If more is needed, maybe neither of these cartridges are the best choice.

The short magnum craze of the early 2000s convinced us of the efficiency of shorter, fat cases. Although rim and base diameter are the same, the .308 case is much shorter than the .30-06 case, thus relatively fatter. It is more efficient, producing more energy per grain of propellant. The .308 is also legendary for accuracy, while the .30-06 seems to have lost that reputation. It is my opinion that, on average, the .308 may be slightly more accurate than the .30-06. But I've never experienced accuracy problems with the .30-06, and I doubt I could prove the theory. Scott Rupp, Editor of *RifleShooter* magazine, used to be on the U.S. Army shooting team. I asked him about this. In his experience in international high-power competition, he didn't think there was a measurable accuracy difference between the two. Per Scott, some competitors preferred the .30-06 because of the velocity advantage.

Both the .30-06 and .308 have been used a great deal in competition. However, for hunting, I don't see either one as a long-range cartridge. In any discussion I can offer, the .308 is at a disadvantage because

My father, Bud Boddington, used this Bishop-stocked Winchester M70 Featherweight in .308 Winchester. Dating to the early 1950s, this rifle still produces marvelous groups.

I took this fine Saskatchewan whitetail at a bit less than 300 yards with a Jarrett .30-06 and a 150-grain Barnes X. The buck was moving across a snow field behind my blind; there was no time to range it, so I had to make a quick judgment and take the shot. As usual, the .30-06 worked just fine.

I've done relatively little hunting with it, certainly in comparison to my experience with the .30-06. I've taken game beyond 400 yards with the .30-06, never with the .308, but I've rung a lot of steel with both at much longer ranges. As I've often said, I'm not into shooting at game at extreme ranges. If I were, I doubt I'd choose either the .308 or the .30-06. Flatter-shooting cartridges make the job a bit easier, and deliver more energy on arrival.

With more velocity and retained energy, the .30-06 has more effective range than the .308, but not enough to take it into a different class. I'm so much a .30-06 fan, and so much *not* a .308 fan, that I've often overlooked the .308 Winchester. So, please remember I said it here: Whether distance or size of game, there is nothing the .30-06 will do that the .308 Winchester cannot do. And the .308 has the advantage of fitting into a short action, translating into a lighter, handier rifle with a shorter bolt throw.

Although he also had a Model 94 .30-30, my Dad did almost all of his big-game hunting with a Winchester Model 70 Featherweight in .308. I still have it, and it shoots exceptionally well. Although the weight savings are real, the shorter bolt throw of a short bolt-action has never been a big deal to me. I've never short-stroked a bolt-action, and the difference in cycling time is minuscule. So, my primary interest in the .308 Winchester has been in other actions besides bolt-actions. I've owned and used semiautos (AR10 and BAR) and lever-actions (both Winchester 88 and Savage 99) in .308 Winchester. There are semiautomatic sporters and lever-actions with actions long enough to house the .30-06, but they are uncommon. So, my personal interest in the .308 has primarily been in actions that cannot house the .30-06.

I used a Browning BAR semiauto in .308 to take this excellent free-range aoudad in Far West Texas. For mountain game, I much prefer the .30-06 to the .308—and I would rather use something faster and flatter shooting than either—but the .308 is an extremely versatile and powerful cartridge.

In the early 2000s, both Donna and I used this left-hand M77 in .30-06 to do a great deal of African hunting. After resting for a few years, it went back to Africa in 2019. Using a standard 180-grain Hornady Interlock load at 2,700 fps, it accounted for this fine Mozambique waterbuck at 275 yards.

Hey, I've already admitted that, between the two, my preference is the .30-06, but a lot of serious shooters prefer the .308, perhaps because it can be housed in shorter, lighter actions, has a bit less recoil, and (whether real or not) has a reputation for better accuracy. My old friend Linda Powell, long at Remington and more recently Mossberg, is a longtime .308 fan. She's not tall, so the short-action advantage is real to her. More important, she *knows* the .308 and shoots it well, most recently to make a very long shot on a Coues deer in Sonora.

Another friend, Ron Silverman, is a die-hard .308 fan and has *four* rifles so chambered. Recently he sent me a detailed and very cogent e-mail about *why* he uses the .308: "It is not the .308 *per se* that I like. I just got started on it years ago. Over twenty years, in many situations, I've learned the accuracy, drop, velocity, and energy with the .308. I know the recoil, I know what it does best, and what I dare not attempt. I have my pet loads; I've marked and tested my data every fifty yards all the way out. With all the variables addressed, if something goes wrong, I can figure out the problem pretty quickly: Scope, bullet, powder, etc. I own the .308 concept and all its variables; it's a whole world for me. And, I practice all the time with all four of my .308 rifles! I could be using the .270, .30-06, or .300 Winchester Magnum . . . in the final analysis, the round doesn't matter to me. That I know, understand, and can deal with the variables of the .308 makes my life of shooting very easy. When I get in the field I am *confident*. Yes, I could do the same things with a different cartridge but, like my father told me, "'If it ain't broke, don't fix it!'"

That's pretty good wisdom from a devoted "one-cartridge man." Ron hunts with us in Kansas, and *all* his deer are well-shot, no tracking required. He makes his .308 talk.

Despite its right-hand action, the Ruger .30-06 I had in Kenya remained my go-to hunting rifle for several years. It made it to Africa twice more before it was stolen, but I've had at least one or another .30-06 ever since. For some time I've been down to just one. It is also a Ruger Model 77, this one with left-hand bolt. During the years I was hosting the *Tracks Across Africa* TV series, I was spending a lot of time in Africa. Donna is also left-handed, but a few inches shorter than I am. I took a bit off the buttstock so she could use it, but not so much that it's disastrously short for me. Between us, we took a lot of African game with that rifle. Although we hadn't used it for several years, I took it to Mozambique in 2019. It performed perfectly, just like it always did.

In 1977, I used the toughest expanding bullet then available, the Nosler Partition. Since then, hunting bullet development has made tremendous leaps. In 1977 we had neither bonded-core hunting bullets nor homogenous-alloy expanding bullets. With today's best bullets, both the .30-06 and .308 perform better than ever.

Compared to .30-caliber magnums, they operate at mild velocities, so excellent bullet performance is routine. There aren't any "bad bullets" for the .308 or .30-06. For most of the filming we did for *Tracks*, Donna and I both shot plain old Hornady Interlock 180-grain lead-core bullets at 2,700 fps. Bullet performance was never an issue. Bullet choice is also about confidence, so if you prefer tougher bullets, be my guest. I've used Barnes X and TSX and Hornady GMX; various bonded-core bullets, including Swift A-Frame and Scirocco; Hornady InterBond; Nosler AccuBond; and Federal Trophy Tip. At .30-06 (and .308) velocities, there just aren't any bad choices, provided the bullets are *hunting* bullets, not match or target bullets. I've also used Sierra GameKing and Nosler Ballistic Tip, fairly soft bullets, with great performance. Likewise, good old Remington Core-Lokt and Winchester Power Points.

For deer hunting, I often shoot 150-grain bullets in both the .308 and .30-06. For elk and African plains game, I normally go on up the scale and use 180-grain bullets. Frequently, I compromise with the 165-grain bullet, a bit faster and flatter than the 180-grain load. In either cartridge, I don't think I've ever hunted with a bullet heavier than 180 grains, and I've never had any reason to.

Now, if I were shooting pachyderms or big bears, you bet I'd load up some heavyweights! Karamojo Bell's last story appeared in *American Rifleman* shortly before his death in 1954. The .308 Winchester was brand new; in this article he wrote that, if he could start hunting ivory all over again, he would choose a short-action .308 Winchester loaded with 220-grain solids. I suspect he might have run into magazine-box length problems in a short bolt-action. If extra-heavyweights are your interest, the .30-06 is superior. However, that is not why I prefer the .30-06. Other than its slightly higher velocity, I have no rational reason to prefer the .30-06 over the .308. It just happens to be my favorite.

The .300 Weatherby Magnum

Chapter 7

In my late twenties, I had a .300 Winchester Magnum on a right-hand Mauser Mark X action stocked in nice Bishop walnut, which was stolen before I ever got a chance to hunt with it. After the burglaries, I was short on rifles and, as the then-new editor of *Petersen's HUNTING* magazine, I was hunting quite a bit. After a stint as president of the Los Angeles Chapter of Safari Club, I was presented with a Weatherby Mark V in .300 Weatherby Magnum with left-hand action. For a time, it was the most versatile centerfire I had, so I used it quite a bit.

Starting over with my rifle collection after the burglaries, I'd made a conscious decision to switch to left-hand (or at least ambidextrous) actions, even though I was accustomed to right-hand bolts and could run them pretty fast. After all, I am left-handed. In the 1980s, availability of rifles in left-hand actions was increasing. So, when asked what rifle I'd like, I specified a *left-hand* Mark V, and never hesitated on the chambering. It had to be a .300 Weatherby Magnum, Roy Weatherby's flagship, and to my thinking the most versatile choice.

Nearly forty years later, I *still* think the .300 Weatherby Magnum is one of the most versatile of all hunting cartridges. Rationally, the same can be said of any of the fast .30-caliber cartridges. When I got my first .300 Weatherby, however, the universe of magnum .30s was smaller. The .300 Weatherby's parent cartridge, the .300 Holland & Holland, was still out there, and was (and still is) a great cartridge. At the time, I'd never seen one, and it would be many years before I used a .300 H&H. Winchester had introduced the .300 Winchester Magnum in

Elgin Gates, the 1960 Weatherby Award winner, took this fine addax in Chad in 1959. Like so many post-war, globetrotting hunters, Gates did much of his hunting with a .300 Weatherby Magnum. This rifle is a pre-Mark V custom Weatherby. (Photo courtesy of Robert Anderson)

1963, intending to replace the old H&H with a shorter, more efficient cartridge that could be housed in a standard-length action.

The .300 Winchester Magnum took off slowly for multiple reasons. The .300 H&H had plenty of history, in this country and around the world, and "replacing" it was offensive to traditionalists. Within months of its introduction, it was caught up in Winchester's disastrous 1964 decision to make changes to its venerable action. Veteran shooters were so outraged that nothing Winchester could do was right. Also, to wring maximum velocity out of its .30-06-length case, the .300 Winchester Magnum had a very short neck. This went against long-held cartridge design theory that stipulated a neck length of at least "one caliber" (meaning, in a .30-caliber cartridge, a neck of at least .308-inch) in order for the case to properly grip the bullet.

Purists argued that the .30-.338 wildcat (.338 Winchester case necked down to .30-caliber), though not as fast, was a "better" and more accurate cartridge. In 1960, one version of the .30-.338 was introduced as the .308 Norma Magnum.

By the 1980s, however, this mess was long past. The .300 H&H was nearly obsolete, and neither the .30-.338 nor .308 Norma Magnum had gone anywhere. The .300 Winchester Magnum wasn't nearly as popular as it is today, but it had become the "standard" fast .30, chambered by all major manufacturers.

The .300 Weatherby Magnum wasn't new, nor was it Roy Weatherby's first commercial cartridge; that honor goes to his .270

Left to right: .300 H&H, .300 Winchester Magnum, .300 Weatherby Magnum. The .300 Winchester Magnum was introduced in 1963 to replace the old .300 H&H. It took time, but the .300 Winchester Magnum eventually became the world's most popular "magnum" cartridge. The .300 Weatherby Magnum was never the most popular "magnum .30" and is no longer the fastest, but it's fast and versatile.

I have used the .300 Weatherby Magnum a great deal since 1983 in several different rifles. This is a standard Mark V, which I used to take a nice free-range stag in Argentina.

Weatherby Magnum. The majority of Roy's cartridges based on the blown-out .300 H&H case (some shortened) were developed in 1944-1945. We Americans love our .30-calibers, and the .300 Weatherby Magnum quickly became the favorite, with factory ammunition available starting in 1948. The .300 Weatherby Magnum is based on the full-length 2.825-inch .300 H&H case, body taper removed and with Roy's "double Venturi" curved shoulder.

My uncle, Art Popham, was a friend of Roy's; they hunted together in Yukon in the 1950s, and Art introduced me to Roy in about 1965. I was a gun-crazy teenager, pestering him with all manner of questions, which he answered with wonderful patience. Uncle Art's primary rifle was not a .300 Weatherby; rather it was a ".300 H&H Improved," with shoulder sharpened and body taper removed, very similar to Weatherby's cartridge.

Roy argued that his distinctive case shoulder enhanced the efficiency of the burning curve. Maybe, maybe not. He also typically chambered his rifles with an unrifled gap or "free bore" between chamber and rifling, to give the bullet a sort of running start before it entered the rifling. Advantages and disadvantages of free bore are still argued, but Roy Weatherby had one thing going for him: Early on, he partnered with the Swedish firm of Norma to make his ammo. Norma loads great stuff, but they also load to slightly higher pressures than American manufacturers are comfortable with. In the 1980s, with Norma ammo, the .300 Weatherby Magnum was *much* faster than the .300 Winchester Magnum—and nothing else came close.

Barrels always vary, but with the recommended 26-inch tube, Weatherby factory velocities were pretty darn close to specifications. Actually, as most handloaders must agree, it's very difficult to handload

Built by Lex Webernick of Rifles, Inc. on a left-hand, stainless Winchester M70 action, this .300 Weatherby Magnum was my "go-to" hunting rifle for many years. Its accuracy is exceptional, and this rifle never changes zero.

I have not been steadfastly loyal to the .300 Weatherby as I have dabbled with numerous other fast .30s. With good handloads, the old .300 H&H is amazing. I used it for this free-range sambar on New Zealand's North Island.

all the way up to the velocities the .300 Weatherby got with Norma factory ammo. In those days I was shooting and hunting almost exclusively with handloads. The first time I used that .300 Weatherby Magnum was in Zambia in 1983, using handloaded 200-grain Nosler Partitions. The largest animals I took with it were roan antelope, wildebeest, and zebra, with marvelous performance. That's what I expected, and although I was new to the .300 Weatherby, I already had great confidence in it.

The first time I had used a .300 Weatherby Magnum was a couple of years earlier, on a Colorado mule deer hunt with Ed Weatherby and Larry Thompson, using a borrowed Mark V. On a very cold, snowy morning, I was on one knob and we glassed a fine buck bedded on another knob on the far side of a flat valley. That was years before laser rangefinders; we studied the buck for a long time using the old (and not very effective) "football field" method. We figured we could fit about five football fields into the valley between us and the deer. So the distance was 500 yards and a bit of change.

I set up a good rest, and almost froze to death before the buck finally got up. Fortunately, he had a very large body, and when he rose and stood perfectly broadside. I'd been studying the shot for a long time but, since the actual distance was a guess, so was the holdover. The only thing in my favor: It was dead calm.

I was estimating three feet of bullet drop, so I held with a lot of daylight over the buck's shoulder. The bullet—I'm pretty sure it was a Partition spitzer—hit just at the very bottom of the heart, almost too low. Larry Thompson and I tracked the buck maybe 150 yards, finding him down, dead. OK, my guesses were educated. Even so, it was a very lucky shot that gave me a lot of confidence in the .300 Weatherby Magnum, confidence that I still have.

These are all awesomely fast .30-caliber cartridges; they are, from left: .300 Winchester Magnum; .300 Weatherby Magnum; .300 Jarrett (wildcat); .300 RUM; 7.82 (.308) Warbird. I have used all these and many other magnum .30s. The .300 Weatherby isn't the fastest and may not be the most accurate, but I have the most history with it and, thus, the most confidence.

No wild sheep in the world requires magnum .30-caliber power, but all hunting requires confidence. The tougher the hunt and the more difficult the shot, the more confidence you want. On the eleventh day of a ten-day hunt, I used a Rifles, Inc. .300 Weatherby Magnum to take this Wyoming bighorn.

Our spectrum of .30-caliber magnums has expanded since then. John Lazzeroni developed his families of short and long fat-cased magnums in the early 1990s, including his massive 7.82 (.308) Warbird; and short-cased 7.82 (.308) Patriot. The .300 Remington Ultra Magnum (RUM) was introduced in 1999, quickly followed by the .300 Winchester Short Magnum (WSM) and .300 Remington Short-Action Ultra Magnum (RSAUM); and the .300 Ruger Compact Magnum (RCM) a few years later. In recent years, we've had a bit of a break from the flood of brave new cartridges, but there's still a trickle, with recent introductions including the 30 Nosler and .300 Precision Rifle Cartridge (PRC). And more, including the .300 Blaser Magnum and .300 Norma Magnum.

I have messed with most of these. In velocities, the shorter-cased cartridges generally fall just one side or the other of the .300 Winchester Magnum. Lazzeroni's Warbird and the .300 RUM have more case capacity than the .300 Weatherby Magnum, and are faster. Both short and long, all of these cartridges are unbelted with fatter cases than the .300 Weatherby Magnum (and its parent, the .300 H&H), except for the .30-.378 Weatherby Magnum, which is much faster, and based on the big, belted .378 Weatherby case necked down. With no argument, I concede some of these are "better" cartridges. Whether faster or slower, fatter cases are more efficient, producing more energy per grain of powder burned. The unbelted cartridges' headspace on the shoulder is more precise than headspacing on the belt. These factors contribute to accuracy, so I concede further that, on average, across a selection of rifles, the newer unbelted .30-caliber magnums are likely to be more accurate. Note: You might have to work hard to prove this. In my experience, quality of barrels, consistency of ammunition, rigidity of action, and bedding are *all* more important to raw accuracy than case design.

Terry Moore and I with a good Montana pronghorn. My Rifles, Inc. .300 Weatherby Magnum was fairly new when I went on this hunt. I already had a lot of confidence in the .300 Weatherby cartridge, so when I made a clean shot at 500 yards—the only shot possible—I gained equal confidence in the rifle.

I took this fine Quebec-Labrador caribou in 2011 with my Rifles, Inc. .300 Weatherby Magnum. This level of power isn't needed for caribou, but on the open, windy tundra, a fast .30-caliber is never a bad choice.

No matter. I have stuck to the .300 Weatherby Magnum as my preferred fast .30. Until Roy Weatherby's passing in 1988, no centerfire Weatherby rifle was chambered to anything other than Weatherby Magnum cartridges, and the major manufacturers respected his propriety to his cartridges and ammunition. Other than custom rifles, the Weatherby Mark V was the only factory rifle chambered to the .300 Weatherby Magnum (and other Weatherby magnum cartridges), and Weatherby's Norma-made ammo was the only source for factory ammo. Since then, much has changed. The Weatherby Vanguard has long been available in several Weatherby and non-Weatherby cartridges; numerous rifle manufacturers have chambered rifles to some Weatherby magnums, and the most popular Weatherby cartridges (especially the .300) are loaded by multiple ammunition manufacturers.

I've never owned a Vanguard in .300 Weatherby Magnum (they come in right-hand bolt only), but I've owned several Mark V .300s in various configurations. All have shot well. With apologies to Roy's memory, and to his successors, my friends Ed and Adam Weatherby, not all of my .300 Weatherby Magnums have been Weatherby rifles.

In the mid-1990s, Lex Webernick of Rifles Inc., then in Utah but long since relocated to Texas, built me a .300 Weatherby Magnum on an uncommon left-hand Model 70 Classic long action in stainless steel. We discussed the rifle quite a bit. Already quite deaf enough, I didn't want a muzzle brake, so I didn't want the rifle too light. He put a medium-contour 26-inch barrel on it, fluted it, and stocked it in a plain, classic-style synthetic stock. This rifle has been both a friend and a favorite, used on a number of important and memorable hunts.

So, why did I have that rifle built in .300 Weatherby? Well, as I said, I'd never seen an accuracy problem with a Mark V in .300 Weatherby.

The Lazzeroni 7.82 (.308) Warbird is the fastest commercially available .30-caliber; it is significantly faster than the .300 Weatherby. While I have used it quite a bit and like it, it hasn't reached "favorite" status. In 2001, I used a 7.82 to take this blue sheep in China at an elevation of 18,000 feet.

The twist-horned markhors are the mountain hunter's Holy Grail. I took this Suleiman markhor in western Pakistan's Torghar Hills and near the Afghan border. I again used my Rifles, Inc. .300 Weatherby Magnum to make a long, tough downhill shot.

The Rifles Inc. rifle didn't disappoint; it's a tack-driver, capable of half-MOA accuracy on good days. Today I also have a super-accurate Kenny Jarrett .300 Winchester Magnum that we'll hear about later. I have had a couple of .300 H&H rifles and, with good handloads, the capability and accuracy of the old .300 H&H are amazing. Also, the smooth feeding of that long, tapered case is marvelous. I have a Lazzeroni rifle in the big Warbird cartridge, which is accurate and definitely the velocity king of all .30 calibers.

Even so, I always come back to the .300 Weatherby. Most important: I'm familiar and comfortable with it, and I have years of handloading recipes to fall back on. As with the 7mm-08 versus the 7x57 and the .30-06 versus the .308, today I'm pretty well convinced that the small velocity edge the .300 Weatherby Magnum has over the .300 Winchester Magnum and the various short .300s isn't enough to matter much. Likewise, the velocity edge that the faster .30 calibers offer over the .300 Weatherby isn't enough to alter their capabilities. The important thing about trajectory isn't a few inches over several hundred yards; it's that you *know* your cartridge's trajectory, can calculate the solution, and have the confidence to make the shot.

I know the .300 Weatherby well, and I have used that Rifles Inc. .300 Weatherby on a lot of wonderful hunts. It was fairly new when Terry Moore, then with Leica, and I took it on a really fun hunt through South Dakota, Wyoming, and Montana. As in many hunting situations, most shots were simple, but I had one 500-yard shot on a Montana pronghorn, a really nice buck. This time, thanks to the laser rangefinder, I knew the range, and I knew the trajectory.

Within the next year or so, I drew a Wyoming bighorn tag and I took the Rifles Inc. .300 Weatherby. It was a tough horseback hunt, cold with lots of snow, and although we saw lots of sheep, we couldn't find any mature rams. One morning my horse zigged and I zagged, and I landed in an area covered with soft, fluffy snow—except for one rock. I finished the hunt taped up with two broken ribs. On the tenth (and theoretically last) day, outfitter Ron Dube went one way and I went another, glassing from different ridges. I spotted Ron signaling to me, and he met me on the horse trail, saying ceremoniously, "The hunting portion of this Ron Dube adventure is concluded. We now proceed to the harvesting."

He'd spotted the unlikely combination of two mature rams and one ewe, way down low. We made a cold camp that night, huddled in horse blankets, and found the sheep bedded in late morning. At 265 yards, the shot was not difficult, and .300 Weatherby power is not essential for any wild sheep. But you'd better have the confidence to make the shot. Over the next few years, I used that Rifles Inc. .300 Weatherby on several mountain hunts in Asia. It made a very long shot on Dagestan tur in Azerbaijan, and that's the rifle I used in Pakistan's Torghar Hills for a Suleiman markhor, one of my most memorable hunts. That shot was 393 yards, but angled steeply downhill, a tough shot.

I took this fine Punjab urial with the Blaser R8 in .300 Weatherby Magnum. Urials are the smallest of the world's wild sheep and do not require such power, but they are small targets and the range can be long.

Early in 2010, I attended a press event introducing the Blaser R8, which we'll also hear about later. I'd used the older R93 and thought it was a great rifle, but I hadn't fallen in love with it. I was headed to Nepal in March, and I was impressed enough by the R8 that I asked to take a loaner R8 on the hunt. The chambering was .300 Blaser Magnum, its velocity falling between the .300 Winchester and Weatherby Magnums. Right out of the box, accuracy was spectacular.

That hunt in Nepal was, easily, my favorite mountain hunt. Tough and high, you bet, but we caught glorious early spring weather, with wildflowers just coming into bloom, and we had a crew of two dozen Sherpas carrying a very comfortable camp. After a two-day trek into the game reserve, we started hunting Himalayan tahr at timberline, about 12,000 feet. I drew a tough shot, about 470 yards, with a strong cross wind. The animal was facing left to right, the wind coming downhill on his tail. I held a little daylight right of the tail, and hit him well on the shoulder.

From there we trekked on uphill, hunting blue sheep at about 16,000 feet. Glassing from one ridge, we found a group of rams on another ridge, just over 500 yards away. The wind was howling on our ridge, so we thought it was an impossible shot, except the grass in the valley below us suggested the wind was much less in between. One ram looked exceptional, and it was much the same shot as I had on the tahr: the animal facing left, wind from left to right. I gave it a little more daylight, and the ram made a few steps and went down.

Oh, yes, I liked that rifle, and I was just fine with the .300 Blaser cartridge. However, Blaser and ammo partner Norma decided not to

My Blaser R8 initially had a .300 Blaser Magnum barrel. When the decision was made to not market the Blaser magnums in the U.S., I immediately traded it for a .300 Weatherby Magnum barrel. For ten years, the R8 in .300 Weatherby Magnum accounted for most of my mountain game.

I was in Mongolia's Altai Mountains in September 2018 when I realized that I might just have taken the ram of my lifetime . . . and I had. Despite my long familiarity with the .300 Weatherby Magnum, I taped a simple range chart to my stock . . . just in case!

market the .300 Blaser Magnum in the United States, and that meant endless headaches obtaining ammo. And, as a gunwriter, there's really not much sense in using and writing about unavailable cartridges. This is why I've never done much with non-standard cartridges, whether wildcat or proprietary. It seems to me we have enough cartridges to choose from and, somewhere in that vast array, there must be a factory cartridge that will do most anything anybody needs to do. By then I liked the Blaser R8 enough that I bought it, but I traded the .300 Blaser barrel for—naturally—a .300 Weatherby Magnum barrel.

If I'd thought it through, possibly I would have "settled" for a .300 Winchester Magnum barrel instead. Two reasons: First, the Blaser barrel was 24 inches. With its longer case and larger powder charge, the .300 Weatherby struts its stuff best with a 26-inch barrel. Second, with newer powders, and the load development that goes with more popular cartridges, the velocity gap between the .300 Winchester Magnum and .300 Weatherby Magnum isn't what it was thirty years ago . . . and, in the shorter barrel, I wasn't going to get full .300 Weatherby velocity anyway.

These things never occurred to me. I was, and am, comfortable and confident with the .300 Weatherby Magnum, and I saw no reason to change. Again, the .300 Weatherby isn't supposed to be as accurate as the "modern" unbelted .30-caliber magnums, but, again, case design isn't the most critical factor in accuracy.

I'm not saying I could win benchrest matches with any .300 Weatherby Magnum, but the Blaser barrel in .300 Weatherby Magnum has been consistently accurate (like all Blaser barrels I've seen), easily capable of sub-MOA groups when I do my part. Since 2011 I've used it a lot, on several African hunts (where the switch-barrel capability is useful), and for what may well be the last of my Asian hunting. These days, I'm mostly using Hornady's aerodynamic 200-grain ELD-X, mostly in the excellent Precision Hunter load. Between the 24-inch barrel and heavier bullet, it's not as fast as some loads. It's rated at 2,960, and I'm actually getting 2,900. But trajectory is just a number, and I know the number.

In 2018, Donna and I, and Joe and Sara Bishop, planned a grand hunt in Mongolia, to include multiple argalis, ibex, and wapiti. Uncharacteristically, Joe forsook his beloved Sako 7mm Remington Magnum, and worked up handloads for a new .300 Weatherby Magnum, thinking he might like an extra edge for the largest of all wild sheep. Sadly, Joe's cancer returned. He was unable to go, and passed away three months later. At his insistence, Donna and I went, and my Blaser with its .300 Weatherby Magnum barrel performed perfectly . . . as it always has, and as the .300 Weatherby Magnum always will.

THE .338 WINCHESTER MAGNUM

CHAPTER 8

Amazing things happened on Donna's Day of the Bear. Specifically, on her Alaskan brown bear hunt that we'd planned for a long time. It was a great experience, but it was over on the first day. Well, that happens. First day is as good as the last, and vice versa. When Mother Nature smiles, it's best not kick sand in her face.

My first brown bear hunt was similar: I got an awesome bear on the first day. I was young and full of . . . *whatever.* Having never before seen an Alaskan brown bear, I wasn't ready to shoot and tried to pass. Fortunately, my guide was good enough, confident enough, and strong enough that he wasn't having any of that. He *knew* what he'd seen. Nearly forty years later, that's a hunt I'd like to do again, but I will never again see a bear as big as I saw in October 1981, just a few hours into the hunt.

But back to Donna's Day of the Bear in May 2013. We were in a little skiff passing the southern tip of Admiralty Island, guide and outfitter Alisha Rosenbruch-Decker (aka "Mutts") at the helm. There was a black dot on a distant beach. It was too choppy to use binoculars. We were headed around the point to a different area, but Mutts immediately turned toward shore.

I glanced around a couple minutes later and she was sharpening knives while steering, her eyes gleaming. That got my attention. "Uh, you're serious about this bear?"

"Oh, yes, that's a ten-foot bear. We're gonna get him if we can." So, that was the first oddity of that amazing day: A quick glimpse from more than a mile offshore, and she was *sure*. It was the most confident and competent instant assessment I've ever seen.

Outfitter Alisha Rosenbruch-Decker, Donna, and I with Donna's massive Alaskan brown bear. Donna took her bear on the southern tip of Admiralty Island using a Proof Research .338 Winchester Magnum. Alisha was concerned about the adequacy of the .338. I agree that the .375 is "better" for the biggest bears, but the .338 works!

Donna was shooting a Proof Research .338 Winchester Magnum, very accurate, and she was shooting it well. When we were checking zero a day earlier, Mutts had commented: "You know, we ask for a minimum of .375 on brown bears." We'd missed that in the fine print, and now it was a little late.

Other than rocks and some driftwood, the beach we were approaching was perfectly clear. But the forest beyond was dark, dense, and ominous. I understood. Nobody wants a wounded bear in that stuff. Alisha was packing a Blaser with a .416 barrel, so I told her, "If you're concerned, back her up." That was a mistake; this was not my hunt, and it was not my business. Being an observer is very hard, and the toughest part is keeping my lip zipped.

The bear was beachcombing. My job was to hold the boat off the rocks while the ladies, in their waders, made the stalk. We found a spot a couple hundred yards out where I could steady the boat while they climbed out.

I had my hands full keeping the boat from *clanking* against rocks in the light swell. I watched while they waded from rock to rock, wind good, closing the gap. Nothing now but to say a little prayer while they set up over twin rocks, Donna on the left, Mutts on the right. The shot was something over a hundred yards, not far. I held my breath.

The bear was quartering away slightly and the shot looked good, behind the on-shoulder into the off-shoulder. The bear rocked with the impact, took a step, and went down hard on his chin, so hard that he dropped out from under Mutts's rifle and her shot went over the top. And that was that. Donna shot again for insurance, but the bear didn't move.

We laid out the hide on clean gravel, and it was ten feet on the nose, no stretching or cheating, huge for the ABC islands. Mutts's assessment

The .338 Winchester Magnum, right, was introduced as a companion to the .264 in 1958. The .264 came in as a version of the Winchester M70 called the "Westerner." The .338's version of the M70 was the "Alaskan," suggesting the game for which the cartridge was designed.

I took this Roosevelt elk with a .338 built by Brown Precision and a 210-grain Partition. Bullets from 200 to 225 grains are fine for elk and lighter game, but for larger game I much prefer 250-grain bullets, which are slower but much harder-hitting.

was the most perfect judgment I've ever seen on a game animal, and it was done from a moving boat at a couple thousand yards.

Later, Mutts told us that they'd had bad experiences with the .338, and this was the first bear shot with a .338 they hadn't had a problem with. I figure this is mostly bad luck. For big coastal bears, I agree the .375 is *better*, but I can't accept that the .338 isn't enough gun . . . as proven with this big boar.

In 1958, the .338 Winchester Magnum was introduced in a version of the Winchester Model 70 called the Alaskan. It's ideal for moose, but I'm pretty sure Winchester's engineers also had brown bear and grizzly in mind when they created the .338. The parallel development was the .264 Winchester Magnum, in the M70 Westerner. The .264 took off like a rocket, but fizzled, especially when Remington introduced the 7mm Remington Magnum in 1962. The

.338 took off slowly because people found out quickly that the .338 *kicked* . . . and not a lot of people needed that level of power.

So, the .338 sort of smoldered along. In time, hunters who needed it accepted the recoil that comes with a heavy bullet at significant velocity. It is popular in both Alaska and Canada among moose and bear hunters, and became a standard among serious elk hunters throughout the West. Trust me, deer hunters don't need it, and although it shoots flat enough for mountain game, sheep and goat hunters definitely don't need it.

Elmer Keith was the major (and most outspoken) champion of the .33-caliber, considering it the "minimum" for elk. He started out using the British .333 bullet (for the .333 Jeffery), but later moved to the American .338, I assume because of better bullet availability. Keith was involved in wildcatting several good .33-caliber cartridges,

Left to right: a .338 Winchester Magnum and a .416 Rigby. I believe a .338 paired with a .416 makes an ideal African battery, but, perhaps because of recoil, few PHs seem to agree. I think the combination provides versatility, power, and just enough redundancy.

Elmer Keith suggested .33-calibers as ideal for deer-size game. This is not true, but provided one can withstand the recoil, fast .33s are unusually versatile. Here, Jack Atcheson Jr. and I pose with a Montana mule deer, flattened with a .338. Atcheson uses his .338 for just about everything, including sheep and goats.

starting with the .333 OKH (Charlie O'Neil, Elmer Keith, and Don Hopkins) on the .30-06 case. Eventually, with Bob Thomson, he created the .338-.378 Keith-Thomson on the massive .378 Weatherby Magnum case. This mighty beast, with slight changes, became the factory .338-.378 Weatherby Magnum in 1998. Keith might have approved, but by then he was long gone.

An interim Keith development was the .334 OKH, using a .338-inch bullet on a shortened .300 H&H case. This sounds suspiciously similar to the .338 Winchester Magnum. Oddly, I don't remember Keith waxing eloquent over the .338 Winchester Magnum, even though it seemed to answer his mail. Having known Elmer, but not wanting to be unkind, I'm a little suspicious. Maybe it was just because it wasn't his idea. Or maybe the .338 just wasn't fast enough to match his concept. The .338 Winchester Magnum is a very credible cartridge, propelling a 250-grain bullet at nearly 2,700 fps. With like aerodynamics, trajectory will be similar to the .30-06 with a good 180-grain bullet, perfectly adequate for quarter-mile shooting, especially at elk-size targets. However, that's nothing like what the .338-.378 can do with a 250-grain bullet up to 3,000 fps.

I've always been very happy with 250-grain bullets in the .33s. After all, a 250-grain .338 bullet has a sectional density (SD) of .313, which is better than the 300-grain .375 bullet's SD of .305. This suggests, all things being equal, that the 250-grain .338 will penetrate at least as well as the 300-grain .375. Elmer definitely preferred heavier bullets, and they have long been available. Winchester had a 300-grain .338 factory load for some time, not popular because it was slow, but heavier component bullets in .338 diameter have been around at least since the 1960s. So, I don't know what Elmer's beef

Jack Atcheson Jr. and I were in Botswana's Okavango in 1985 when I took this Zambezi sitatunga using a left-hand Brown Precision .338 Winchester Magnum with a 210-grain Nosler Partition bullet. While Jack has used his .338 all over the world, I have not, but I consider the .338 among the most versatile of all cartridges.

Dave Leonard and I with a big Alaskan grizzly that I took with a Kimber in .325 WSM. It worked, but I believe the .338 Winchester Magnum would have performed better with its higher velocity, more bullet weight, and greater frontal area.

was with the .338 Winchester Magnum (if there was one). Doesn't matter, because this is my story, not his!

In the mid-1980s, Chet Brown made me a lovely .338 Winchester Magnum on a left-hand Remington action, dolled up a bit with a Sako extractor in one of his early synthetic stocks. It was fairly light, handled like a dream, and I used it a lot for moose, elk, caribou, deer, black bears, and I took it to Africa several times.

I don't often think of the .338 as an African cartridge, but that depends on what you're doing and what you pair it up with. If you can kill a big bear with a .338, and you surely can, then you can kill a buffalo with one. Again, going back to the sectional density comparison, a 250-grain .338 will penetrate as well as a 300-grain .375. Load up 275- or 300-grain bullets, and it will penetrate better. A Namibian game ranger who handled PAC elephants in and around Etosha National Park told me he used a .338 with 300-grain solids, and those are large-bodied elephants. I shot just one buffalo with a

.338, using a 250-grain Swift A-Frame, and it was down and dead on the spot, no insurance needed.

There is just one major issue: In a lot of jurisdictions, the .338 is not legal for buffalo. It's often stated that the legal minimum is .375. This is not always true; some countries don't have legal minimums for various types of game and, of those that do, the minimum is more likely to be the European 9.3mm (.366-inch) rather than .375. However, if there's a minimum, then whatever it is, it must be observed. So, on safaris where dangerous game is on the menu, the .338 may not be legal, so you can use it for plains game, but you have to pair it up with something else for dangerous game.

I'd feel silly pairing up a .338 with a .375; the two are just too similar and redundant in performance. In both of my *Safari Rifles*

The selection of fast "medium magnums" isn't large. Left to right: .325 WSM; 8mm Remington Magnum; .338 Winchester Magnum; .338 RUM; .340 Weatherby Magnum. I have used all these and more, and I believe in them. The .338 Winchester Magnum isn't the fastest, but it's the most popular, combining power with acceptable recoil.

I also had a significant fling with the .340 Weatherby Magnum. Faster and flatter-shooting than the .338 Winchester, it's a fine cartridge. The problem with all the fastest .33s is severe recoil, but if you can handle them on a sustained basis, they're awesome. I took this Kamchatka brown bear with the .340 Weatherby Magnum and a single 250-grain Partition bullet.

books, I suggested that a .338 paired with a .416 (or similar) might make a perfect two-rifle safari battery. Only a couple of the PHs surveyed agreed, but I still think that makes a wonderful match: Major separation of power, but a bit of redundancy in a pinch. I've used the .338/.416 battery a couple of times, and it's pretty effective. The .338 is a powerful cartridge, and using it in Africa as the "light" rifle assumes you can shoot it well. Too many PHs see hunters show up with rifles they fear and don't shoot well; it's possible that for them, alarm bells go off when clients bring anything above .30-caliber, especially for plains game.

So far, I've pretty much limited this discussion to the .338 Winchester Magnum, which is a longtime favorite. However, I haven't been loyal or steadfast, so I need to expand this discussion to the class of "medium" cartridges between .30-caliber and 9.3mm or .375. Man, I have messed with a *bunch* of cartridges in this arena. I spent a *lot* of time with the 8mm Remington Magnum. It's a wonderful cartridge, obviously with much more case capacity than the .338, thus potentially higher velocity. The 8mm I used most had a 28-inch barrel, so I was getting the full velocity. I took it to Africa a couple of times, on several Asian mountain hunts, and it accounted for multiple bull elk on this side of the pond.

With the long barrel and an aerodynamic 220-grain bullet, I'm pretty certain it's a better long-range elk rifle than any .338 ever made. But I go through these phases; sometimes they last for years. Sooner or later, I come to my senses and am honest with myself. I'm *not* an extreme-range hunter; it's fun on the range, but not my thing in the field. When I was a kid, long before rangefinders, an honest 400-yard shot was a pretty long poke. Still is, but with the tools we have today, 400-yard shooting is often practical. When conditions allow, I'm okay with pressing a couple hundred yards beyond that, provided the equipment and shooter are set up for it. But, regardless of what we read and see on TV, I'm not going to snipe at an unwounded game animal at 700 or 800 yards. Never have, never will.

By careful study of charts, and by using the extra-long barrel with max handloads, I had the 8mm set up to deliver a ton of energy at 600 yards, which no .338 Winchester can ever do. However, I missed the only *really* long shot I ever attempted with the 8mm—I shot right over the top of the biggest bull elk I've ever had a chance at, something just over 500 yards. My fault, not the rifle's, but I'm pretty sure I would have made that shot with one of my .300 Weatherby rifles. So, it's a *faux pas* that still haunts me. Fortunately, there aren't many like that, otherwise I'd never get any sleep at all.

Although beautifully stocked, that 8mm was long. That didn't bother me, nor did the recoil; the gun was heavy, and I had a mercury tube in the butt to counterbalance the long barrel. Eventually, though, the weight did bother me. The rifle weighed about twelve pounds, too much to carry in tough country. Also, there's the matter of bullets. The 8mm has never been popular in America, so bullet selection has always

I shot this massive Livingstone's eland in Zambia in 1996 with an 8mm Remington Magnum. Around the turn of the millennium, I used the 8mm Remington Magnum a great deal. An underrated cartridge, it may be a better elk cartridge than the .338, but with limited bullet selection, it's just not as versatile.

been limited. We got a boost when the 8mm Remington Magnum was new back in the late 1970s, and another small boost in the early 2000s thanks to the .325 WSM (also a darned good cartridge). But most of the available bullets are 180 to 200 grains, with just a shrinking handful of 220-grain bullets. Col. Charles Askins was America's greatest 8mm proponent, and even Charlie lamented that the fastest 8mms really needed good, heavy bullets in the 250-grain range. With today's low-drag projectiles, I can shoot bullets from 200 to 225 grains (and beyond) in my fast .30s. Thanks to greater popularity and proliferation of .338 cartridges, including fast numbers like the .338 Lapua, the .338 offers a wide and rich bullet selection, while the 8mm is sharply limited. The 8mm Remington Magnum is still an effective and much underrated cartridge, but it makes even less sense today than it did when I was using it a lot, a period that ended twenty years ago.

Now, I've said that there isn't much you can't do with a fast .30-caliber. This is true, but I'm a believer in frontal area (as was Elmer Keith). Larger-diameter bullets transfer more energy on impact and therefore "hit harder." Our standard metric of foot-pounds of energy relies heavily on velocity, and bullet diameter is not part of the equation. Elmer Keith liked "pounds-feet" or momentum as a substitute for foot-pounds, but this seems more applicable to handgun cartridges. John Taylor's "Knock-Out" values consider caliber, but were intended to reflect the initial blow of a solid, non-expanding bullet. With expanding bullets, you need a subtle blend of penetration, expansion, and weight retention. To my knowledge we *still* have no index to reflect and properly compare these things, but I remain convinced that, given a proper blend of penetration, expansion, and weight retention (and always with appropriate shot placement), larger-caliber bullets hit harder.

It's a point that is almost impossible to prove, but especially with bullets at similar velocity, I'm convinced the 8mm (.323-inch) bullet hits harder than a .308-inch bullet, and .338-inch bullets hit even harder, and transfer more energy upon impact. This is not important with deer-size game. A .30-caliber slug is a big bullet on any deer. It becomes more important on elk and big bears, which are larger and tougher than deer. It is also important with Africa's plains game, because of the great size variance. For me, it has also seemed important on medium-size animals that are especially tough, such as black bears and wild swine.

I have a long history with "medium" cartridges between .30 and .375. My multiple flings with the 8mm are just part of this. I also love the .35-calibers, a bullet diameter that is mostly an American phenomenon. Some .35s are limited in range (and utility) either by velocity or sighting equipment. However, at ranges appropriate for the cartridge and its rifle platform, I'm absolutely certain the .35s hit noticeably harder than lesser calibers, even if velocity and energy are considerably less.

I like the old .348 Winchester, even though its Winchester Model 71 platform is primarily limited to iron sights. I haven't used the .35 Remington much, but it's a legendary deep-woods deer

I used a Proof Research in .338 Winchester Magnum to take this good black bear. For the biggest bears, the .338 is probably "on the edge," but it's a wonderful choice for black bears which, at their largest, are as big (or bigger) than most interior grizzlies.

cartridge. I've used the .358 Winchester quite a bit, an underrated cartridge with mild recoil and velocity allowing use to perhaps 250 yards. At first blush, I'm impressed by Winchester's new .350 Legend, designed for use in the formerly "shotgun only" deer states that now allow straight-wall centerfire cartridges. The Legend uses 9mm (.357-inch) bullets, and is AR-compatible. A bit faster than the .35 Remington, it's a 200-yard deer cartridge. Because I apply for permits in now straight-wall states, I have a .350 Legend in a Mossberg Patriot bolt-action. I've taken several feral hogs with it and, like all the .35s, it hits hard with a resounding *whack* when the bullet strikes.

The .35 Whelen is easily the most versatile .35, capable of meaningful velocity with 250-grain bullets. It is effective and powerful, yet recoil is mild. I've used it for moose and elk as well as hogs and black bears, and I keep threatening to take a .35 Whelen to Africa, but I have not. The almost-obsolete .350 Remington Magnum is much the same in power and performance as the Whelen, but can be housed in a short bolt-action for a shorter, lighter rifle.

Missing from the mix is a readily available "fast" .35. There have been some in the past. The .350 Griffin & Howe on the .375 H&H case was loaded by Western in the 1930s, and the .350 Rigby Rimless Magnum (1908) was popular for a time. The belted .358 Norma Magnum, still loaded by Norma, looks like a powerful and effective cartridge, but it's so rare that I've never seen one. Layne Simpson's .358 Shooting Times Alaskan is based on the 8mm Remington Magnum case necked up, no doubt a great cartridge, but it has remained an uncommon wildcat. Hunting bullet selection in .358 diameter isn't bad, but since most .35-caliber cartridges are limited in velocity and range, there are few "extra-heavy" and fewer "high BC" .35-caliber bullets.

So, between .30 and .375, for genuine hunting versatility in all types of habitat and terrain, we pretty much have to return to the .338, which has the widest selection of both cartridges and bullets. I have never used the old .33 Winchester, the original .338-inch cartridge introduced in 1902 in the Model 1886 Winchester, which was dropped in 1940. I have also not used the .338 Federal, a nice little cartridge based on the .308 Winchester case. Nothing against it, but I figure that's what my .35s are for.

I keep coming back to the .338 Winchester Magnum because it is powerful and versatile, and easily the most popular of what I think of as "medium-bore" cartridges between .30 and .375. There *are* much faster .338-caliber cartridges, definitely extending range and versatility. I don't consider myself recoil-sensitive, but when you go up in velocity from the .338 Winchester Magnum, recoil goes up fast. In the early 1990s I had quite a fling with the .340 Weatherby Magnum, a marvelous cartridge that shoots flatter and delivers more energy than the .338 Winchester. I used it on a grizzly hunt in BC,

I took my best woodland caribou in Newfoundland with a .338. Detractors suggest the .338 doesn't shoot very flat. In actual fact, depending on bullet weight, it shoots about as flat, or flatter, than the .30-06, which is not damning with faint praise.

and in 1992 I took a monstrous Kamchatka brown bear with a single 250-grain Partition. The bear was quartering toward me; the bullet entered the front shoulder and exited the off hip.

In North America, we typically plan a hunt around *one* key animal. So we do our range time, get ourselves prepared, and we go forth and try to make that one perfect shot. Twice, however, I took that .340 to Africa. In Ethiopia in 1993, it was the only rifle I had, with a variety of game on license. I was shooting it every day, and that made a big difference. Fortunately, I didn't become afraid of it, but I realized that, on a constant basis, the recoil was objectionable, and I never used it again. A decade later I hunted with the .338 Remington Ultra Magnum, which is even faster and more effective, but generates a lot of recoil. Although I've used them on the range, I haven't hunted with the fastest .33s, Lazzeroni's big .338 Titan, the .338-.378 Weatherby Magnum, or the .338 Lapua, and I have no desire to. As Clint Eastwood said (as Dirty Harry Callahan in *Magnum Force*): "A man's got to know his limitations."

So, once again I'm back to the .338 Winchester Magnum. Although its reputation for recoil retarded its success, I don't consider the .338 a hard kicker. That's me, perhaps because I spend a fair amount of time shooting powerful cartridges. You may think differently. Also, I lost a lot of hearing when I was young, so I avoid muzzle brakes like the plague because of the increased blast. The fastest .33s *need* muzzle brakes and they work, but I can't afford to lose another decibel. Sooner or later, if I have a brake, I know I'll forget to put the muffs on. So, if recoil is such that I really need a brake, I retreat to a cartridge with less recoil. We are all different in recoil tolerance, but I don't need a muzzle brake with a .338 Winchester Magnum of moderate weight.

When it comes to .338 bullets, over the years I've mostly been a 250-grain guy. With the great hunting bullets we havc today, you don't always need that much weight. Lighter bullets increase velocity, yet reduce recoil. The bullet Donna used on her brown bear was a 225-grain Hornady Interbond, and it gave perfect performance. We would have used a 250-grain bullet, but at the moment they were unavailable. For Africa, I'm still most likely to use 250-grain bullets, but for lighter game I often use 200-grain bullets or compromise with 225-grain. Recoil is noticeably milder.

I'm not an "every year" elk hunter, I may never hunt another moose, and nobody does a lot of hunting for big bears. So, I don't use the .338 a great deal. I haven't had a whole bunch of them, but it's a cartridge I can't imagine being without. Right now, the only .338 I have is a barrel for the Blaser R8, and it is very accurate. Mark Bansner has a left-hand Sako action with a belted magnum bolt face that he's making into a synthetic-stocked .338 for me. That's a rifle I'm looking forward to, and when it's finished, I'll plan an appropriate hunt.

The .375 H&H Magnum

Chapter 9

Holland & Holland's .375 Belted Rimless Magnum, the cartridge we know as the .375 H&H Magnum or just the .375 H&H, was not the first cartridge to use a .375-inch bullet. Neither was it the last, nor the most powerful. The .375 H&H is not the only .375 I've used, and it's not the slowest or fastest. However, the .375 H&H was my first .375. Half a century later, it is my favorite, and it's still one of the most useful and versatile across the entire spectrum of sporting cartridges.

Bullet diameter .375-inch is a convenient 9.5mm metric, with at least one European 9.5mm blackpowder cartridge. Some references state that an impetus for the development of the .375 was the growing popularity of the 9.5x57mm Mannlicher-Schoenauer. Maybe, but the 9.5x57mm MS was a mild little cartridge only slightly more powerful than 9x57mm and 9.3x57mm Mauser, and although no cartridge references (nor the records they are based upon) are perfect, the 9.5x57 MS (also called 9.5x56 MS) may not have been introduced until 1910.

By that time, Holland & Holland had already tried once, and failed, with the .400/.375 Belted Nitro Express (1905). This little cartridge was based on a .40-caliber blackpowder case necked down to .375, with a belt added. Adding a belt to a cartridge, both as a headspacing index and for case head reinforcement, had been proposed as early as the 1890s, but the .400/.375 was the first belted cartridge. Never mind; it flopped. Using a 270-grain bullet at 2,175 fps and a 320-grain bullet at 2,000 fps, it was much too similar to the 9x57 and 9.3x57 Mauser cartridges (as well as the 9.5x57 MS cartridge, although it probably didn't exist yet).

Donna took this fine muskox in Greenland with an MGA .376 Steyr. The .376 Steyr is not as powerful as the H&H, but it will do almost anything the H&H will do, with much less recoil.

Exactly what they were thinking in 1905 is unclear, but in 1912 they tried again, and this time they got it right. The word "magnum" is taken from the French word for an extra-large bottle of champagne. In British cartridge nomenclature (which is almost as inconsistent as ours), "magnum" suggested a larger (faster/more powerful) cartridge on an existing bullet diameter already used by that company. So, despite all the hallmarks, the .416 Rigby was never called a magnum because it was the first .416-caliber cartridge created by Rigby (or anyone else). As Holland & Holland's second .375-caliber cartridge, however, the .375 Belted Rimless Magnum was thus a magnum in every sense of the word, and especially in 1912, when smokeless powder velocity was still new and not fully explored.

Original loadings were an incredibly fast, light-for-caliber 235-grain bullet at 2,800 fps, a 270-grain bullet at 2,650 fps, and a 300-grain bullet at 2,500 fps. Light .375 bullets are still available for handloading and, with modern powders, can be pushed even faster, but the 235-grain factory load wasn't popular and didn't last too long. The 270- and 300-grain bullets remain standard and most common and, although propellants have improved considerably in the last century, the original velocities have held up pretty well. "Standard" velocities today are generally quoted at 2,690 fps for the 270-grain bullet and 2,530 fps for the 300-grain bullet.

As much as I love the .375 H&H, I have seen tremendous variance in factory loads. I've seen velocities as low as 2,400 fps with "good" American 300-grain factory loads rated at 2,530 fps. I don't think many game animals would notice the difference, but if you are trying to put a solid through an elephant's skull, it's important that you get reasonably close to the velocity (and therefore energy) you *think* you are getting. On the other hand, especially with older

I was very young when I took my first ram, a Stone sheep. It was 1973 and I was using my .375 H&H with a right-hand Mauser action. No one can argue that this was a particularly good choice, but it speaks to the marvelous versatility of the .375 H&H.

PH Cliff Walker and I with an excellent Selous Reserve buffalo, which I took in 2000 using a .375 Remington Ultra Magnum. The fastest .375s like the RUM hit with about the same energy and authority as a .416, but their recoil is significantly greater than that of the .375 H&H.

loading manuals, I have had no trouble achieving 2,600 fps over a chronograph with 300-grain bullets. This was often aided by a 25-inch barrel (one inch longer than standard).

Reloading manuals change over time and not all, especially in the past, have been based on accurate pressure data. So, you won't catch me quoting unpublished loads, or loads from outdated manuals. A quick check of my own current loading manuals (I have them all) indicates that most top out at the velocities previously quoted, but there are still some recipes that will give you a bit more. As always, approach "maximum recommended" velocities with caution, working up in half-grain increments and checking carefully for pressure signs. But standard velocities are good enough, and a couple dozen fps one way or the other, with any bullet weight, aren't worth worrying about.

Some fifty years ago, my dad's friend, Jack Pohl, owned E. C. Bishop & Sons in Warsaw, Missouri, "Gunstock Capital of the World." Jack had a full-length Mauser action with magnum bolt face. He barreled and stocked it in .375 H&H. The barrel was good and stiff, the rifle fairly heavy. If it kicked a lot, twenty-year-old me didn't notice! I thought it was wonderful.

I first used it for pronghorn and mule deer in Wyoming in 1971, and for my first elk in 1972. In August 1973, Dad and I went on a combo moose/caribou/goat hunt in British Columbia. I had just completed Marine Corps Officer Candidate School (OCS), so it was kind of an early graduation present. Or, maybe (not suggesting Dad was devious), a thanks for doing what I was supposed to do. My Pop was a wonderful guy and great dad, but from an early age I understood that there were three things I must accomplish: I was

This lineup represents most of the .375 cartridges. Left to right: .376 Steyr; .375 Flanged Magnum; .375 H&H; .375 Ruger; .375 Weatherby Magnum; .375 RUM; .378 Weatherby Magnum. The .375 H&H is not the fastest and thus not the most versatile, but its recoil is moderate. This is probably why it has been the most popular "medium bore" for more than a century.

I was in northern Cameroon in 2004, and my only rifle was a Weatherby Mark V in .375 Weatherby Magnum, which I used for everything from duikers to buffalo, including this huge-body western hartebeest. Problem was, when shooting from field positions, I couldn't stay away from the scope. After multiple scope cuts, I removed the scope and went to iron sights. Despite the wonderful versatility of the fastest .375s, recoil is severe. After this safari, I went back to the .375 H&H and .375 Ruger.

expected to be an Eagle Scout, earn a college degree in *something*, and get a commission in one of the services. Dad got his Eagle in 1939, just before he turned eighteen. In 1942 he took an early out from college so he could fly in the Navy, did his time as a decorated F6F Hellcat pilot, and went back to school after the war, completing his undergrad and law degree in one jump in 1948.

So far, I was ahead of the game: I got my Eagle in 1966, and was set to graduate from Kansas University and become a Marine Second Lieutenant in May 1974. I'm sure I disappointed him in other ways at other times, but in August 1973 the latter two requirements were scheduled, so we went to British Columbia. Dad took his .308 Model 70 Featherweight. I took the .375. From a distance of a half-century, I cannot evaluate my thinking (other than flawed). I had a .264, and I had a .270. In my defense, I can only say I was a beginning shooter during the first magnum craze, and I drank the Kool-Aid!

The hunt was arranged by Jack Atcheson Sr., a wonderful guy, hero of the Chosin Reservoir fight, and a mentor since I was about fifteen. The hunt cost $1,200 for goat, moose, and mountain caribou (such hunts cost a little more today). We hunted with Frank Cook, a rough and tough guy, and in 1973 (before quotas), holder of perhaps the best Stone sheep area in northern B.C. I had just come from OCS with my head properly shaved, at a time when western Canada was still full of draft dodgers. We bought licenses on the way, and showed up with $25 sheep permits in addition to the tags we were supposed to have. Frank Cook, admiring my short hair, said, "Well, if that boy wants a ram, I'd probably need another five hundred bucks." (Again, I think Stone sheep cost a bit more today.)

So it was that, in 1973, I took my first goat, sheep, caribou, and moose with the .375 H&H. In retrospect, I had better choices, but the point is, it *worked*. Using a little 4X scope, I missed my ram with my first shot, but rolled it with the second when it started to run. Why would twenty-one-year-old me think he had made anything other than a perfect choice? I was handloading for the .375 at the time, but that rifle shot exceptionally well with a

I used a .375 Ruger with 250-grain GMX bullets to take a very large polar bear in 2016. The .375 Ruger is a great cartridge, producing just a bit more velocity than the H&H. It is not appreciably "better," but I chose it for this hunt because the Mossberg rifle in .375 Ruger was available with a stainless steel barrel and action and laminate stock, a combination better suited to tough Arctic conditions than my walnut-and-blued steel .375 H&H rifles.

Remington semispitzer 270-grain load, so that's what I was using. Enough gun? I think so!

Nine months later, just after I graduated and got commissioned, Dad and I went bear hunting in the Kootenays with Ed Langlands. Again, that was before quotas, and a grizzly was on license. Dad and I each shot a couple of black bears, his falling equally as dead with his .308 as mine did with the .375. From the outset, with trails and passes blocked from a heavy snowfall, grizzly seemed unlikely, but in the last few days, on horseback, we penetrated into a hanging valley with open slides. After we glassed a grizzly, I went on the stalk alone, plowing up through deep snow.

That was decades before rangefinders, and, brash kid that I was, I hadn't nearly the experience I thought I had. The bear was far above me, feeding along an open slide. I figured 300 yards, but who knows? I grabbed a fistful of alder saplings for a rest, took a couple of breaths, and held just above the hump. It's amazing, but the bear, hit well, hurtled down the slope toward me. I shot again, hit again (in a front paw!), and then the bear hung up in alders a hundred yards above me. It was not a big bear, not at all, but it was a boar, and I still have the rug.

So, why, in my early twenties, shouldn't I have considered the .375 H&H the most versatile and magically endowed cartridge in the world? The worm turned badly in 1977, in Kenya, when I wounded my first buffalo. Thing is, I shot it badly, too far forward, essentially through the brisket. Worse, following conventional wisdom at the time, I used a 300-grain solid. That's only part of the error. At that time, as young people do, I credited myself with more experience

Although their ballistic coefficients are poor, light .375 bullets can be pushed very fast from the H&H case, reducing recoil and flattening trajectory over normal game ranges. I took this elk on the Jicarilla Reservation with a Sako .375 H&H using a 240-grain Trophy Bonded Bearclaw at 2,900 fps. With lighter bullets, the .375 H&H is awesome for elk.

This Mozambique "swamp buffalo" dropped quickly to a single 300-grain DGX from a .375 H&H at a range of about 100 yards. One-shot kills are never certain on African buffalo, but I have experienced as many with the .375 H&H as with larger cartridges.

than I had. I was totally confounded by close-cover hunting. The bull reacted little (and was probably hurt only a little); he ran to the right and away and, as the dense bamboo closed around his broad, black rear, I had my cross hairs on that rear.

I think it's an exaggeration to say that I froze, but it's accurate to say that I didn't have a clue what to do. I should have shot, anywhere, and a solid up the bum would have helped but, like so many Americans in a similarly unfamiliar situation, I admired that first shot, waiting to see what happened, and then did nothing. PH Willem van Dyk understood what had happened. He knew his job, was good at it, and tried to help, but when he aimed at that broad, black bum and pressed the trigger on his over/under Krieghoff .458, both barrels went off.

I heard a horrible sound like a bell ringing, and glanced around to see Willem in the middle of a backward somersault, his rifle doing an "endo" in the air. That was certainly distracting, but it was not to blame for the lost buffalo, because I had already "admired" my first shot and failed to fire the second (and critical) follow-up.

So there followed some years when I questioned the efficacy of the .375 H&H for buffalo. I was simply young and dead wrong. The .375 H&H is plenty of gun. You need a good bullet (preferably 300 grains), but I've taken a lot of buffalo with 270-grain bullets from the .375 H&H. Mostly, you need good shot placement, and for most of us, this is easier with the .375 H&H than with more powerful cartridges. I have taken African buffalo with a *lot* of different cartridges, almost all more powerful than the .375 H&H. But I know I've taken more buffalo with the .375 H&H than anything else.

It is plenty of gun. If you do things right, and the buffalo accepts the bullet in the proper frame of mind, a pure one-shot kill is, in my experience, just about as likely with a .375 H&H as with a much more powerful cartridge. This is not something one should dwell on: You place the first shot as well as you can. The buffalo will do what it will do; *you* must do as you must, and continue to shoot if needed. A couple years ago, my friend Zack Aultman and I were watching a big herd in Mozambique, both of us hunting with .375 H&H rifles. He saw a bull off to the left, detached from the herd. He shot it well, then again, and then again. The herd didn't move, so when his bull was down, it was my turn. We spotted a nice bull on the right edge of the herd, standing clear. I shot it, and it took two steps, and went not just down, but upside down. Same cartridge, similar bullet, not better shot placement—just not the same buffalo.

I have much more experience with buffalo than elephants. In fact, I have only shot a couple of elephants with .375s, and I still have reservations about the .375 for elephant, especially when we're talking about the really large-bodied Botswana-type elephants. Far more experienced elephant hunters have sworn by the .375, and I'm certain that it will work, given perfect shot placement. However, my interest with the .375 is buffalo, not elephants. Given a choice, when hunting elephants I will always carry a bigger gun.

In March 2021, Donna used her Blaser R8 with a .375 H&H barrel to take this awesome sitatunga in Uganda. Although this is an exceptionally large-body sitatunga, .375 power probably wasn't needed. However, it was a tough shot through papyrus, and even perfectly hit sitatungas are hard to recover in deep swamps. The idea is to hit them hard and anchor them, and the .375 H&H did exactly that.

There are much faster .375-caliber cartridges that deliver more energy than the H&H. Under the right conditions you can *see* the effect of the increased energy. I have never hunted with the .378 Weatherby Magnum, as it is really too ferocious for me. However, I have taken multiple buffalo with both the .375 Remington Ultra Magnum and the .375 Weatherby Magnum, both of which are a couple hundred feet per second faster than the H&H, with a thousand more foot-pounds of energy. I can *see* the added energy, it makes a difference, but I can also feel the added recoil. I had quite a fling with the .375 Weatherby Magnum, carrying it as my only rifle on several safaris. It worked, but (as with the .340 Weatherby Magnum in the previous chapter), I decided it was too much of a good thing and went back to the .375 H&H.

My only experience with less powerful .375s is with the .376 Steyr. We have one in an MGA rifle, light, handy, with moderate recoil and, I suppose, at least 90 percent of the performance of the H&H. It would be great for bear and is buffalo-capable, but it's so uncommon it probably doesn't warrant further discussion. That said, I've had more than a fling; rather, a long-term affair, with the .375 Ruger.

When the Hornady-developed .375 Ruger was introduced, I was spending a lot of time in Africa filming the *Tracks Across Africa* television series. Both Hornady and Ruger were sponsors, so I did a *lot* of hunting with the .375 Ruger. I was beside Steve Hornady when he took the first buffalo to fall to the cartridge. I've used it for several buffalo and a lot of other game. Mine is an early left-hand walnut-stocked Hawkeye, used throughout southern Africa. In 2008, it was the only rifle I took to northern Cameroon, where it accounted for a fine Central Africa savanna buffalo. And it took my personal all-time favorite African animal: A spectacular Derby eland, taken with a 250-yard shot after a tough, all-day tracking job.

So I'm a fan of the .375 Ruger. The primary design parameter was to equal the H&H, using the same .532-inch rim, but without a belt, so a standard magnum bolt face could be used. The result was a cartridge a bit fatter but able to be housed in a .30-06-length action. The .375 Ruger is a model of case design efficiency; it's actually about a hundred feet per second faster than the .375 H&H, which surprised its designers. With the shorter action, the Hawkeye is much lighter than most .375 H&H rifles, so the .375 Ruger has more recoil. Even so, it's tolerable. In 2016, I hadn't used a .375 Ruger for several years, but I borrowed one in a Mossberg Patriot to take on my polar bear hunt. That's another advantage to the .375 Ruger: Manufacturers lacking an action long enough to house the .375 H&H can chamber to it, which was part of the reason for its development. In stainless and synthetic, the rifle was perfect for awful Arctic conditions, and of course the cartridge was fine. Honestly, in all ways I can think of, I have to concede the .375 Ruger is a "better" cartridge than the

PH Mark Haldane and I in Mozambique with my fine Livingstone's eland. The .375 H&H and eland go together like peas and carrots. The shot was over 300 yards, and while many H&H loads can easily handle this distance, I was using a 300-grain DGX, a blunt-nose bullet with a steep trajectory curve. It's crucial to know the trajectory!

H&H. However, it does not have the availability or tradition of the .375 H&H.

As usual, I've not been steadfastly loyal. At this moment, I have two .375 Ruger rifles, the left-hand M77 and a No. 1 single-shot. I also have two .375 H&H rifles, a Blaser barrel with open sights and a CZ M550 Mauser on a left-hand action. To break the tie, I also have an MGA in .376 Steyr. All are excellent rifles. All modern .375 cartridges are versatile, at least for game up to buffalo. The faster .375s are perhaps better for elephant, although I lack the experience to know, and have no desire to learn.

This I do know: The .375 H&H is adequate for any buffalo that walks, and it shoots flat enough and hits hard enough for anything up to that. There are many things it is not perfect for. In fact, in the entire world, the only animals I can think of that the .375 is truly *perfect* for are eland, lions, the largest bears, and tigers. Obviously, I have no experience with tigers and never will, but I accept history. Eland are larger than buffalo, but not as tenacious. The biggest coastal brown and polar bears are as big as Cape buffalo, and as tenacious. Lions are not nearly as big, but you must take into account what a lion might do to you if you mess it up. That's why the .375 is perfect for lion.

In North America, the .375 remains a primary choice for the biggest bears, and although useful for this and that, it is essential for nothing else. Now, in any reference that says .375, unless otherwise specified, you are free to interpret it as your own favorite .375-caliber cartridge. There are faster cartridges with more modern case design than the H&H. But, in terms of shootability and availability, I always circle back to the .375 H&H. There is nothing I need to do with a .375-caliber cartridge that I can't do with the H&H.

THE .416 RIGBY

CHAPTER 10

The .416 Rigby was developed in 1911, with the first rifle delivered in August of 1912. Some consider the cartridge to be John Rigby's greatest contribution to gunmaking. I'm not so sure of this, but the .416 Rigby has definitely been one of the firm's great legacies. Although it was not common knowledge until Rigby's recent relocation to London, it now appears that John Rigby and Peter Paul Mauser collaborated both on the magnum Mauser action to house the .416 Rigby, and on the development of the cartridge itself.

The bullet diameter is interesting, at least as mysterious as Winchester's choice of .277-inch for their famous .270. There was no history of a .416-caliber cartridge, neither in England nor on the Continent. In Europe, the .404 Jeffery (.423-inch bullet) carried the designation 10.75x73mm. There were other 10.75mm cartridges before and after the .404's 1905 introduction, and some references suggest that the .404 Jeffery was a collaboration with the German firm of Schuler. There were also a couple of 11.2mm metrics (bullet diameter .440-inch), both apparently developed by Schuler.

A lot of British cartridges used the smaller land-to-land diameter rather than the groove-to-groove or bullet diameter. The .416 Rigby is literal: .416-inch is the nominal groove diameter, and .416 is the bullet diameter. There is no trace, anywhere, of another .416-caliber cartridge, and there would not be another factory .416 for more than seventy-five years, when the .416 Remington Magnum was introduced in 1988. There is one that is very close, the Swiss 10.3x60R, intended as a target cartridge and based on the .450/.400 2⅜-inch blackpowder

My first .416 was the wildcat .416 Hoffman. In 1985, I used this rifle to take my first elephant, a massive tuskless bull in Zimbabwe's Matetsi. I made a through-and-through, side-on brain shot with a 400-grain Barnes Super Solid bullet.

case. It was loaded in England, and is still used by some Swiss hunters because of the weird rule in some cantons (counties) that stipulates a minimum of .40-caliber for hunting. The 10.3x60mm uses a .415-inch bullet, which is pretty close, but my conversion table yields 10.54mm as the equivalent of a .415-inch bullet. There were other metrics designated 10.25mm and 10.5mm, but none of them used a .416-inch bullet.

So the bullet diameter is a John Rigby original. You can play with a calculator as well as I can: There is .083-inch (eighty-three-thousandths) between the .375 and .458 (the bullet diameter of John Rigby's .450 3¼-inch. Split the difference between the two and you get .415-inch. That's pretty close, so you can say that, within a thousandth, the .416 is halfway in bullet diameter between the .375 and the .458. That makes a lot of sense today, but it doesn't seem logical in a 1911 context. Holland & Holland's .400/.375 (1905) was a flop, the 9.5x57mm (1910, according to most references) barely existed, and H&H's great .375 was also a 1912 release.

I'm not a conspiracy theorist, so I'm not suggesting there was industrial espionage between Rigby and H&H. However, the .350 Rigby Magnum came out in 1908. It was a success, but part of Rigby's interest in working with Mauser on a larger action included creating a cartridge that would max out that true magnum Mauser action. The British gun trade was not large and, although it's purely an assumption, a lot of the players must have known each other (which has always been the case in our own firearms industry). So, just maybe, during a slow moment on a grouse moor, or over a gin and tonic at the club, sometime in 1911, somebody let it slip that the H&H team was working on a cartridge to cure the .400/.375's chronic anemia.

Whatever made John Rigby decide on the .416-inch bullet diameter, the cartridge was done right (as was the .375 H&H). Al-

Four great early twentieth-century cartridges, left to right: .350 Rigby Rimless Magnum (1908); .375 H&H (1912); .404 Jeffery (1905); .416 Rigby (1911). John Rigby's .416 is clearly the big brother to his .350; both are rimless, unbelted, sharp-shouldered cartridges with little body taper, and both were obviously ahead of their time.

The .416 Taylor was a popular wildcat in the 1970s and 1980s. I used one in the early 2000s because the left-hand Ruger M77 action couldn't handle the longer .416 cartridges. I made a miraculous shot in the Cameroon forest in 2008 using the .416 Taylor when I took this prized yellowback duiker from more than 200 yards down a forest road. The short .416 Ruger quickly made the .416 Taylor unnecessary.

though he designed rimmed (flanged) cartridges, it appears John Rigby believed in unbelted rimless design and shoulder headspacing, as did Peter Paul Mauser. The .416 Rigby isn't just a modern case design; it was decades ahead of its time, not only unbelted rimless, but with most body taper removed, a sharp shoulder, and generous (but not overly long) neck. It *still* looks like a modern case design; in fact, seventy-five years later, it would be the basis for the .338 Lapua Magnum.

The original load suggested a 410-grain bullet at 2,370 fps, yielding 5,100 ft-lbs of energy. These remain Federal's specifications with Woodleigh bullets, but more common today is a 400-grain bullet at 2,400 fps, also a bit over 5,000 ft-lbs. The massive case is capable of much higher velocity. The .416 Weatherby Magnum is based on the .378 Weatherby Magnum case. Norma factory loads for the .416 Weatherby are rated at 2,700 fps, and current loading data in some manuals take .416 Weatherby handloads up to that velocity.

Although case capacity is much the same, you won't find loads like that for the .416 Rigby. The case was extra-large from the start, to keep pressures down. Even today, the .416 Rigby is held to moderate pressure, with a SAAMI specification of 47,100 psi; the .416 Weatherby, on the other hand, is loaded to a maximum of 65,000 psi, a huge difference. With that giant case, you can load the .416 Rigby well above standard velocity. Some people do, but recoil goes up fast, and the .416 Rigby has always performed just fine at its original velocity.

It's an interesting cartridge in that, until recently, its legend has far outstripped its actual use. The .416 was retained as a Rigby proprietary and the actual rifles were uncommon. Between 1912 and 1939, Rigby made only 189 .416 Rigby rifles, a very small number.

I briefly experimented with a .350 Rigby Rimless Magnum. Although uncommon today, the .350 Rigby was a fine medium-bore cartridge. Sadly, the barrel on this rifle was "reclaimed" and had more wear than appeared; accuracy was marginal and I had to give up on it.

I took this lovely bongo, my first, in the C.A.R. in 1997 with a London-made .416 Rigby. It was a gorgeous rifle, but the left-hand, American-made action was plagued with mechanical problems. I had no confidence in the rifle, so I have been searching for another for more than twenty years.

Over the years, some Continental and American custom rifles were so chambered, but ammunition was also a Rigby proprietary, expensive and not always easy to come by. Roy Weatherby introduced his .378 in 1953 and the .460 in 1957. The .460 pretty much coincided with Kynoch's gradual discontinuance of the big Nitro Express cartridges. This actually gave the .416 a slight rebirth in America; it was a simple matter to turn the belts off of .460 Weatherby Magnum brass and full-length resize to .416 Rigby. Although hardly known as a big-bore guy, Jack O'Connor had an American-made .416 Rigby; like many others, he used .460 Weatherby brass.

Although never common, the .416 Rigby was famous, with knowledgeable and well-known users including CDR David Blunt, J. A. Hunter, George Rushby, and Harry Selby. Although he was even less of a big-bore guy than O'Connor, Walter Bell ordered a *pair* of .416s in 1913, and used at least one of them in West Africa after World War I. Generating fully 5,000 ft-lbs at the muzzle, the .416 Rigby had (and has) enough stopping power for the largest game. And, with its faster bullet of smaller diameter, in my experience it provides deeper and more reliable penetration than the slower big-bore Nitro Express cartridges. Also, with higher velocity, it is more versatile than the big bores. In this regard, it's a bit like the .375: In a pinch, you can do almost anything with it. On medium game, it is not as versatile as the .375, but it's better for the big stuff in all ways.

I was young when I started reading Ruark, so of course I knew that Harry Selby used a .416 Rigby, as did Peter McKenzie, Ruark's fictional PH in his best novel, *Something of Value*. John Taylor died a pauper in London, and regrettably never saw what an often-reprinted

Left to right: .416 Rigby; .460 Weatherby Magnum; .416 Weatherby Magnum. Roy Weatherby's big .460 was essentially a belted version of the .416 Rigby. When ammo was scarce, .416 Rigby owners could make brass by turning the belts from .460 Weatherby cases. Thirty years after the .460, in 1989, Ed Weatherby created the .416 Weatherby by necking down the .460 case.

Here I am preparing to shoot an old buffalo bull in Mozambique. This was the longest shot I have ever made on a buffalo, about 160 yards, executed with a Rigby Big Game .416 Rigby and Leupold 2–7x33mm scope. The buffalo dropped to a single 400-grain Swift A-Frame.

classic his *African Rifles and Cartridges* would become. Taylor spent much of his time in Africa living almost as a hermit, just beyond the reach of authority. Considering the geography and lack of communications at the time, I have to question how many of the rifles and cartridges he wrote about actually passed through his hands, and how much he extrapolated from the experience of others, such as Fletcher Jamieson's .500 Jeffery, a rifle so rare that Jeffery is thought to have made only twenty-six! No matter, his book is wonderful and, although he was primarily a double-rifle guy, he gives great (and well-deserved) accolades to the .416 Rigby, completing a paragraph with, "I just cannot speak too highly of the .416."

Taylor states several times that he had a .416 Rigby and used it a lot, so I accept that he did. However, clear into the 1980s, despite its fame, the .416 Rigby was at best uncommon. Part of the problem was the extra-large magnum action it required was as scarce as finished rifles and loaded cartridges. But then something else happened: The .416 was resurrected by good old American wildcatters. Developing non-standard cartridges is almost unique to American handloaders. The practice is called "wildcatting," the resultant cartridges referred to as "wildcats." Developing a non-standard cartridge involves a lot of work and considerable expense, requiring custom dies and chamber reamers.

Modern bolt-actions can withstand much higher pressures than the .416 Rigby is loaded to. And .416 Rigby ballistics can be generated in much smaller cases, which can be housed in smaller and more available actions. Many wildcatters messed with .416s on various cases, but the two best known are the .416 Taylor and .416 Hoffman.

American wildcat developments have been critical to the current proliferation of the .416s. Left to right: .416 Hoffman; .416 Remington Magnum; .416 Taylor; .416 Ruger;.416 Rigby. George Hoffman's wildcat led to the .416 Remington. Robert Chatfield-Taylor's .416 almost became a factory cartridge more than once, but it was made redundant by the stubby .416 Ruger. The granddaddy, the .416 Rigby, may not be the most practical .416, but it's the one with the most tradition and charisma.

In 1988, I used an open-sighted Dumoulin in .416 Rigby to take this lion in Tanzania's Masailand. This began my long search for a left-hand .416 Rigby, a search that has not yet concluded.

The .416 Taylor was developed in 1972 by American gunwriter Robert (Bob) Chatfield-Taylor. Taylor wasn't especially prolific and isn't well-remembered, but he knew his stuff. I have an amazing stack of correspondence between Taylor and Jack O'Connor, from a time when people actually wrote letters. Some are short notes, but many are long and chatty, in all a couple hundred between late 1957 and December 1975. I understand Taylor died of a heart attack shortly thereafter, but beyond what I can glean from his letters to O'Connor, there isn't much information on him.

His .416 Taylor is based on the .458 Winchester Magnum case necked down, thus able to be housed in a .30-06 length bolt-action. It became a fairly popular wildcat, and almost made it into factory form at least twice. John Wootters had one in the 1970s and loved it. Much later, in the early 2000s, I had one and found it a wonderfully effective cartridge. In that short case it was difficult to get a 400-grain bullet all the way to 2,400 fps, but you could come close enough.

Texan George Hoffman was among the relatively few Americans to become a successful African PH, and he loved the .416. His .416 Hoffman cartridge is based on the .375 H&H case necked up, and easily reaches full .416 Rigby ballistics.

In the 1980s the .416 Hoffman was a popular and much-discussed wildcat. It was the basis for the .416 Remington Magnum (1988), but Remington chose to use its own 8mm Remington case. Hoffman never forgave them, but there is one benefit: .416 Remington ammunition will chamber and can be safely fired in a .416 Hoffman chamber, but not the reverse.

The big .416 revolution came in 1988. In the space of just a year, Federal introduced a new American factory load for the .416 Rigby, Remington introduced its own .416, and in mid-1989 Weatherby unveiled the .416 Weatherby Magnum. By that time, I was seriously

In 1993, I used a right-handed Dakota in .416 Rigby to take a huge Masailand buffalo; to this day it is my best-ever. On buffalo, the .416 isn't necessarily "better" than the .375, but it often achieves more dramatic results, with more versatility than is possible with the true big-bore cartridges.

With greater velocity and less frontal area, the .416s generally provide deeper penetration on elephants than the traditional Nitro Express big bores. I loaded up a right-hand-action Rigby Big Game rifle with solids to take this marvelous old Caprivi tusker. It will probably be my last elephant.

besotted with double rifles (thank you, Mr. Ruark), but I had already recognized that I was much more effective with a bolt-action rifle that could readily wear a scope.

The .416 made a lot of sense, and still does. My first .416 was a Hoffman, built in 1985 on a Remington action by Randy Brooks of Barnes Bullets. I used it for my first elephant, and I took several buffalo with it. Light, handy, and in a synthetic stock, it was my concept of a "swamp rifle" for hunting in the Okavango. Problem is, the rifle was too light. At barely six pounds, it was ferocious. It destroyed scopes and mounts like they were going out of style.

Since then, I've owned a number of .416s, and I'm pretty sure I've hunted with *all* of the .416-caliber cartridges. In addition to those already mentioned, these include Krieghoff's .500/.416 rimmed cartridge, the .416 Ruger, and Lazzeroni's short (and powerful) 10.75 (.416) Maverick. I've also used a number of similar cartridges, including the .400 H&H, .411 KDF, .404 Jeffery, and .425 Express. Somehow, I've never squeezed the trigger on a .425 Westley Richards. Among all of these, we can split hairs over a few thousandths in bullet diameter, and a few dozen feet per second in velocity, but all of these are essentially equal in performance on game.

Although the performance is magnificent, there is no magic in the .416 Rigby "formula" of a 400-grain bullet at 2,400 fps (or 410-grain at 2,370, if you prefer). The .400 H&H, .500/.416, .416 Ruger, .416 Taylor, and .404 Jeffery, all with a 400-grain bullet at about 2,350 fps, are equally adequate for buffalo and, with solids, will penetrate an elephant's skull from any angle. Add a few hundred feet per second, and performance is even more spectacular, but recoil goes up sharply, which is too much of a good thing for many of us.

You can take your pick. As I'm sure I've written before, the .416 Remington Magnum probably makes the most sense. It's easily chambered in any .375 H&H-length action, with inexpensive ammo available from multiple sources and, for those who *do* like to split hairs, it achieves the full traditional velocity of a 400-grain bullet at 2,400 fps. The .416 Remington Magnum is loaded to a maximum

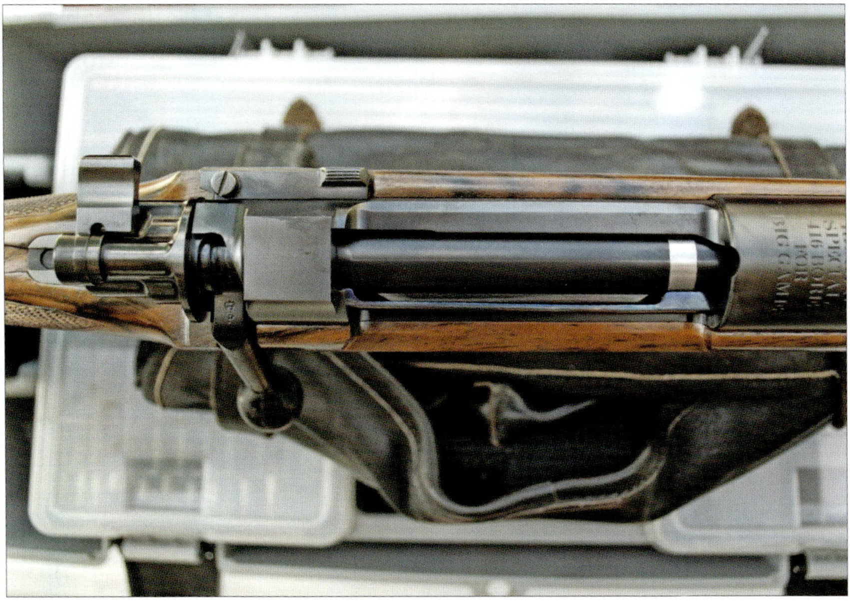

Rigby's new Big Game .416 bears the faithful roll-mark on the front receiver bridge: "Rigby's Special .416 Bore for Big Game." An awesome and relatively affordable rifle, it's sadly available only in a right-hand action.

of 62,400 psi, a lot more pressure than the Rigby. There is a rumor out there of sticky extraction with the .416 Remington Magnum. This might have happened in African heat. I can't dispel it, but I've also been unable to verify it. I've used the .416 Remington on late hunts in the Zambezi Valley and Mozambique, and in Cameroon, all when temperatures were well over 100 degrees Fahrenheit. I've never experienced extraction problems, and none of the many PHs I've asked have actually *seen* this. Sure, it could happen with overly generous handloads or cartridges left in the sun. But I'm pretty sure it's neither a common nor inherent problem. If you just want a .416 for its performance, get a .416 Remington Magnum.

As we've already seen, however, I place value on history and tradition in my cartridge choices. So, my favorite is the .416 Rigby. Performance on game is no better than that delivered by at least a dozen other cartridges, but none come close to the legend and lineage of the .416 Rigby. It does have drawbacks: Ammunition, though readily available today, is heavier, bulkier, and more expensive than most of the others. Thanks to CNC machining, the extra-large magnum action the Rigby case requires is more available than it has ever been, but these actions are larger, heavier, and more expensive than standard actions. Rifles chambered to .416 Rigby are also a bit larger and heavier, and generally more expensive. The only real bargain in a .416 Rigby was the Ruger M77 Safari Magnum. It carried a premium as American production rifles go, but was still the most affordable .416 Rigby rifle *ever.* Regrettably, Ruger no longer makes the magnum action, but there are still some out there, and prices remain reasonable.

Even more regrettably, Ruger never made that action in left-hand version. Left-hand magnum bolt-actions exist, but they're scarce and

In ascending order of velocity, these are the most common .416 cartridges available today. Left to right: .500/.416 Nitro Express; .416 Ruger; .416 Remington Magnum; .416 Rigby; .416 Weatherby Magnum. All are perfectly capable of doing anything anyone needs to do with a .416.

pricey. Which, in a nutshell, is why I don't have a .416 Rigby right now. Instead, I have a .404 Jeffery on a left-hand Montana action. The .404 can be housed in a .375 action (just barely); the .416 Rigby cannot.

In the 1980s and 1990s, I had *two* left-hand .416 Rigby rifles on full-size magnum mirror-image actions, but both were delivered with serious mechanical issues. I fixed the problems and hunted with them, but my faith was shaken and I didn't keep them long. I've borrowed and hunted with two of the new Rigby Big Game rifles in .416 Rigby. One was a single-square-bridge, thus an open-sighted rifle; the other a double-square-bridge with detachable scope in addition to express sights. Both were awesome rifles: accurate, mechanically perfect, with marvelous handling qualities. I shot multiple buffalo with each, and, with the double-square-bridge, what was probably my last elephant.

The Rigby Big Game is not inexpensive, but it's in the same range as a Dakota or other semi-custom rifle on a big action, and it's a Rigby, so it is history in your hands. I'd have bought that scoped rifle without hesitation—part of me wishes I had—but it wore a right-hand bolt, and I'm just not gonna go there. Sadly, the Big Game is made in right-hand actions only. Rigby does offer their "bespoke" full-up custom bolt-actions in left hand, but they're a bit above my pay grade! I'm sure I'll have another left-hand .416 Rigby one of these days; it's moving up on the bucket list. But for now, the search continues.

The .450/.400 Nitro Express

Chapter 11

It's generally accepted that the .470 Nitro Express is the most popular of the big-bore British Nitro Express cartridges. That is certainly true today; the .470 dominates in new double rifles, and .470 ammo is available from many sources. Historically, I'm not so sure. The British gun trade was complicated. There were dozens of small shops, and the larger firms had proprietary cartridges; by 1910, there were eleven big-bore Nitro Express rimmed cartridges between .450 and .500, all similar in performance on game. Also, the majority of British double rifles were shipped not to Africa, but to India. In older rifles, my guess is the .450/.400, considered perfect for tigers, outnumbered any single one of the big bores.

There were two .450/.400 cartridges, both chambered by numerous makers. In British cartridge nomenclature, the larger parent case is often listed first, followed by the actual (nominal) caliber. So, .450/.400 means a .450 case necked down to about .40-caliber. The .450/.400 3¼-inch was based on an existing blackpowder case, converted to smokeless in the early 1890s. The .450/.400 3-inch (aka .400 Jeffery), with a shorter case, was introduced by W. J. Jeffery in 1902.

Blackpowder cases didn't need to be as strong, and there were extraction problems with weak cases in the initial years of smokeless powder. John Rigby's 1898 .450 3¼-inch cartridge was the first large-caliber Nitro Express cartridge specifically designed for smokeless powder; the .400 Jeffery was probably the second. Interestingly, an Australian correspondent told me that he has an 1899 Jeffery rifle that is nitro-proofed and the chamber is .450/.400 3-inch, but is not

This is the first Cape buffalo I took with a .450/.400 3-inch and Hornady's new load, using a Ruger No. 1. This was in Zimbabwe's Zambezi Valley, and the bull ran fifty or sixty yards before going down.

marked ".400 Jeffery." This suggests that Jeffery was chambering to the cartridge for some time before formally naming it.

The two versions are not interchangeable; the shorter Jeffery cartridge has a thicker rim. Ballistics are similar but not identical; both use a 400-grain bullet, but the longer cartridge was always a bit faster. The .450/.400 3¼-inch was rated at 2,150 fps, energy 4,110 ft-lbs. Traditional loads for the Jeffery cartridge were rated at 2,100 fps; Hornady's current load is rated at 2,050 fps, with energy yield of about 3,800 ft-lbs.

I've never had a .450/.400 3¼-inch rifle, but I certainly wouldn't shy away from an older gun so chambered, if it fit and the price was right. However, I prefer the shorter case simply because load density is better with modern powders. In performance on game, they're much the same: perfect for buffalo, yet with adequate penetration for elephant.

Both are available today, with the 3¼-inch ammo loaded by Kynoch and Norma, and the .450/.400 3-inch by Hornady. Largely because of the cost and widespread availability of Hornady ammo, new .450/.400 3-inch rifles are common, but I'd be surprised if even one .450/.400 3¼-inch double has been made in fifty years. Almost all modern double rifle manufacturers chamber to the .450/.400 3-inch, and Ruger has made quite a few No. 1 single-shots in that chambering.

Years ago, I had a lovely .450/.400 3-inch boxlock by Birmingham maker Thomas Turner. That is the double rifle on the dust jacket of my *Safari Rifles* book, but the Kynoch cartridge box doesn't match the rifle!

A vintage .450/.400 3¼-inch rifle by Wilkes was used to take this Zambezi Valley bull. Historically, both the 3-inch and 3.25-inch versions of the .450/.400 were chambered by numerous makers. The longer case may have been more popular, but the 3-inch version is far more popular today. The two are very similar in performance on game, and the shorter case gives better load density with modern propellants.

PH Paul Smith guided Donna to her first buffalo, also taken with the Ruger No. 1 in .450/.400 3-inch. This is a spectacular Zambezi Valley buffalo. Recoil level of the .450/.400 is mild, with marvelous power and amazing penetration.

I never hunted with that rifle, and didn't think about the cartridge much until the early 2000s, when I was in the Zambezi Valley with Steve Hornady. He was interested in expanding his line of large-caliber ammo, so I suggested he might consider resurrecting the .450/.400 3-inch.

Why? Well, the .470 had been the dominant double rifle cartridge since Federal started loading it in 1988. Most of the other big-bore Nitro Expresses were available one way or another but they all had something in common: They were 5,000-ft.-lb. cartridges, with 5,000-ft.-lb. recoil. They are not fun to shoot! The little .450/.400 is a 4,000-ft.-lb. cartridge, thus with much less recoil, but significant capability. Per John Taylor, the .450/.400s penetrated at least as well as the big-bore Nitro Expresses, which they should: sectional density (SD) is about the same as the 500-grain .458 bullet (.340 versus .341). Velocity is similar, but frontal area is smaller, so there is less resistance and at least equal penetration. Great performance, with much less pain.

Hornady went home and began some research. In 2005, we had a Ruger No. 1 in .450/.400 3-inch on safari with a brand-new Hornady factory load. There is a technical difficulty with the .450/.400s, discovered quickly by the Hornady engineers. Most of the Nitro Express cartridges can vary a bit in bore diameter, probably due to some combination of period manufacturing, transition from blackpowder, and the fact that the British gun trade was essentially a cottage industry, with parts sourced from multiple small shops. It appears that the .450/.400s vary more than most. References state the .450/.400 3¼-inch is supposed to have a .405-inch bore, while the .450/.400 3-inch (.400 Jeffery) is supposed to have a .411-inch bore. Having almost no experience with the longer cartridge, I can't speak to the .450/.400 3¼-inch. However, older .450/.400 3-inch rifles have turned up with bores from as tight as .408-inch to as loose as .412, although .409 to .411 appears most common.

Bore variance with Nitro Express cartridges is not a secret. I knew of it, and have often written that, with older rifles, it's a good idea to

Left to right: .450/.400 3-inch Nitro Express (.400 Jeffery); .450 3¼-inch Nitro Express; .404 Jeffery. The .450/.400 is based on the .450 case necked down to .40-caliber. Introduced in 1902, the .404 Jeffery was designed to emulate .450/.400 performance in bolt-action rifles.

Older accounts are near-universal in agreement on the .450/.400's adequacy for elephant. With less frontal area, high sectional density, and similar velocity, it stands to reason that it penetrates at least as well as the true big bores.

have the bore inspected and measured by a competent gunsmith, especially if a double comes into your hands with no history or knowledge from a previous owner. Although perhaps I should have been, I wasn't aware that the .450/.400 3-inch had a predilection for so much bore variance. When I had the Thomas Turner .450/.400 3-inch rifle, I loaded (original) Barnes bullets sized for the .411 KDF with no problems.

To bring out a modern load, Hornady had to compromise. Undersize is clearly safer than oversize, so Hornady settled on .409-inch, which is the diameter all current rifle makers are using for .450/.400 3-inch barrels. With older rifles, first be certain you know exactly what you're dealing with. At modest Nitro Express pressure, a very slightly oversize bullet shouldn't cause significant problems, especially if the barrels are worn a bit. Undersize bullets alleviate pressure concerns, but even a thousandth undersize can create accuracy problems, especially in a worn barrel, and bullets a couple thousandths undersize are almost certain to shoot poorly.

This came home to me in spades with a lovely Holland & Holland double in .303 British that belonged to Joe Bishop. References vary on whether the .303 is supposed be .311 or .312. Bullets in both diameters exist, and so do barrels. The rifle was regulated with the old 215-grain bullet, which is hard to find. I started with old 215-grain Winchester ammo, and the bullets keyholed. I was horrified, thinking I had an expensive wall-hanger on my hands. The micrometer showed Winchester used .311-inch bullets, and as it turns out, the barrels on my rifle are .312. Dr. Richard Hale, a friend from the Boone and Crockett Club, had some old Peters ammo with 215-grain bullets and a small cache of Remington 215-grain component bullets. Apparently, Remington/Peters used .312-inch bullets for their .303 ammo. Since these match my rifle's barrels, the .312-inch bullets shoot just fine.

So, it's an unfortunate fact that .409-inch Hornady bullets intended for the .450/.400 3-inch may not shoot well in older rifles with looser bores. There are .410 and .411 rifle bullets and, although

In the swamps of the Marromeu Reserve in Mozambique, I shot this buffalo bull on the edge of a herd with a hundred-yard shot using the Ruger No. 1 .450/.400 3-inch and a 400-grain Hornady DGX bullet. It was a one-shot kill.

there isn't much to be done about undersize bullets, oversize bullets can be swaged down. I had a brief fling with a .318 Westley Richards, a lovely rifle with a right-hand bolt and a lot of right-hand cast in the stock. The bullet diameter is .330; I swaged down .338 bullets and they shot just great. Today there is usually a solution for most ammunition problems, but it can take some work.

Anyway, in 2005, Donna and I took a brand-new Ruger No. 1 in .450/.400 3-inch to the Zambezi Valley. By then, I was decades past any misguided concerns about the adequacy of the .375 H&H for buffalo. I figured 4,000 ft-lbs were, well, 4,000 ft-lbs; the .450/.400 is much slower than the .375, but has a heavier bullet with greater frontal area, and energy yield is similar. Theoretically, the .450/.400 should perform at least as well as the .375.

But that's theory, and I had no experience with the cartridge. I did have a lifetime of reading under my belt, and history is universally kind to the .450/.400. Nobody ever said they are as powerful as the true big bores. Nor, with less energy, are they supposed to be. But they loom large in the hunting history of both Africa and India. Walter Bell, champion of small bores, used a .400 Jeffery double on safari after World War I, although he didn't care for the recoil. John Taylor wrote about both .450/.400s, considering them adequate for elephant. Jim Corbett's preferred tiger rifle was a double .400 Jeffery, a rifle now in the collection of Bill Jones. Other than the man-eaters that made him famous, Corbett wrote little about his personal hunting exploits, but one must speculate that, during his long career in India, Corbett's .450/.400 must have accounted for gaur and other big game.

So, there was no reason to question the efficacy of the .450/.400 and I did not, but I was curious. Absent a repeating action, Ruger No. 1 rifles can be very light, especially for powerful cartridges. The only real way to mitigate this is with denser wood, which is hard to control, or a thicker barrel. The Ruger No. 1 Tropical has a really stiff barrel, adding welcome weight. In .450/.400 3-inch, with scope

Three .450/.400 3-inch loads, left to right: Hornady 400-grain DGX; Hornady 400-grain DGS; original 400-grain Kynoch. The older "style" for solids was a gently tapered meplat; current research suggests a flat-pointed meplat may promote better straight-line penetration and transfer more energy on impact. Either way, the .450/.400 provides deep penetration.

The Ruger No. 1 .450/.400 3-inch with the Heym 88B double rifle in the same chambering. Both have accounted for their share of dangerous game; they represent two great choices in a wonderful cartridge.

added, the rifle weighs a bit over nine pounds; for me, recoil was very mild, more of a firm push than a jolt.

We were in the Sapi safari area, east of Mana Pools. One morning, we caught a nice herd of buffalo feeding along a narrow sand river. After a bit of creeping around, we caught a lovely old bull feeding on the far side, the wind perfect. The shot was close, forty or fifty yards, broadside. The bull took the bullet hard, turned, and ran up a bare slope, but there was no way I could get the single-shot loaded in time for another shot before we lost sight of him. We clambered across the wash, Andy Dawson ready with his William Evans .470. No problem; the bull was down and dead sixty yards up the slope, absolutely no need for a follow-up shot.

A few days later we moved down the Zambezi, across Chewore to the Dande North safari area, to hunt with Paul Smith, Dawson's partner in Chifuti Safaris. They had a spare buffalo on quota, rare in those days, so I struck a deal for Donna to take one. She'd already shot the .450/.400 on the range and found it easier to shoot than a .375. With similar gun weight, recoil foot-pounds are about the same as a .375. But, since the .450/.400 is much slower, recoil *velocity* is less, which has much to do with *felt* recoil.

Late the first afternoon we found where a huge herd had crossed the track and fed up a bare ridge. The spoor was from the morning, too late in the day to follow, but we came back and started on the tracks early the next morning. By then we were a full day behind them. I figured it could be a long day, but unless lions get into them, big buffalo herds don't travel far or fast; within two hours we found them spread out along a steep hillside. Paul spotted an incredible bull, but he was in a tight knot of other bulls, and as we watched he bedded down into a black wad of buffalo. We spent several hours within eighty yards, waiting him out, but when he got up, there was no shot.

In 2008, Donna used the Heym .450/.400 3-inch with Hornady DGS solid bullets to take this Botswana tusker. The .450/.400 is a sensible minimum for elephants, and a whole lot more fun to shoot than the big-bore Nitro Express cartridges.

Gordon Marsh took this fine Mozambique swamp buffalo with his scoped Sabatti .450/.400 3-inch and using a Hornady DGX bullet. All current double-rifle manufacturers are chambering to the .450/.400 3-inch. Unless one plans to do a lot of elephant hunting, the .450/.400 is the most sensible cartridge in a new double, with light recoil and great performance.

The herd eventually spooked and they split up. With no other choice, we followed one splinter group, catching them in a brushy valley two ridges away. There, feeding by himself, in the wide open, was the same big bull! Paul took Donna a bit closer, while the trackers and I hung back. I think her shot was over a hundred yards, and strongly quartering away. We found the bull dead at the head of the valley, maybe eighty yards away. Donna's follow-up solid was not necessary; her bull was *down*.

Those first, still-experimental .450/.400 loads were made with cobbled-together bullets, but performance was perfect; the softpoints showing good penetration, a lot of expansion, and surprising weight retention. Donna's follow-up solid, an insurance shot from behind, didn't exit. Recovered, it could have been loaded and fired again. Over the next couple years, Hornady's "Dangerous Game" line progressed to the DGX and DGS bullets, and now to the bonded version. The bonded-core bullets are "prettier" when recovered, but I've never seen anything but superb bullet performance from the .450/.400, consistent hallmarks of plenty of weight for caliber, and moderate velocity.

It took a bit more time, but the various double-rifle makers quickly began chambering rifles to the .450/.400 3-inch. In 2007, we had the first Heym double in .450/.400 3-inch in the Zambezi Valley. I used it for a nice buffalo bull, making good hits with both barrels at about a hundred yards, and Dawson and I collaborated on a charging PAC (Problem Animal Control) elephant bull. The next year, in 2008, Donna used the .450/.400 on a fine Botswana elephant. Shooting steeply uphill at six yards, her frontal brain shot was a bit to the side and failed, but it turned the elephant, and she executed a perfect going-away hip shot with her second barrel. We caught up quickly, and she finished the job.

I don't have a lot of experience with the .450/.400 on elephants, and am unlikely to acquire much more, as I think my elephant-hunting days are over. However, I believe it is plenty adequate, and I remain convinced that the .450/.400 is near perfect for buffalo. Because of frontal area and bullet weight, it is better than any .375. With much less energy, I don't think it hits quite as hard as the .416s, and shouldn't penetrate as well. But it does its work calmly and efficiently, and with much less recoil.

Gordon Marsh, in Mozambique, zeroing in his scoped Sabatti double in .450/.400 3-inch. All current double-rifle manufacturers are chambering to this caliber. Unless one plans to do a lot of elephant hunting, the .450/.400 is the most sensible cartridge in a new double.

Because of range, recoil, and limited sighting equipment, most of us never really know how accurate our big-bore rifles are (or are not). We don't worry about it too much, nor should we, since shots at dangerous animals are always close. Even so, I have found the .450/.400 3-inch to be accurate. On the target is a five-shot, hundred-yard group with the scoped Ruger No. 1; the paper plate group is fifty yards with Heym double, without a scope. Both rifles show plenty of accuracy for any likely task for the cartridge.

The basic .450 case pretty much maxes out the Ruger No. 1 action; it will house the .450/.400s and the .450 3¼-inch Nitro Express. Ruger No. 1 rifles have been converted to .470 and other cartridges based on the .500 Nitro Express case, but it's custom work that requires hogging out the bottom of the action to make room. I've had two No. 1s in .450/.400 3-inch, and also a No. 1 in .450 3¼-inch. The latter rifle is very accurate, but even with the heavy-contour Tropical barrel, it is too light and recoil is pretty dramatic. The .450/.400s, with much less power (and recoil) and more steel in the barrel, are very comfortable to shoot. In the strong Ruger action, you *can* increase velocity quite a bit, but I've generally loaded it to 2,150 fps, bringing it up to 4,100 ft-lbs of energy.

I've mounted scopes on both the Ruger single-shots. Our Heym .450/.400 double could be adapted to optical sights with relative ease, but I've left it with open sights only. This does limit range and versatility but, of course, it depends on what you want to do with the rifle. For elephant hunting, I'm happy with open express sights because ranges are so short: Twenty-five yards is a long shot. For buffalo, you're definitely better off with an optical sight; if not a scope, at least a red-dot sight.

In 2017 I was in Mozambique with my friend Gordon Marsh, whose Wholesale Hunter store and website is one of the larger Sabatti dealers. Gordon had his Sabatti double .450/.400 3-inch with him. That was one of those wonderful years when outfitter Mark Haldane had a handful of unsold buffalo on quota. Gordon shot two, one with his .375 and a second with the scoped .450/.400. That rifle shot so well, and was so easy to shoot, that we passed it around. I shot a buffalo with it, and my friend and frequent videographer Matt Young used it for his first buffalo.

The .450/.400 is, without question, my favorite double rifle cartridge. It always depends on what you intend to do with your double, of course. If you're serious about elephant hunting, then one of the big bores is a better choice. The .470 is by far the most popular and available today, followed by the .500 3-inch, which probably gives you just a bit more. Of the big-bore group, my pick is the original .450 3¼-inch for three reasons: the smaller base can be housed in a trimmer action; the straight case allows a bit better load density with modern powders; and it uses readily available (and inexpensive) .458-inch bullets.

But if your interest lies primarily in hunting buffalo, then the .450/.400 3-inch is the way to go. It's a lot more fun to shoot than the larger cartridges, so you'll find yourself shooting it more and becoming more proficient. Power is enough for any large bovine that walks, *anywhere*, and with good 400-grain solids, it will do just fine on elephants as well.

Part Three
My Favorite Rifles

I've owned a lot of rifles and used many more. Some that I wish I'd hung onto slipped through my hands, and there were many others I wish I'd bought and didn't, often because I simply couldn't afford them. Then again, knowing how fickle I am about buying, selling, and trading guns, even if I'd been able to come up with the scratch, I might not still have some of them today. Truth is, the rifles I can't imagine parting with are few in number, and they are genuine favorites.

Some are very nice rifles; others are over-the-counter factory jobs. Exactly why they fall into the "favorite" category varies. One thing is constant: All are either left-handed or at least "almost" ambidextrous. Not all of their chamberings match my favorite cartridges and, in some cases, are not a single rifle, but a type or model. Most are exceptionally accurate, but some are simply "accurate enough" for their intended purpose.

All of my favorite rifles fit me well and handle easily and smoothly. Note, again, these are my *favorites. It's not necessary in the least that* you *agree, let alone approve. Chances are you've already noticed that my taste in cartridges runs toward the traditional, and my preferences in hunting rifles follows right along. None of my "favorites" are rifles that I've used throughout my life and hunting career. Since I have a habit of buying, selling, and trading rifles, some represent upgrades or improvements to guns long gone, possibly even a culmination of several rifles I've long admired and coveted. One way or another, I have a long history with all of these, and when I'm done, I expect to pass them along. Let's just hope at least one of my grandchildren turns out to be left-handed.*

Serengeti Westerner

Chapter 12

On 23 December 2003, a 6.6 earthquake rocked California's Central Coast, with some of the worst damage occurring in our little town of Paso Robles, twenty-four miles from the epicenter in San Simeon. The drop-ceiling in my office collapsed on my desk, breaking some glass but mostly making a mess. A few weeks passed before I got to the bottom of the pile and found a small stack of unopened mail.

No bills, no checks, but there was a letter from a grocery store in New Jersey, addressed in an older man's shaky hand. Inside was a note on an invoice sheet, in the same handwriting. "No, this is not a bill," it read. "I have a left-hand Parker Ackley Santa Barbara action that I was always going to use to make a special rifle. I thought you might be interested."

Now *my* hands were shaking as I reached for the phone! Parker Otto "P. O." Ackley (1903–1989) was a prolific gunsmith, custom gunmaker, and experimenter. If there's a cartridge case that he didn't neck up, down, or sideways, I don't know what it might be. He is probably best remembered for his "improved" cartridges, increasing powder capacity (and thus velocity) by removing body taper and changing neck length and angle. One of Ackley's self-imposed rules for an improved cartridge was that standard ammo could still be used. I had a .35 Whelen Ackley Improved for some time, and right now I'm messing with a .280 Ackley Improved, which has become one of the most popular of Ackley's many designs.

Years ago, when commercial Mauser actions were scarce, Ackley imported a line of Santa Barbara actions from Spain. Opinions vary

The Santa Barbara action was a Spanish-made Mauser action. Nobody ever claimed it was among the best Mauser actions, but Parker Ackley imported them in a time when new Mauser actions were scarce, and almost unheard-of in mirror-image left-hand. It took some smoothing to make it work. "P. O. Ackley" on the right side of the receiver makes it extra cool!

on these; they probably weren't the best-ever Mauser actions, but also not the worst. Doesn't matter to me; I knew of them, but I'd never owned one, and I'd never even seen a left-hand Ackley action, although it had been rumored that some were made. I called the gentleman, told him I'd misplaced his letter, and asked if there was any chance he still had the action.

He did, and he wanted $350 for it. I offered to send a check immediately. He kindly suggested that he should send the action first, and if I liked it then I could pay him. Oh, yes, I liked it: It was standard length with a belted magnum bolt face, in the white, with "P. O. Ackley" engraved on the right side. And, yes, I sent a check!

The action sat on my desk for quite a time because I wasn't sure what I wanted to do with it. I think I was between .338s at the moment, so that was my immediate inclination. Over in the corner, and also covered with earthquake debris for some time, I had a high-grade 6.5mm barrel. This was before the Creedmoor craze; *good* 6.5mm barrels were scarce. I got it from friend Marv Quillen, who talked Butch Obermayer into making him a match-grade 6.5mm barrel, and one more for me. I can't remember what Marv had in mind, maybe a 6.5mm-06, but for a long time I wasn't sure what I wanted to do with mine. The answer should have been obvious.

The .264 Winchester Magnum was introduced in 1958 in a 26-inch-barrel version of the Model 70 called the "Westerner." The cartridge took off like a rocket . . . for just a few years. It was overbore capacity, and was hard on barrels. Worse, Winchester put a bit of blue sky in the initial velocity figures, and word started to get around that the .264 wasn't quite as fast as they promised. In 1962 Remington introduced the 7mm Remington Magnum, which was almost immediately viewed as more versatile than the .264 (and it is). Like all things Winchester, the .264 took another hit with the pre-1964/post-1964 shift. Taken

One of the specialties of Serengeti Rifles was to make laminates by essentially slicing a gunstock, then putting it back together with resin, gaining the strength and stability of laminate, yet retaining the warmth and beauty of good walnut. You have to look pretty hard to see the telltale lines of a laminated stock.

The barrel of the my "Westerner" is an extra-good tube from Obermayr. Accuracy has been consistently excellent from the start, even with vintage factory loads. Due to long decreasing popularity, there's been little development in .264 loads for fifty years. Fortunately, this rifle doesn't need fancy ammo to strut its stuff.

altogether, the .264 fizzled as quickly as it soared; it's really a wonder it didn't become completely obsolete before 1970.

Dad got a .264 in 1966, a little-used rifle from the widow of a guy he knew. It came with a lot of ammo and reloading dies and bullets. I used it for most of my hunting for the next several years. That rifle was an early Remington Model 700 with 24-inch barrel. I didn't have a chronograph back then, so no matter that I never got the velocity I thought I was getting. I still thought the .264 was magic.

That rifle, restocked by Bishop, was one of the rifles I lost to burglars. By then I knew I'd hoodwinked myself: Despite the .264's real or imagined faults, in a 24-inch barrel I wasn't getting anything I couldn't get out of a .270. But I still carried a soft spot for the .264, and I vowed I'd have another one someday, with a proper 26-inch barrel. At different times, I actually bought a couple of pre-1964 Westerners. They had right-hand actions, of course, which meant that I didn't get attached. Although I intended to, I never hunted much with either of them . . . I sold them before I got around to it.

The solution was there, gathering dust in my office: An unusual left-hand action with the correct length and bolt face, and an unchambered 6.5mm barrel that, by all rights, should shoot well. So, the folks at Serengeti Rifles in Montana (regrettably now scattered to the winds) made me a left-hand "Westerner," with a 26-inch medium contour barrel, on one of the laminate stocks that was their specialty. They started with a nice piece of walnut, cut it into slices, and then put it back together as a laminate. You have to look really hard to see that it's a laminate; at first glance, it appears to be good, solid walnut. Seems like that's almost the best of all worlds: You get the warmth and beauty of a nice walnut stock, along with the added strength and weather-resistance of laminate.

At nine pounds, it's not a light rifle, but the stock is good and straight, and it handles well. Original Winchester specs for the .264 called for a 140-grain bullet at 3,200 fps. It would be awesome if you could really get there, but that's almost impossible with safe handloads, and current 140-grain factory loads have long since been downgraded

This Wyoming mule deer was the first animal I took with the Serengeti .264. The .264 never was quite as magical as Winchester claimed in 1958, but it was designed with Western big game in mind, and it's still a solid choice for everything up to elk.

to 3,030 fps. Still, with 140-grain bullets it's no trick to get to about 3,050 fps, and 129- or 130-grain bullets can be pushed quite a bit faster.

Despite all the things that were supposed to be wrong with the .264, it has a pretty good reputation for accuracy. I haven't messed with enough .264s to have an opinion, but this one is very accurate (with that barrel, it should be). It's a sub-MOA rifle all day long with most loads, and on occasion with some loads, I can cut that in half.

Winchester dubbed their original .264 the "Westerner," which to me implies hunting elk. With a 140-grain bullet at over 3,000 fps, the .264 (and all similar 6.5mm cartridges) are very much elk-capable. However, Winchester also seemed to see the .264 as a crossover varmint/deer cartridge, loading a very fast 100-grain bullet. When I was a kid, I used my .264 on prairie dogs. Spectacular, but the .264 is too powerful and has too much recoil for varmint shooting, and there's no way I'm going to pour that many bullets down the barrel of this one. I have never used the .264 for elk, although one day I might. Mostly I've used it for deer-size game, and found it wonderful.

As is true with most of my favorite rifles, I don't use my Serengeti .264 all the time. That's part of the baggage that goes with gunwriting: We don't often choose what we must write about, or have a choice of what we use. There have been a lot of times when I've left the Serengeti .264 in the safe when I might have taken it. But it's been a lot of places! When the rifle was brand-new, I took it on a mule deer hunt in Wyoming, which seemed a great start for a "Westerner." We were hunting on my friend Tom Arthur's ranch near Saratoga, and the day before the season we saw a wide, wonderful buck that Tom and ranch manager Mark Jones knew about, with some nontypical tines that had earned it the name "Stickers."

Donna and I both had tags—her first mule deer—so we tried to find that big nontypical buck for her. Tom and Mark sort of knew

With its laminate stock and 26-inch medium contour barrel, the Serengeti .264 isn't especially light. Against that, trigger pull is excellent and it's extremely stable and easy to hold steady in field positions.

Jack O'Connor was probably right about the .264 when he said that it wouldn't do anything his .270 couldn't do. However, it has the advantage of 6.5mm bullet aerodynamics, and it shoots fast and flat. I took this Blanford urial sheep, a very small sheep, in southwestern Pakistan from about 300 yards with the Serengeti .264.

where that buck lived. We glassed all the likely (and unlikely) places, no sign of him, and the unspoken concern was, with opening day come and gone, how many bucks we should pass; there was no guarantee that Stickers hadn't gone onto a neighbor's or public land, and was already in somebody else's freezer.

Although unavoidable, none of this was good thinking. Stickers was right there, somewhere under our noses. Eventually, Donna shot a very nice typical 4x4. We had just loaded her buck when Stickers popped up out of a draw and bounced over a ridge into a brushy pocket.

Sundown was coming fast before we saw him again, feeding up out of that pocket toward a ridge. Mark and I made a careful approach, getting into position about 275 yards out with the light going fast. The hard part was getting steady; the ground rolled too much and the buck was too low to rest the rifle over my pack, always my fallback position. I had my African shooting sticks, but the shot was much too far to stand over sticks. I unscrewed the legs to make a low tripod and propped up my pack for an elbow rest. The buck was quartering away, and he took about two steps after receiving the 140-grain bullet. It wasn't my best-ever mule deer but, at the time, it was my best in a very long time, in country where my "Westerner" was perfectly at home.

Not long after that, I used the .264 to take a wonderful whitetail at Zack Aultman's place in Georgia, a quick shot down a long lane through the Georgia pines, not enough time to be sure of what he was carrying, just an impression that I'd better take the shot *now*. I was reasonably sure of the shot, but those long lanes are like South Texas *senderos*; there are few landmarks and it's hard to keep perspective. It took a while to figure out where the buck had been standing, and there was no blood. He'd run hard to the left, and I was pretty sure a deep-cut set of tracks were his. I made a quick cast along them and there he was, just a few dozen yards away, one of those few animals that just gets bigger the closer you get. With thick, mahogany-colored antlers, he scored well into the 160s, easily my best Southern whitetail.

The Serengeti .264 served me well on two hunts in Pakistan as well. Down in Baluchistan, it was perfect for the small-bodied urial sheep and Sindh ibex, and of course perfect for Asian gazelles. I also used it up in the Himalayas of northern Pakistan, where it accounted for a huge-bodied Himalayan ibex, the size of a Shetland pony. Hitting at longer distance wasn't an issue; fast 6.5mms shoot *flat*. At some ridiculous elevation in the Hushe Valley, shooting at nearly 400 yards steeply uphill, I hit this big ibex three times—or was it four? I didn't know for sure if I was hitting him at all until he went behind a bush and started sliding down the mountain.

At that point I had used various .270s for some of my Asian mountain hunting, with perfect satisfaction. Depending on how you prefer to make the argument, a fast 6.5mm is a little bit better than

A tough situation in Hushe Valley, northern Pakistan: Deep snow, high altitude, a big ibex far up in the rocks at 350 yards. This is the Himalayan ibex, one of the largest wild goats. The .264 performed just fine, but my "note to self": This may be close to the sensible upper limit of game size for a 6.5mm.

a .270, or not quite as good. Either are fine, but after that experience in northern Pakistan, I went back to a fast .30-caliber for the larger-bodied Asian sheep and goats. That doesn't mean I like that Serengeti rifle less, or that I still don't have a soft spot for the .264.

The Serengeti Westerner has also been to Africa several times. That hearkens back to a Charlie Askins story written when the cartridge was new, titled "The .264 Winchester Magnum in Africa." In a time when bag limits were much higher, Askins took a *lot* of various antelopes with the .264, reporting excellent results. I thought it would be fun to reprise that, and it was! In Namibia, I used it for smaller antelopes like springbok; and on up to hartebeest, gemsbok, wildebeest, and zebra. There were no problems at all, great bullet performance with both 130- and 140-grain slugs, and in open country, such a flat-shooting cartridge simplifies shooting. I had drawn the line; I knew I would *not* be hunting eland with the .264, but I was pretty happy with it all the way up to zebra. Just one thing: My impression was that larger, tougher animals were more likely to require a bit of tracking than if they'd been shot with a larger caliber and heavier bullet.

I also took it to South Africa, on a specialized hunt for brown hyena. That's one of the tough ones; I'd tried before without success. Just before I left the States, PH Tino Erasmus told me he had a big male feeding at a bait, so he was anxious to get the hunt going. I landed in Johannesburg early in the morning, receiving my gun case, but not my duffel with the ammo. I doubted we could find .264 Winchester Magnum loads, and we couldn't, but the Safari and Outdoors store had dies, Nosler brass, and bullets. I picked up a sweater, heavy socks, and other must-haves for a winter night hunt while my friend and store manager Benand Els loaded up some ammo on a "demonstrator" loading press. We got to Tino's place just in time to check zero, and I shot a huge brown hyena that evening.

I won't try to make a strong case for resurrecting the .264. In fact, I can always make a case for choosing *popular* cartridges, just in case you run out or get separated from your ammo! Thanks to the popularity of

I took this double of excellent Kalahari springboks with my Serengeti .264 using a 130-grain Nosler AccuBond bullet. I am hard-pressed to argue that the .264 is "better" than other 6.5mms, .270s, and 7mms, but it's effective on the full run of plains game.

the Creedmoor, there's a much better .264 bullet selection today, and all 6.5mm cartridges have received a shot in the arm. Even so, the .264 Winchester Magnum is "on the rocks," with almost no new rifles so chambered, and a dwindling selection of factory loads.

Even so, it's a fast and effective 6.5mm cartridge. It seems to me that a 140-grain bullet at roundabout 3,000 fps is the 6.5mm "sweet spot." This is *much* faster than the mild 6.5mms such as the 6.5x55, .260 Remington, and 6.5mm Creedmoor, but not as loud nor as overbore capacity as the 26 Nosler and 6.5-.300 Weatherby. The combination of the 140-grain bullet at 3,000 fps is not unique to the .264; the 6.5-.284 Norma and wildcat 6.5-06 will almost get there, and that's exactly what the 6.5mm PRC and Weatherby's new RPM generate. So, if you wanted a fast 6.5mm sort of like mine, then the 6.5mm PRC is probably the most practical horse to ride.

On the bench with the Serengeti .264. Although called "magnum," the .264 is actually a mild-mannered cartridge to shoot, especially when combined with a sensible gun weight and the 26-inch barrel that this cartridge needs. The Serengeti Westerner weighs about 10.5 pounds with a full-size scope, and that is just about right.

I recently realized that I hadn't handloaded for the .264 for many years. Thanks to the popularity of the 6.5mm Creedmoor, bullet choices have greatly expanded. The .264 is overbore capacity, not the kiss of death, but it needs extremely slow-burning propellant and a long barrel, both for best accuracy and to reach full velocity.

PH Barry Burchell and I with the Hartmann's mountain zebra I took in southern Namibia. The .264 performed just fine, but zebra and elk, both tough and weighing perhaps 800 pounds, are probably at the sensible limit for any cartridge using a 140-grain bullet.

My gun case arrived in South Africa but my duffel bag did not, and the hunt was to commence immediately. No .264 ammo could be found (no surprise), but Safari Outdoor in Pretoria had dies, cases, and bullets, so we quickly whipped up fifty rounds. I used them to take a brown hyena that very evening. Here Benand Els is quickly loading up my .264 ammo.

Most manufacturers gave up on the .264 decades ago, so there are few choices in factory loads. Uniquely, Nosler loads multiple "flavors" with bullets from 100 to 140 grains. Of these, this rifle likes the 130-grain AccuBond, a fast and effective choice for deer-size game.

I believe the 6.5mm "sweet spot" is the ability to push a 140-grain bullet to about 3,000 fps, gaining great downrange performance, power for anything and everything up to elk, and acceptable recoil. Left to right are the primary factory "140 grains at 3,000 feet" 6.5mm cartridges: .264 Winchester Magnum; 6.5-.284 Norma; 6.5mm PRC; 6.5mm Weatherby RPM. The old .264 certainly isn't the best, but all of these are similar in performance.

My Serengeti .264 could possibly be rechambered to 6.5mm PRC. The PRC is shorter, so you'd have to take a little bit off the chamber end and rethread the shank for the shorter cartridge, but I think it could be done. I gave it some serious thought . . . for maybe five seconds. My .264 does everything any 6.5mm PRC could possibly do. Because of that excellent barrel, it shoots as well as I could reasonably expect any PRC to shoot. This comes under the heading of "if it ain't broke, don't fix it." The .264 will never again be as popular as it was in its first years of production, but it's still a good hunting cartridge. I intend to keep my .264, and although I don't use it all the time, I will most certainly continue to hunt with it.

Great .270s

Chapter 13

For almost fifty years, I've had one or another rifle chambered in .270 Winchester. Coincidentally, this is just about as long as Jack O'Connor used his .270s. Like me, and to use the military term, O'Connor had at least one "break in service" when he did not own a .270. (His was in the 1930s; mine in the late 1980s). For sure, I haven't championed the cartridge nearly as much as Professor O'Connor did, but I do have a long familiarity with the .270.

I think the first animal I took with a .270 was a black bear (my first), in the spring of 1973. When I was a kid, Dad and I went West for mule deer, and I knew nothing about whitetail hunting. My first experience with whitetails was in the fall of 1974, when I was stationed at Quantico. Virginia was "shotguns only" for deer, but I took a rare three-day weekend and dashed down to North Carolina, which was rifle country. So it was that I took my first-ever whitetail with a .270; by dumb luck, it was a really nice buck for the time and place.

Since then, my periods without a .270 have been short, and corrected as quickly as possible. In Chapter Four I wrote about that Dakota .270 I had for a long time. I used it a lot, and I probably should have kept it. But after Dakota founder Don Allen passed away in 2003, the company was acquired by an odd character; after I got to know him, I didn't want to write about his company. (That's not the only time I've sent some good guns down the road because of a particular personality.) I also had a Browning A-Bolt .270 for a while, a great rifle that shot like gangbusters. There's no good reason why I don't still have it, except that a friend needed a left-hand rifle for one of his kids.

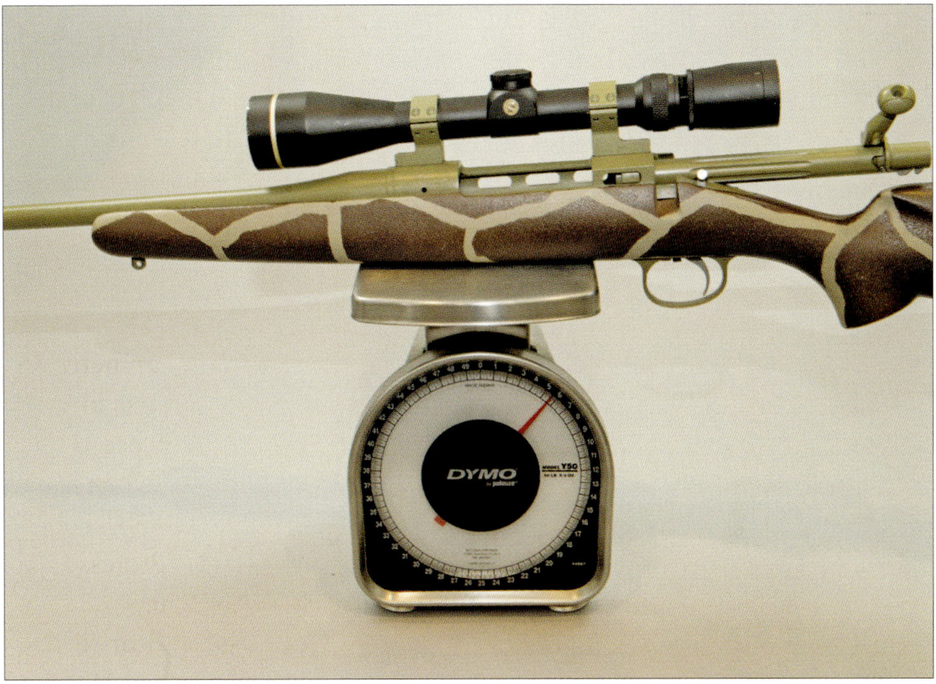

Donna's MGA .270 Winchester that is built on a skeletonized Remington M700 action. With a Leupold 3.5–10X scope attached, it tips the scale at 5.7 pounds. Although I find it almost too light for stable shooting when out of breath, it's a joy to carry in tough country.

Right now, Donna and I have three .270 Winchester rifles, and I don't see any of them going anywhere. One is a .270 barrel for the Blaser R8, accurate and consistent. I think Donna has used it more than I have, but we've both used it quite a bit. In fact, on two different actions, that Blaser .270 barrel has provided good service on all of the six continents that offer hunting opportunities.

Another .270 is really Donna's rifle, although we've shared it. It was built for her by Kerry and Carol O'Day of MG Arms in Spring, Texas. MGA's specialty is building exceptionally light rifles that shoot well. Donna had been doing most of her hunting with a left-hand Ruger M77 .30-06, and doing fine. Although she'd proven over and over that .30-06 recoil is not a problem for her, I still thought she'd be better off with a lighter, more compact rifle.

I also figured the .270 would be more versatile for her purposes, with less recoil. Yeah, that's a different spin on "versatile." Even Jack O'Connor conceded the .30-06 was more versatile than his .270, and he was right, but it depends on what you're doing and where you are. The .270 always shoots flatter and, in Africa, we almost always have something more powerful available for anything the .270 can't handle. We settled on the .270 Winchester for Donna's MGA rifle, after considering that, in a really light rifle, a .30-06 would have a lot of recoil.

The rifle started with a left-hand Remington M700 action, action and bolt handle skeletonized. Metal finish is Cerakote in sort of an olive drab, with the stock painted in a cool and distinctive "giraffe" pattern. The rifle has a blind magazine in a very light synthetic stock, with slender 22-inch barrel. With two-piece alloy bases and one-inch

The MGA .270 is extremely accurate and, for a very light rifle, amazingly nonfinicky. One of the loads it consistently likes is Hornady's inexpensive American Whitetail with plain old 130-grain Interlock bullets.

Leupold 3.5–10x42mm scope, total weight is less than six pounds. The rifle is definitely a joy to carry. Accuracy has been consistently marvelous; with loads the rifle doesn't like, groups open to a bit over an inch. With loads it likes, half-inch groups aren't uncommon. Because the rifle is so light, recoil is considerable, certainly not less than a .30-06 weighing a couple pounds more, but a sub-six-pound .30-06 would be downright unpleasant!

Let me make a side note here: *None* of our favorite rifles have muzzle brakes. They work and, like many gunmakers, the MGA folks recommend them. I avoid them, figuring I'm already deaf enough and don't need to lose any more hearing. These days, I keep sound-magnifying Walker earmuffs in my daypack, and I take them into deer stands with me. But, sooner or later, I know I'll take a shot and forget to put them on. That's always an error, but with a muzzle brake, it's a *bad* mistake.

When the rifle was brand-new in 2007, Donna used the MGA .270 for pronghorn, mule deer, and her first elk (proving, once again, that the .270 is just fine for elk if you place your shot properly). One of the first times we took it overseas was to Turkey in 2009. Donna wanted one of those monstrous Turkish wild boars, and I was going to hunt Anatolian chamois. I figured a .270 was all we really needed, so the plan was to share her MGA. She got a huge boar, so big it looked like a grizzly, and after a tough and lucky hunt in deep snow, I got a chamois. The Asian races of chamois, the Caucasian in southern Russia and the Anatolian in Turkey, are usually the two most difficult of the various races of chamois.

In between hunting boars in the rugged hills inland from the Black Sea, and going toward the Iranian border for chamois, we added a hunt for stags in the high country west of Ankara. In Asia, where much hunting is on a quota system, you never know what opportunity might come along. Outfitter Kaan Karakaya had a leftover permit for the big Anatolian stag (also called mid-eastern red deer). The price was good and, theoretically, we had time. Donna said OK, so I said OK.

Overlooking a Georgia power line right-of-way with the MGA .270, we're all set to go. Now, if a buck would just step out!

What we didn't know was that the rut was over and the stags had quit roaring. Things weren't looking good, and on our last morning the mountains were cloaked in dense fog. We were sitting on a knoll, hoping it might clear. Almost on command, a window opened in the clouds, and a big stag stepped out of the mist. The Turkish stags are some of the largest-bodied of the red deer, the size of North American elk, and the distance was 400 yards. I was shooting Hornady's brand-new GMX bullet, and the clouds were closing in again. I shot, and kept shooting. From the first shot I was sure the stag would go down, but I was losing visibility fast. We saw him stumble, and then clouds closed in and we had to find him by feeling our way. I'd held at the top of the shoulder, and I'd printed a nice, tight four-shot group, with three of the bullets exiting.

Over the next few years that rifle accounted for a lot of game in many places, mostly with Donna on the trigger, but sometimes me, because it never changed zero, and a really accurate .270 is *useful!*

By 2015 she'd taken a couple of chamois and a second tahr in New Zealand, and had the bug for mountain game. We did a backpack hunt in Alaska's Brooks Range with Eric Salitan of Bushwhack Alaska, a good outfitter. Unfortunately we got completely weathered out, no shots fired, no opportunities.

With friends Joe and Sara Bishop, we planned a hunt in Mongolia for September 2018, intended to be my longtime hunting partner's last "big hunt." Donna would have taken her MGA .270, but we met up with Kerry O'Day on a hunt in Texas and he insisted on taking it home with him for refurbishing. After a decade of hard use, it needed some TLC. That meant it wasn't available for Mongolia, so Donna wound up using the .270 barrel on her Blaser R8 action. Just a few weeks before the hunt, Joe's cancer returned and he was unable to go. Always practical, he insisted that Donna and I go, and we did.

On the last day of the 2018 Safari Club Convention I found Donna at Dave Leonard's Mountain Monarchs booth, booking a Brooks

Donna and Zack Aultman pose with a nice Georgia whitetail that she took on his power line the evening before with the MGA .270.

On a snowy day in eastern Turkey, I used Donna's MGA .270 to take this Anatolian chamois. The Asian chamois populations are probably the most difficult to hunt of the several races of chamois.

Range backpack sheep hunt with her friend Lisa McNamee. I piddled around base camp at Bettles with Brother Dave, while we listened for satellite updates. On the sixth day Donna took a gorgeous Dall ram with her refurbished MGA .270. A couple days later, hunting separately from a different spike camp, Lisa also took an awesome ram.

While writing this chapter, Donna and I were hunting on Isla de Carmen, off the coast from Loreto in Baja Sur. I wasn't hunting, but Donna and son-in-law Brad Jannenga were, both for the *weemsi* subspecies of desert bighorn, Brad with a bow, Donna with her MGA .270. On the third day, Brad made an awesome forty-two-yard frontal shot on a *big* ram. Donna's hunt was more difficult, but on the sixth day she shot a fourteen-year-old ram with massive bases, carrying the mass throughout, with both horns broomed back. After much effort and some challenges, her shot was a set-piece situation, 270 yards from one ridge to another, across a rocky canyon. I suspect she'll keep using that MGA .270, but whether I'll be allowed to borrow it is becoming questionable.

A *true* custom rifle, built from scratch for the owner, is a rare bird, especially if the owner happens to be me. But that doesn't mean I don't admire finely crafted firearms that were built for somebody else. My old friend and mentor John Wootters had a couple of gorgeous rifles made by custom maker Joe Balickie, a longtime leader in the American Custom Gunmakers Guild (ACGG). One was a Winchester Model 88 .308 in awesome walnut, with all the flaws of the imperfect Model 88 wonderfully corrected. Balickie and Wootters were old friends, and Joe was there on a couple of hunts on John and Jeannie Wootters' South Texas ranch. Joe Balickie's trademark was slim, trim, beautiful wood, and his rifles shot straight. I long coveted

Donna was in northwestern Colorado with Mark Jones when she took this elk—her first—using the MGA .270. The .270 is probably on the marginal side for elk, but it's on the right side of the margin.

My .270, made by Balickie, is based on an unusual left-hand Carl Gustav action. Built some thirty years ago, the rifle is super-accurate and not finicky, but it especially likes homogenous alloy bullets; the top right group was shot with 130-grain GMX.

a rifle that he'd made, especially one of his lever-action Model 88s, which few custom gunsmiths ever messed with. At the time, his work was far above my pay grade . . . and then Joe retired.

Not so long ago, Joe, now in his eighties, contacted me. He had a .270 he'd made decades earlier on a left-hand Carl Gustav action. The client he'd built it for had passed away, so he had it on consignment from the family and thought I might be interested. Honestly, I'd never seen a Carl Gustav left-hand action, but I was already hooked. He said to me, "Typical Balickie stock." (This meant "spectacular.")

I asked, "Joe, do you know if it shoots?"

Classic Balickie: "Well, it did when I built it!"

He named a price, although I still hadn't seen the rifle, and there were no photographs. "Gee, Joe," I said, "that seems a bit steep."

I didn't hear the *harrummphh*, but it was there: "Well, hell, it would be a lot more if I was still working."

The MGA .270 was almost new when Donna used it for her first pronghorn, an excellent Wyoming buck. I believe the .270 is perfect for pronghorn.

This kudu was running across a brushy valley in southern Namibia when I pasted it with the Balickie .270. A rifle's handling qualities are hard to describe and vary from person to person. With this rifle, that's the difference between good and great: It comes up fast and shoots straight.

I couldn't argue with that, so I quibbled no further and sent Mr. Balickie a check, still having no idea what the rifle looked like!

The Carl Gustav action is very smooth, but also tight and positive. The stock is, well, Joe Balickie: excellent walnut, probably English, very slim and trim, perfect inletting and checkering, classic and classy, 22-inch barrel, apparently shot very little with almost no wear and tear and obviously well cared for.

At five feet, nine inches, I'm Joe Average in size, so standard factory stock dimensions tend to fit me pretty well. And, unless the person a custom rifle was built for is unusually short or tall, a lot of custom rifles also fit me. This Balickie rifle fits like a glove and handles wonderfully.

In a custom rifle built for someone else there are almost always little things (and sometimes big things) I would have done differently. This one has a blind magazine, and I prefer a floorplate. With

Donna's .270, the blind magazine reduces weight, and light weight was a goal. Habitually, I load and unload bolt-actions from the top, rarely opening a floorplate, so it's really just a matter of preference; it doesn't keep me from liking the rifle, but I'd have done it differently. And, drop-floorplates are easier to keep clean.

It also has a checkered steel buttplate with a trap. Buttplate compartments are cool, but I wish I knew what this one was for! The recess is 2.25 inches tall, 1 inch wide, and 2.25 inches deep. It won't hold .270 cartridges or a segmented cleaning rod, but I suppose it would hold a pull-through cleaning rod. So, although it's a nice touch, it's an oddity.

The rifle came with a vintage Leupold 2–7X scope with one-inch tube in equally vintage two-piece Buehler mounts. My first thought was that I'd update the scope, perhaps with a 3–9X or 3.5–10X like Donna has on her .270. Fortunately, I figured I'd better shoot it first! The first group, Hornady factory ammo with 130-grain GMX,

In January 2021, Donna used her MGA .270 with a Hornady 130-grain Interlock bullet to take this awesome old desert bighorn. The hunt was on Carmen Island in the Sea of Cortez, the shot about 250 yards.

printed a bit less than a third of an inch, just a couple inches low and left. The old scope responded perfectly and came into zero, so I figured I'd better leave it alone. With 22-inch barrel, the total weight with scope and mounts is 7¾ pounds, a nice weight that Professor O'Connor and I agree is pretty close to just right.

As I'm sure we all know, O'Connor did much of his later sheep hunting with his "No. 2" .270 by Al Biesen, on a Featherweight Model 70 action. Jack had no compunctions about taking this and other nice rifles stocked in good walnut on tough hunts, but perhaps that's because synthetic sporter stocks were very uncommon in his day. Me, I'm not about to take this Balickie .270 on a serious mountain hunt!

I have hunted with it, and will hunt with it more; I can't imagine owning an accurate, reliable sporting rifle and *not* hunting with it . . . but I'm careful where I take it. So far, I've used it mostly for feral hogs and deer hunting. In June and July of 2018, the Balickie

Taken in January 2021, this Alabama whitetail is certainly no giant, but he's going to be very tasty, and he was dropped in his tracks at 200 yards with the Balickie .270. In my world, sometimes *the rifle is more important than the game or the hunt.*

I was 400 yards away when I shot this huge Anatolian stag in central Turkey with the MGA .270 and using Hornady's then-new GMX homogenous-alloy bullet.

The perfect handload for the Balickie .270 is still a work in progress, but it's responding well to good old IMR 4831 with both 130- and 140-grain bullets. This group was fired with 130-grain Swift Scirocco, an excellent tipped-and-bonded bullet.

I took this excellent red hartebeest in Namibia with the Balickie .270 at 300 yards. The rifle came with a vintage 2–7X Leupold scope. My first thought was that I should replace it with a somewhat larger and more modern scope, but it shoots so well I'm probably going to leave it alone!

The Balickie .270, all set to go up into a tall whitetail stand. I have pledged to be careful where I take this rifle. It's not going to see any sheep hunting, but it's ideal for a lot of deer hunting.

rifle and I spent a full month in Namibia. The country is rocky and often dusty, but in their winter, rain is unlikely, so it's a place where you can take a nice rifle without undue risk. Namibia is also a place where an accurate .270 really shines! I made a couple of longish shots on gemsbok and hartebeest, and took a nice kudu bull running through a brushy valley. The rifle was *fun* to use, the older scope adequate. And, as always, its .270 Winchester cartridge lived up to its reputation.

I will *not* take the Balickie rifle to Central Africa, nor to the swamps of coastal Mozambique, no more than I'd take it on a tough mountain hunt. Fortunately, there are lots of places I *can* take it. I suppose you could say it is sort of the culmination of a search for a near-perfect .270, made better by long friendship with the artist who made it. I call it a favorite, and I trust it completely. In time, I'm sure it will become an old friend.

A 7x57 Stalking Rifle

Chapter 14

Looks are important to me in hunting rifles. My preferences run toward the traditional: Straight, classic buttstocks, slim and trim fore-ends. The practicality of rustproof metal and the strength and durability of laminates and synthetic stocks have undeniable appeal. Even so, in my heart of hearts I prefer good walnut with cut checkering and blued steel.

I'm less picky on certain details. My longtime boss and longer-time friend Ken Elliott believed that scoped hunting rifles should also wear iron sights. His reasoning (I think) wasn't so auxiliary irons were available if a scope failed; it was more a matter of *completeness.* I must not agree because most of my hunting rifles (including my favorites) have plain barrels. I have had scope (and mount) failures, but I've also had iron sights break and bend. Most of my large-caliber rifles wear iron sights, and I'm pretty religious about knowing how they shoot. Even so, only a couple times in my entire hunting life have I purposefully removed a perfectly good scope in favor of irons, and once when I did, it was a mistake.

I was in northern Cameroon, shooting a .375 Weatherby Magnum. Theoretically I had plenty of eye relief, or at least I thought I did. At the bench at home, there was no problem, but in hundred-plus degree heat, with lots of sweat, only a thin cotton shirt, and hard, fast recoil, I received multiple scope cuts. Toward the end of the hunt, I had only a buffalo license remaining so I took the scope off. Up until that point we'd been up close and personal with buffalo almost every day. I'd held off because of Cameroon's odd licensing system (two "Class A" animals, three "Class B" and so forth). The shot

I borrowed a vintage .275 Rigby stalking rifle to take this roebuck in England. This is very similar to a .275 that Walter Bell might have owned, but, like so many older rifles, it was originally "iron sights only," later modified to scope use.

I got was nearly a hundred yards, which is far for open express sights (at least for me). Predictable outcome: The buffalo was wounded, hit a bit far forward. We got him without drama, another hundred-yard shot up on a low ridge. That was back when I was still 20/10 in both eyes; today I would never consider removing a functioning scope in favor of irons, or shooting at a buffalo at a hundred yards without a scope. I still enjoy hunting with iron sights, but I'm careful about where I use them. Today I hunt mostly with scopes, with reflex (red-dot) sights as a close-range alternative.

Even so, *some* rifles really need iron sights in order to be complete, whether I'm actually going to use them or not. My Todd Ramirez 7x57 stalking rifle is one of those. The "stalking rifle" is a form of hunting rifle that I have admired (and coveted) most of my life.

The connotation is obvious: A rifle intended for closing on game, creeping and crawling as required. Not so obvious: "Stalking" is the proper English term for hunting four-legged game from deer on up. "Shooting" refers to birds and small game, while "hunting" is reserved for riding to the hounds. In the British Isles deer are a cash crop. Antler quality is unimportant. The best bucks and stags are often spared for breeding; the approach for a close shot or "stalk" is everything. So, the proper "stalking rifle" was developed more than a century ago, based primarily on pursuing roebuck and red deer in the Scottish hills and English countryside.

The rifle needs to be light and handy, the cartridge versatile and powerful enough for the biggest stags. Extremely flat trajectory and long-range power projection doesn't matter because the goal is to get as close as possible; the long distances we routinely shoot today are still considered "unsporting" by many professional game keepers throughout the British Isles.

From the collection of Bill Jones, this Holland & Holland falling-block single-shot was built in 1898 for Frederick Selous. Chambered in 6.5x53R, it's a classic "stalking rifle," and I used it in northern Namibia to take this excellent Angolan black-faced impala.

My beautiful Dakota Model 10 falling block single-shot certainly fills the bill as a "stalking rifle," which I used to stalk this 6-point roebuck in Scotland. The rifle is roll-marked ".275 Rigby," identical to the 7x57.

The stalking rifle didn't have to be a bolt-action. Bill Jones's Holland & Holland falling block in 6.5x53R, built in 1898 for Frederick Selous, is definitely a stalking rifle. So is my Dakota Model 10 falling block, roll-marked .275 Rigby. However, the most classic form probably emerged as a bolt-action.

Rigby's pre-World War I exclusive agreement with Mauser gave the firm an edge, and their fast 140-grain load for the .275 Rigby was perfect for stalking, powerful enough for any red stag, and fast and flat-shooting for the day. As we know, .275 Rigby stalking rifles weren't restricted to use at home. Walter Bell comes to mind; he bought six .275 Rigby rifles. Jim Corbett's .275, now in the Rigby collection, must be one of the most famous of all sporting rifles. I've held that rifle; touching it sent goose bumps up my spine. The late Fred Duckworth, colorful character and career African PH with experience all over the continent, spent his early years in India. He once told me a story of, as a young boy, going north to the "hill country" (now Pakistan) and watching his father take a markhor with his .275 Rigby.

These early stalking rifles were almost all iron-sight-only rifles, usually with express-type rear sights with multiple folding leaves, although aperture sights weren't unusual. As such, they were stocked accordingly with lower combs. Most bolt-action receivers, certainly Mausers, can easily be drilled and tapped for scopes, and many early rifles were so modified. However, as originally stocked, the combs are often too low for proper cheek-weld with scopes. As scopes came into common use, combs were raised for use with scopes. This is the form of Rigby's new Highland Stalker, a beautifully made and classic stalking rifle. Considering what it is and where it comes from, it is reasonably priced.

This is another situation where being left-handed causes problems. I've admired the classic stalking rifle throughout my adult life, but I've never seen a vintage example with left-hand bolt. Like

Rigby's current London-made Highland Stalker is a faithful reissue of a traditional British "stalking rifle." Its two primary nods to modernity are that the receiver is adapted for scope use and the comb is higher for proper cheek weld with a low-mounted scope. My only problem with the Highland Stalker is it is right-hand bolt only. This rifle is roll-marked ".275 Rigby/7x57."

The first animal I took with my Ramirez 7x57 was this South Texas whitetail. It came running to antler-rattling, put on the brakes, and went down in his tracks to a single 140-grain InterBond bullet. Fast-handling and versatile, this rifle remains my favorite for whitetail.

the Rigby Big Game, the Highland Stalker is right-hand only. No matter; I have a southpaw stalking rifle. It is not only a favorite rifle; it is the only rifle I have ever owned that was completely built "from scratch" to my preferences and specifications.

It was crafted nearly twenty years ago by Texas custom maker Todd Ramirez, a youngster then, but then and now, an amazing talent. From the ground, the concept was to re-create a proper stalking rifle, certainly not because that's the "best" configuration for a sporting rifle, but because that's what I wanted.

We discussed chamberings. By the early 2000s there were a lot more choices than there were in 1912. Briefly, I thought about .30-06 and considered .270, but in keeping with the configuration of the rifle, I decided it must be a 7x57, always useful and, even then, a longtime favorite. Todd asked if I preferred roll-marking ".275 Rigby." I decided not; to do so would have been pure ego and, after all, the rifle would be a Ramirez, not a Rigby. Practically, 7x57 brass is common. At that time, .275 Rigby brass was unavailable, and I've hunted a number of countries where cartridge headstamps must match the rollmark on the rifle. Hornady now offers ".275 Rigby" brass and loaded ammo. My Dakota single-shot is so marked, but I'd make the same decision today: 7x57 is good enough. (Interestingly, Rigby's new rifles are marked ".275 Rigby/7x57.")

I spent time in Todd's shop, looking at wood, discussing details, Todd taking careful measurements. The rifle is built on a left-hand Granite Mountain CNC-machined Mauser clone, with a five-shot magazine box with floorplate release in the trigger bow. We decided against left-hand cast in the stock; I'm not used to it, and dead-straight fits me just fine. The butt has a shallow but traditional sculpted cheekpiece, with the straight comb just high enough to accommodate a low-mounted scope. The rifle wears New England

The 7x57 and .275 Rigby are identical and interchangeable. Hornady offers ammo and brass headstamped either way, an important detail for international hunters, since some countries require that cartridge headstamps match the roll-mark on the barrel.

Based on a Granite Mountain left-hand Mauser clone with five-shot magazine capacity, the Ramirez rifle has a custom detachable scope mount. Although I have used several scopes on this rifle, it typically wears a bright 1.75–6X Schmidt & Bender. (Photo by Michael Anschuetz)

express sights with hooded bead-on-ramp front with one standing and one folding leaf rear sight.

Older rifles often had a bunch of folding leaves; I had a Westley Richards .318 with folding leaves to 500 yards, but I figured that was optimistic and, considering my vision even twenty years ago, silly. Also, I intended to use it with a scope, and that's the way it is stocked. As a result, I have to scrunch my face a bit to get properly down on the iron sights—but that's the way it has to be. It is impossible to stock a rifle so that the cheek weld and sight picture are equally comfortable and perfect with both iron sights on the barrel and with a scope mounted on the receiver.

The stock is excellent walnut, stained dark as I requested, the checkering incredibly fine and perfectly executed. The fore-end, with ebony tip, is short, in keeping with the 22-inch barrel, and leaving plenty of room for a barrel-mounted forward sling swivel. The butt plate and pistol grip cap are skeletonized, with the exposed wood checkered. This was not a mistake because the fit and checkering are perfect. However, the buttplate is the most fragile and thus perhaps the only impractical aspect of the entire rifle. I have to be extremely careful where and how I set it down.

The stock has recoil lug bolts with escutcheons, and the action is double-square bridge. The detachable scope mount is of Todd's design, spring-loaded plungers on the bases that mate perfectly into the bridges. The scope rings and cocking piece shroud are color-case-hardened; the rest of the metal magnificently blued except for the jeweled bolt sleeve and nitre-blued long Mauser extractor. Todd and I discussed engraving, but that really isn't my thing; other than

When planning my 7x57 stalking rifle, I spent a lot of time in Todd Ramirez's shop choosing wood, taking measurements, and going over details. A possible error may have been the ordering of a skeleton butt plate; this is the most fragile and vulnerable part of the rifle. I must be very careful where and how I set the rifle down.

Checking zero in Victoria, southern Australia. Although I make slight variations to the loads of 140-grain bullets, I can't remember the last time I had to adjust the scope.

the checkered bolt handle, there is almost no embellishment. This rifle doesn't need it; it's gorgeous and perfect just the way it is.

Todd built both one-inch and 30mm scope rings, so I've gone back and forth with a 3–9X Swarovski and a 2–7X Leupold with one-inch tube, but mostly it wears a 30mm 1.75–6X Schmidt and Bender. The latter scope is the heaviest of the three; with it in place, the total rifle weighs 7¾ pounds, easy to carry and heavy enough to be stable for fast offhand shooting.

To keep it at that weight, the barrel is fairly slender. Accuracy was *always* good enough for any purpose I might have for a 7x57, but it took a while to break it in properly. At first, I was concerned that it seemed a bit finicky. After some shooting, it settled down nicely, easily sub-MOA with decent loads. More importantly, it is *consistent*. I haven't adjusted the scope for years. Of course, I check zero—but it's always ready to go hunting. I am *not* profligate with my expenditure of ammo in this rifle, but that's an advantage to cartridges like the 7x57 at moderate velocity: I'd have to work hard to wear out the barrel. Mostly I shoot 140-grain bullets, sometimes 150-grain, but rarely heavier, although I still have a small supply of 175-grain Barnes Super Solids loaded up just in case I have a Karamoja moment! If I ever do, the express sights are perfectly zeroed for close range.

Let's get real: I'm careful where I take it, an inherent drawback to any nice rifle stocked in good wood. It was fairly new when Donna and I took it to New Zealand, where we did some really tough walk-up hunting for Himalayan tahr and free-range red stag. It did just fine, but since then I have not taken it up any sheep or goat

The Ramirez rifle has seen honest use all over the world, but I haven't taken it up many sheep and goat mountains. Donna used it to take her first Himalayan tahr on a tough hunt in New Zealand, but since then, I have tried to keep it away from rocks.

The slender barrel took quite a bit of time to break in—enough that, for a time, I was concerned. I needn't have been; once broken in, its accuracy has remained consistent and excellent. The group on the right: 100 yards with 140-grain Interlock bullets and scope, a bit high; the group on the left was with 175-grain Barnes Super Solid bullets, just right at 50 yards with iron sights.

mountains. Therefore, I haven't taken it to either Alaska or Asia, where conditions are usually especially tough on good rifles, and I haven't taken it on any horseback hunts.

Elsewhere, it's been used fairly hard. The fit is perfect, because it was genuinely fitted to me, making it fast and lively. It's a "go to" whitetail rifle, and it's been to Argentina and Australia, as well as several times to Africa and Europe. Typically, I think of it for situations where shots are unlikely to exceed 300 yards. As far as size of game, I don't really worry about that. It's plenty of gun for red stag and any African antelope short of eland. I have not taken it elk hunting, simply because so much American elk hunting is second only to sheep and goat hunts in toughness.

The first time I used it was on a whitetail hunt in South Texas, on the Killam family's huge Duvall County Ranch. I haven't taken many whitetails by rattling. Although a South Texas specialty, conditions have to be right, but when it happens, it's magic, and it happens *fast*. Michael De Witt, a genuine rattling expert, was on the "horns" when a gorgeous, chocolate-racked buck with heavy antlers came dashing out of a prickly pear thicket.

I usually carry a grunt tube, a great way to stop a buck, at least for an instant. But Michael gave his signature cat *meow* and the buck put on the brakes. The Ramirez rifle was ready, came up smoothly, and I dropped the buck with a frontal shot, center of the chest, quicker than it takes to tell.

That was the first buck I took as a result of rattling, just one of many firsts for the Ramirez rifle. Over the years, it's accounted for a lot of animals I'd never taken before. That's sort of par for the course in international hunting, where a lot of animals are unfamiliar.

The Ramirez rifle has its share of these, but a favorite "first" to its credit includes the first whitetail taken on our Kansas farm, certainly

This is the largest feral hog I have ever seen; it has good tusks, too. It was taken on a hunt with dogs in Argentina. With a frontal shot at very close range, the big boar went down on the spot.

I took this fine southern greater kudu in Namibia with a single 140-grain Interbond bullet, which went in one shoulder and out the other. It was a fast shot at close range . . . exactly what the rifle does best.

not our biggest buck, but the hardest-won. Nothing had been done with food plots or management for years, and I knew little about our deer. Even so, I passed some nice bucks the first few days and figured this would be a snap. Then the moon got bright and deer movement slowed to a trickle.

Despite hard hunting, by the next-to-last day of the season I was worn out and discouraged. I almost didn't go out that afternoon, but I went down to our (then one and only) tower stand. Maybe I was a little late, because I hadn't even started up the ladder when an 8-point stepped into our fledgling food plot about 150 yards away. Like several bucks I'd passed over the previous ten days, he was OK, but a bit young. The decision not to shoot was already made; I was just about to climb on up to the stand when I realized he wasn't looking in my direction, but off to the right, into the woods. Resting the Ramirez rifle against the ladder, I spotted the *second* buck, not huge, but much older, with a heavier rack. I stood frozen for long seconds, then shot him when he stepped out of the woods.

A year or two earlier, Donna also used it for her first whitetail. We were hunting on Jack Fields' *Dos Angeles* ranch, along a beautiful winding stream that served as Pinto Creek for some of the *Lonesome Dove* filming. Jack had a marvelous herd of blackbuck on that ranch, so I'm not sure if we were really hunting whitetails or just *hunting*, but just past sundown Jack spotted a very nice, mature whitetail slipping along some riverine brush. Deer season was open and Donna had a license, so she grabbed "our" 7x57 and dropped him. At that stage she'd been to Africa with me a couple of times, but she'd never shot a deer of any kind. Jack congratulated her on a great shot, and it was. She said something like, "Thanks, I've been practicing on impalas!"

In my younger days I was more of a magnum maniac. There was a time when, despite the teachings of Walter Bell and Professor O'Connor, I might have questioned the power level of the 7x57 for game such as red deer, elk, and greater kudu. Those days have been over for a long time. I think it was 2005, in Namibia with my old friend Dirk de Bod, when we came up onto a little bench and I spotted a magnificent kudu bull staring at us from some thick stuff, with just a small window on his shoulder wide open. Dirk instantly said those magic words, "Take him!"

I raised the Ramirez rifle and shot him offhand, absolutely certain of the shot, seeing the cross hairs steady on the shoulder, one-third up from the brisket.

At the shot, he crashed off into the brush, vanishing instantly. Long seconds passed before Dirk, equally certain, said quietly, "Craig, you missed."

We stepped into the thorn, me going to the left, Dirk to the right, both of us perplexed. Turns out there had been *two* kudu bulls, and each of us had fixated on one and had not even seen the other! We regrouped and found mine, stone dead twenty yards away, with a 140-grain InterBond having gone through the top of the heart and out the far shoulder. Neither of us have any idea which was the bigger bull, but we still laugh about it.

I'm notoriously hard on equipment, but I've managed to be pretty careful with this rifle. The wood bears a few honest scratches and dings, and the bluing has gone silver in a couple of places. Todd Ramirez keeps asking me to send it back so he can clean it up, but I'm having none of that; the wear is honorable, part of the rifle and its history . . . and there will be more.

The Blaser System

Chapter 15

We've already seen that my tastes in rifles generally run toward the traditional. This is greatly complicated by my being left-handed. If I were right-handed, I'd probably have at least a few pre-'64 Model 70s, maybe a couple of vintage Mausers. Or, at least I hope I would! Actually, I've owned several of each, but they were all sort of "trading material" that didn't stay around very long. I *can* operate a right-handed bolt, so I hunted with some of these, but none progressed into the "frequent use" category, let alone became favorites. Even so, I have a tremendous soft spot for the looks, lines, and *feel* of classic sporting rifles.

It is therefore amazing to me that I have become such a fan—and frequent user—of the Blaser system, which is very much a "system" and not just a rifle. It was not love at first sight! Back in 2003, one of my editors asked me to take a look at the switch-barrel Blaser R93. Introduced in Germany in 1993, the R93 quickly became fairly popular in Europe, but in the early 2000s the rifles were almost unheard-of in the United States. As I recall, the barrels on that test rifle were .22-250 and .270. Accuracy was excellent, and the modularity was impressive: Switching barrels was fast and simple, and the unique detachable saddle mount was wonderfully repeatable. The cocking piece took some getting used to, and I could see that, with practice, the straight-pull bolt would be very fast. I was impressed, but not ecstatic. In retrospect, I realize now that I just didn't "get it." That test rifle had a right-hand bolt, and there was no way left-handed me could properly appreciate the straight-pull action while operating it with the wrong hand.

The first time I hunted with a Blaser R8 was in Nepal in April 2010. Outfitter Mahesh Busnyat points, below, to my one and only "check zero" shot on the first day. Ten days later, I used the .300 Blaser Magnum barrel to take this big Himalayan blue sheep at a bit over 500 yards.

Operating a right-hand Blaser left-handed isn't nearly as fast as having the bolt on the left side. I can now handle right-hand Blasers just fine—but only after I became familiar with Blasers with a left-hand bolt. Of course, the stock on my initial test rifle was also right-handed, and very European in design. The workmanship was excellent, the mechanics amazing, but I didn't have a burning desire to run out and buy one.

Apparently, a lot of folks appreciated the rifle more than I did. Between 1993 and 2017, Blaser produced more than 200,000 R93s, a huge number for a rifle in its price range. By end of R93 production, its successor, the R8, had been on the market for a decade, reaching 100,000 in 2015. There are significant mechanical differences between the R8 and R93 with limited parts interchangeable, but the operation is essentially the same. In Spain in 2012, I borrowed a right-handed R93, using it for wild goats on Mallorca and Beceite ibex on the mainland. This was no problem, because by then the R8 was already an old friend, and I had become completely sold on the Blaser system.

The R8 was introduced in Europe in 2008, and in early January 2010 was unveiled to a group of writers at an event in Texas. Wisely, they had one available with a left-hand bolt. Like the R93, the R8 is a straight-pull, operated by direct back and forth action of the bolt handle. Lockup is accomplished by a fourteen-lug radial collet that locks into a barrel recess when the bolt is fully in battery. The concentric 360-degree lockup almost certainly contributes to accuracy, and the system is very strong. The R93's radial lugs have more bearing surface than the Mauser's two large dual-opposing locking lugs, and the R8 locks up with about 50 percent more bearing surface than the R93.

The R8 has a unique detachable magazine that includes the trigger assembly at the bottom rear, making the R8 two to almost two and a half inches shorter than conventional bolt-actions with the same barrel length. Although ingenious and an obvious extra safety measure, I wasn't all that excited about the magazine system: Lose the magazine and you've got no trigger (I will come back to that!). I

Prior to 2010, I had never hunted with any Blaser rifle. There are many of the older R93s still in use. Though few parts are interchangeable, the operation is similar to the R8. Since then, I've borrowed several R93s. I took this Beceite ibex in Spain using an R93 in 7mm Remington Magnum.

was a lot more enthusiastic about the new stock. Although the first R8s wore stocks that were still somewhat Germanic in lines (it is, after all, a German rifle), this R8 stock was completely redesigned, with a higher, straighter comb and a wider, deeper butt that handles like a dream and really soaks up recoil.

As I wrote earlier, I borrowed one for a hunt in Nepal, with left-hand bolt and stock, and, initially, barrels in .300 and .338 Blaser Magnum. Note, please, that this was a major concession: The hunt was not sponsored by anyone; I was paying for it, and there was no advantage to taking a brand-new whiz-bang.

I don't usually go off the deep end over a brand-new and unfamiliar rifle, but I *liked* the R8. I still do! Fortunately, I got the rifle long before the hunt. Both barrels shot extremely well, and I spent a lot of range time becoming familiar with the magazine and the cocking lever. This last is critical: It takes a fair amount of thumb pressure to cock the mainspring, and a little bit of muscle memory to learn how to rock it down to de-cock. Everybody who uses a Blaser is probably going to mess this up a bit at first but, with practice, it quickly becomes second nature.

After the hunt in Nepal, I bought the rifle with both barrels, but when Blaser and Norma decided not to market the Blaser Magnums in the U.S., I traded them in for a .300 Weatherby Magnum and .338 Winchester Magnum barrel. I haven't used the .338 barrel much, but with the .300 Weatherby Magnum barrel I've used the Blaser for almost all of my Asian hunts since 2010, in Kyrgyzstan, Mongolia, Russia, and Pakistan,

The only problem with the rifle was that, although it fits me like a glove, the stock was too long for Donna. We solved that by getting her one, with the stock cut down a bit. Trust me, there were lots of

In 2010 I used my then-new R8 with .338 Blaser Magnum barrel to take this European brown bear in Romania. Although the first shot was fine, this was the first time I truly appreciated the speed of the straight-pull action. This was the only time I used the .338 Blaser Magnum barrel; when Blaser decided not to market the Blaser Magnum barrels in the U.S., I traded the .300 barrel for a .300 Weatherby Magnum barrel and the .338 barrel for a .338 Winchester Magnum.

Donna used a .308 Winchester barrel on her R8 to take this waterbuck out on the floodplains of coastal Mozambique. Donna usually uses a .270 barrel, but she decided on the .308 for this hunt, specifically to gain more bullet weight for use on large antelopes.

choices: R8 barrels are chambered to forty-odd cartridges from .222 Remington to .500 Jeffery! We kept it simple, initially getting her barrels in .270 Winchester and .375 H&H, and later acquiring a .308 Winchester barrel. At an event at FTW Ranch, I shot an R8 with a .500 Jeffery barrel. That's one of the most brutal cartridges I know of. I have no desire to own one of those barrels, but the Blaser stock is so well-designed that it wasn't all that bad.

I'm sure they must exist somewhere, but I've never seen a Blaser barrel that wasn't extremely accurate. I've been to the Blaser factory at Isny; their barrels are made on a huge hammer-forging machine, and they make them very well. All of our barrels shoot tight groups, but I suppose what I like best and most about the Blaser system is it *works*. I can change the barrels back and forth and configure either Donna's rifle or mine for just about anything. The magazines aren't "one size fits all," but for cartridge "groups." The bolt head is similarly interchangeable for different case head diameters, but we keep it a bit simpler, using Donna's bolt with the .308 and .270 barrels, and my bolt for the three belted magnums. The "saddle" scope mounts are equally interchangeable, going back and forth between barrels. It is an extremely repeatable detachable mount, so precise that I haven't seen any shifts in point of impact. However, when you change a scope from one barrel to another you must always zero the rifle.

Historically, I've never been enthusiastic about switch-barrel rifles. Here in North America, we typically prepare a rifle for a hunt—usually for just one animal—so there's no need. Also, we have few restrictions on firearms ownership. In a lot of European countries firearms ownership is limited, so it's handy to have one action with multiple barrels. In part, that's why the Blaser is so popular, almost dominant, among serious European hunters.

Because of the variety of game, African hunting is different. You might hunt buffalo in the morning and impala in the afternoon, or

At a shooting course in Texas, I made a center-punch shot using an R8 with a .500 Jeffery barrel. No one can say the .500 Jeffery is fun to shoot, but the ergonomics of the R8 stock are so good that the huge cartridge is almost manageable.

On a hunt in Mozambique, I reconfigured the left-hand bolt and scope from my R8 with a .300 Weatherby barrel to the "camp's" R8 with a .416 Remington Magnum barrel. Despite a scope change, no zero adjustment was needed; the next day I shot a buffalo with the .416, then switched it all back again.

you might run into a world-record duiker while hunting buffalo. Game animals aren't going to stand around while you change barrels, which is one of the conceptual issues I have with switch-barrel systems: How do you know which barrel should be in place at a given moment? We've taken one Blaser or another with multiple barrels to Africa on a couple of occasions. Where we hunt in Mozambique, we go to the swamps to hunt buffalo, and there isn't much out there besides buffalo. So, when it's time to go to the swamps we put on the .375 barrel; for plains game, we put on a different barrel.

Most of the time, we set up the Blaser with whatever barrel seems most appropriate for a certain hunt, and that barrel and scope stays on the rifle. But here's an example of how interchangeable the Blaser system really is. In camp in Mozambique, the outfitter had a right-handed R8 in .416 Remington Magnum as a camp gun. Donna was hunting with our Montana Rifles 9.3x62 and I had my Blaser with .300 Weatherby Magnum barrel. I wanted to go to the swamp to hunt buffalo, so no problem: I took my left-hand bolt and popped it into Mark's .416. Then, I took the scope off my .300 barrel and put it on the .416 barrel. When switching scopes like that, you need to feel the tightness as you lock the mount into place. The front mount was fine, but I needed to tighten the rear mount screw about a quarter of a turn. Then, to the range.

I bore-sighted and it looked close enough. The rest was pure luck: With a scope zeroed on a different barrel chambered to a different cartridge, the first shot from that .416 barrel hit the exact center of a bull's-eye target at fifty yards. There was no point in wasting any more ammo; I shot a nice buffalo with the outfitter's action and barrel . . . and my bolt and scope.

With multiple barrels, magazine assemblies, two bolts, and two actions, we have to be careful to make sure we have all the pieces in the right places. Generally, it's pretty simple, but barrels vary in diameter. Our .375 barrel is heavy, and the barrel channel on my fore-end won't accommodate it. So, if I want to use the .375 barrel,

I took my first ram in Mongolia with a steep downhill shot from a horribly cramped position in a howling wind. The ram was a massive-horned old giant; the Altai argali has the largest body of any sheep.

I have to switch out my fore-end for Donna's. And be sure not to lose the magazine!

We were hog hunting in Texas, Donna with her Blaser, me with a Steyr .30-06. My friend Conrad Evarts was filming the hunt, so they dropped Conrad and me off in a blind in a side-by-side four-wheeler and took Donna on to a blind about a half-mile away. Amazingly, we had cell service. Conrad and I were just getting situated when Donna called: She'd lost her magazine!

We thought it through; she was pretty sure it had been on the seat of the four-wheeler next to her, probably on the right side. I told her to start my direction while Conrad and I headed her way. The trigger on that assembly is gold-plated. I started walking slowly along the right edge of the track, staring at the ground. I doubt I'd gone two hundred yards when I saw something glittering: the magazine. No harm, no foul—we both shot pigs that evening. That was early in our experience with the Blaser, and it was a good object lesson, so far never repeated.

Once you get the hang of it, the straight-pull action is very fast, requiring much less hand movement than any rotating bolt-action. Throughout much of Europe, organized drives are one of the most common hunting techniques, and fast shots matter. Over there, semiautomatics are often restricted, so speed of operation is another reason for the Blaser's incredible popularity in Europe. I took the R8 with the .270 barrel and an Aimpoint red-dot sight on a driven boar hunt in Sweden in 2019. On the last day, a big hog came from behind, running hard and fast. I hit him more than once and got him stopped, but I shot four times. It wasn't a spectacular display of shooting. Europeans do this all the time and they're better at it than we are, but with a conventional bolt-action I might have gotten off a second shot, no way three or four.

After a full decade of using the Blaser, I'm comfortable with it, and I have my moments. I was in a pop-up blind on a bluff in Alberta on a very cold January morning, looking down at a moose carcass on a frozen river. I'd been on this bluff a year earlier, same frozen river but different moose carcass. That had been a long, cold week, no wolves

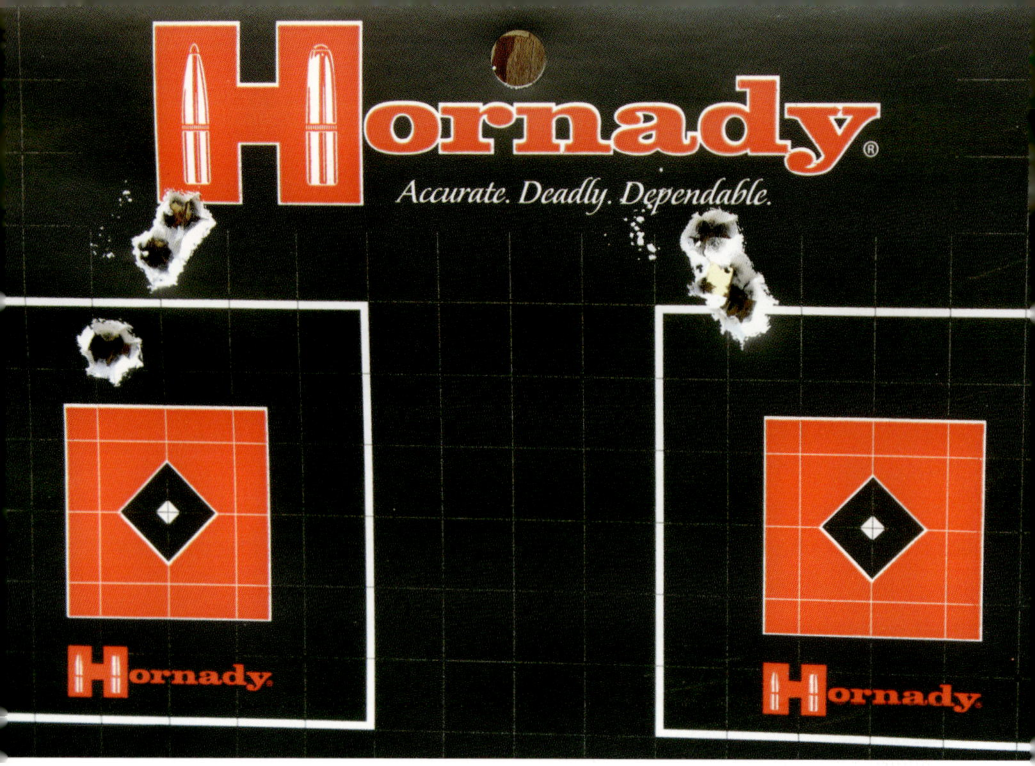

These days, changing scopes is almost like adapting to a new rifle! For a hunt in Mongolia in 2018, I set up my rifle with a new Zeiss 4–16x50mm scope, spending time on the range with the iPhone app and fine-tuning to zero. These are a couple of final groups with 200-grain ELD-X in the .300 Weatherby barrel. Almost there!

It's amusing that I had to go all the way to Mongolia to take a really big elk. This is an Asian wapiti, visually indistinguishable from our elk, taken near the Kazakhstan border. It was a tough hunt but not a tough shot, about 200 yards with the Blaser R8 with a .300 Weatherby Magnum barrel.

Although both of us used Blaser R8 rifles, Donna and I used opposite approaches for the 2018 Mongolia hunt, I using a .300 Weatherby Magnum barrel and large Zeiss scope and she using a .270 Winchester barrel with a medium-size 3–9X scope. Both concepts worked just fine. The photo shows my sheep horns next to the sheep shot by my wife.

seen, but I figured outfitter Trent Packham knew what he was doing. I returned a year later, and this was the first morning. I'd practiced the drill as soon as it got light. Shooting sticks were propped by the window, knife open in the snow so I could cut the window net and get the barrel out. The moose was exactly two hundred yards below me. Cut the net, get the barrel out, fore-end on the sticks.

I decided to read, which is just about the only way I can sit still in a blind. I try to read just a few lines, then look. I don't think I'd finished a page when I glanced up and saw three wolves trotting up the river. In the lead was a monstrous black wolf, trailed by a smaller black wolf and a big gray. I cut the net and slowly got the barrel out. I saw the first wolf go down hard, the other two reversing and streaking down the river. The second black wolf hadn't gone ten yards before I got thc cross hairs moving ahead of it. This one somersaulted onto the ice, and I just plain got lucky with the third, a going-away shot well down the river. I was shooting the R8 with .300 Weatherby Magnum barrel, a lot of gun, but I know it well. I *probably* could have made the first shot with a lot of rifles, but the next two were pure Blaser.

When Donna and I went to Mongolia in 2018, she took her Blaser with .270 barrel, and I took mine with, of course, the .300 Weatherby barrel. We both took big Asian wapitis as well as argalis, the world's largest wild sheep. I'm not prepared to say that the .270 Winchester is the perfect tool for either animal, but she knows the cartridge and she knows her Blaser. And I knew my Blaser and its cartridge.

None of our shots were particularly long, but there's a huge amount of pressure on a hunt like that. Whatever shot you draw, you must make it; you cannot expect a second chance. There's no substitute for a rifle you know well and trust. As my late friend Joe Bishop intended, the Mongolian hunt was the mountain hunt of a lifetime . . . and we got good rams. I was happy we entrusted this hunt to our Blaser R8s. They didn't let us down.

Synthetic-stocked versions weren't available when we got our Blasers. At the start, mine had really good wood, Donna's a bit

The Blaser is very much a modular system, and not just the barrels. The most visible difference between the R8 (shown) and the older R93: The R8's trigger assembly is integral to the detachable magazine (better not lose it!). Bolt heads can be interchanged, and various magazine inserts are used for various "families" of cartridges.

Switching Blaser barrels takes about one minute. With the bolt open, simply undo the two hex-head, fore-end bolts, remove the barrel, put in the next barrel, and re-tighten the bolts. Unless removal is desired, the scope remains with the barrel. Checking zero is always best for confidence, but I have rarely seen any zero shift from switching barrels.

Attaching and reattaching the unique Blaser saddle mount is simply a matter of ensuring good tension on the rocking levers on the left side. This is an exceptionally repeatable system, but, in changing a scope from one barrel to another, an adjustment is made using a blade screwdriver on the right side: one-eighth of a turn to good thumb-pressure tightness.

In March 2021, Donna used the Blaser R8 with .375 H&H barrel to take this excellent Nile buffalo . . . forty inches wide, good bosses, everything. *We were hunting in Uganda's famous Karamoja district up in the northeast corner.*

With switch-barrel rifles, one must think through the scenarios with genuine practicality. On this safari to Mozambique and Namibia, Donna and I packed one Blaser action, .308 Winchester and .375 H&H barrels, two bolts with different bolt faces, proper magazine inserts, and screwdrivers. Everything fit into the tidy Blaser takedown case.

I figure my crowning achievement with the Blaser R8 was taking these two wolves (plus one more) on a subzero day in Alberta. All three were on the move, 200 yards the closest shot. I'm certain I couldn't have gotten off three shots with a rotating-bolt rifle.

I took this marvelous southern nyala in Mozambique with the Blaser R8 and a .300 Weatherby Magnum barrel.

plainer. Today, after a decade of hard use, both rifles show quite serious wear. We haven't spared them! Mine, especially, has been up a lot of mountains, some of the toughest and steepest in the world. One of these days they need to be sent to the Blaser USA shop in Texas for some cleanup. But I'm reluctant to turn loose of either. What if we need them?

Ruger No. 1

Chapter 16

William Bannerman "Bill" Ruger (1916–2002) was a firearms genius for the ages, a name to be whispered along with John Moses Browning and Peter Paul Mauser. Combining classic lines with sound design and modern manufacturing, his credo was to build good-quality firearms that would appeal to hunters and shooters, and bring them to market at reasonable prices. He was not error-free; his single-shot Hawkeye pistol was not popular, and the .256 Winchester Magnum cartridge it used is almost forgotten. Usually, though, he read the market right.

Many of Bill Ruger's guns were based on his personal interests, as both a hunter and a shooter. He revered the .416 Rigby, and his extra-large Safari Magnum bolt-action was a long-term project. Ruger probably knew he wouldn't sell a whole bunch of them, but his rifle brought the .416 Rigby to the American market at the most affordable price ever. A significant number were made, and it's really a shame the volume wasn't enough to keep it on the market. Another rifle type that Ruger admired was the classic British single-shot, perhaps most typified by the internal-hammer Farquharson falling-block action. I've always wanted to own just one original "Farkie." Maybe I still will, but they're as pricey as double rifles today.

My guess is Bill Ruger owned several, and studied them intently. His Ruger No. 1 single-shot is essentially an improvement on the Farquharson action, with several variations (including my favorites, Tropical and Light and Medium Sporter) unabashedly cribbing on traditional British lines. The improvement, however, is real: Most older (and many modern) single-shots are extractor guns, meaning

The configurations of the Ruger No. 1 that I like best—purely for looks—are the Light and Medium Sporter and the Tropical, with Alexander Henry fore-end and barrel-mounted forward sling swivel stud. This is a Tropical in .450/.400 3-inch.

that the extractor starts the fired case out of the chamber, but does not eject it, and it must be manually plucked from the chamber. Bill Ruger alone figured out how to engineer and incorporate a powerful and reliable ejector. *Then* he added a quarter rib, not just for looks and to act as a base for the rear sight, but to incorporate his simple and strong scope mounting system.

The Ruger No. 1 was introduced in 1967, making the cover of *Guns & Ammo* in November of that year (and again in November 2017, marking its fiftieth year). In 1967, there were almost no single-shot hunting rifles on the market, and a lot of folks thought Bill Ruger had lost it. The No. 1 is expensive to manufacture, and has always been a premium product in the Ruger line. Numbers have never been large, but more than a half-century later the No. 1 is still in the Ruger line, and the versatile action has probably been chambered to more cartridges than any single-barrel (meaning not switch-barrel) production firearm.

The ethos of "one shot, one animal" resonates with many of its fans. I suppose it must appeal to me because I've owned and used

Ruger No. 1 rifles for most of those fifty-odd years. However, my primary attraction to the Ruger No. 1 doesn't run that deep or require long contemplation of hunting ethics. I simply think it's the best-looking production rifle ever made!

My "go to" varmint rifle is a heavy-barreled No. 1 in .204 Ruger, which is non-traditional with its stainless steel action and barrel and laminate stock. However, the looks I like best are found in the Tropical and Sporter versions, which have an Alexander Henry fore-end and forward sling swivel stud on a barrel band.

Around 2008 I worked with Ruger on a special run of No. 1 rifles, 1,250 rifles each in five cartridges. We chose the Tropical and Sporter versions with the cool Alexander Henry fore-end, chambered to 7x57, .300 H&H, .375 Ruger, .450/.400 3-inch, and .450 3¼-inch. The .375 Ruger, although a great cartridge, is an anomaly; I would have preferred .375 H&H in this grouping of classic cartridges. The .375 Ruger was new,

I took this very nice Wyoming pronghorn in 1978 with my first Ruger No. 1 in .243. It was acquired in the late 1960s, so it was a very early No. 1. I used this rifle for pronghorns, deer, and a whole lot of prairie-dog shooting.

I took this greater kudu on a horseback hunt with Ant Baber, and I was using a No. 1 in .375 Ruger. Riding a horse while pursing game is one of few situations where a single-shot isn't ideal, for the rifle must be carried empty in the saddle scabbard and with the action closed, so one must fumble for a cartridge after dismounting and tying the horse.

and I got outvoted. Otherwise, Ruger did a wonderful job and included some No. 1 firsts: matte metal finish, upgraded express sights, and Ruger-supplied detachable Warne scope rings. Wood was upgraded, but wood varies a lot with No. 1s. Most wear pretty good sticks, but there are exceptions both ways. My .300 H&H has gorgeous wood and so does the .450 3¼-inch, but my 7x57 looks like it was stocked from an orange crate. No matter, I have all five of mine with unique serial number. Although it took a while, I've hunted with all of them.

Much as I love it, the Ruger No. 1 is not perfect. Accuracy varies quite a bit. A two-piece stock is usually not conducive to extreme accuracy, and the fore-end is attached to the barrel via a screw into a barrel fixture. This is not an uncommon arrangement, but it can play havoc with barrel vibration. My experience is that heavy-barreled No. 1s tend to be very accurate, while slender barrels (like the Light Sporter) are often finicky, with vertical stringing common as the barrel heats up. I had a Light Sporter .270 for several years, but it was inconsistent and I finally gave it up. My 7x57 (also a Light Sporter) is also finicky, but it groups well with loads it likes.

Most No. 1s are plenty adequate for their purposes, but you never know until you go the range. My .300 H&H is a Medium Sporter configuration, with 26-inch tube, not as slender as a Light Sporter, but the barrel is long and thin. Even so, it's the most accurate No. 1 in a big-game cartridge that I've ever owned, capable of quarter-inch groups on a good day. My friend Gordon Marsh has a Ruger No. 1 in .270 Weatherby Magnum, a most uncommon Ruger chambering. He picked it up on Gunbroker for a good price. With a medium barrel, it turned out to be another tack-driver, consistently printing one-hole groups. Super-accurate No. 1s are not necessarily uncommon, but when you find one, hang onto it!

I owned this Light Sporter in .270 in the early 1980s. Many light-barreled No. 1s show vertical stringing as the barrel heats up. This particular rifle was bad for that, so I didn't keep it long. I used it for some deer hunting and to take this mule deer of the southern race, now often called Pacific Coast blacktail.

I shot this sitatunga in extreme northwestern Zambia with Ruger No. 1 in .300 H&H. I was using a 200-grain Sierra GameKing bullet.

Heavy-barreled No. 1s, whether in Varmint or the stiff-barreled Tropical configuration, usually shoot very well. When we get to .375s and larger, we often don't get too concerned about nickel-sized groups because, for hunting purposes, they just don't matter. And, with heavy recoil and low (or no) magnification scopes and sights, we often never learn how well our big bores really shoot (and don't care). Both .450/.400 No. 1s I've owned shot extremely well, but, honest, I'm not sure about the .450 3¼-inch. It's brutal enough off sticks, and no fun at all off the bench. It seems to shoot OK, and that's good enough.

This year I've done some hunting with a No. 1 in .280 Ackley Improved in Medium Sporter configuration. It's not my rifle (yet); it belongs to Lee Newton, avid Ruger collector, but I'm hoping he'll let me buy it. It's showing some vertical stringing but it's not extreme, and I think it just needs some careful handloading. The .280 AI is an interesting cartridge, probably one of P. O. Ackley's best improvements, almost the equal of the 7mm Remington Magnum, but with an unbelted case and more compact ammo.

There are two inherent advantages to the single-shot action. First, one size fits almost all. The Ruger No. 1 has been chambered to a host of cartridges, from .22 Hornet and .218 Bee all the way up to .458 Lott and .450 3¼-inch (which is the maximum base and rim diameter the rifle can handle without custom work). Other single-shot actions, including original Farkies and the Dakota Model 10, have been made in various sizes, up to and beyond .600 Nitro Express.

Second, absent a magazine and repeating mechanism, the single-shot is much shorter than any repeating rifle. My No. 1 in .300 H&H with 26-inch barrel is *exactly* the same overall length as my Joe Balickie .270 with 22-inch barrel. Nobody likes unwieldy rifles but, all other things being equal, I prefer longer barrels; you wring out more velocity, and depending on the rifle, longer barrels sometimes offer better balance. With single-shots, you get three to four inches of extra barrel length essentially for free, with no increase in overall length.

Alabaman Gordon Marsh is also a No. 1 fan. He picked up this rifle secondhand, a medium-weight barrel in .270 Weatherby, an uncommon No. 1 chambering. This rifle proved exceptionally accurate, producing tight groups with just about all the bullets he's tried.

Single-shots have advantages and disadvantages. Advantage: Extra barrel length without extra overall length! The author's 26-inch barreled No. 1 in .300 H&H is exactly the same overall length as his 22-inch-barrel .270. Disadvantage: A single-shot rifle is either fully loaded and ready, or completely empty, with no magazine in reserve.

The Ruger No. 1 is not my only single-shot rifle. I've had Thompson/Centers with various barrels for decades, and I've had break-open Harrington & Richardson rifles and a couple of Sharps reproductions. And I've been a fan of the elegant Dakota Model 10 since it was introduced. Back in 1996 I shot a couple of buffalo with a Dakota single-shot in .375 Dakota, and in Tanzania in 2010 I shot a number of animals with a Dakota M10 in 7mm Remington Magnum. I always wanted one, but, to be honest, I could never figure out what chambering.

As sometimes happens, the answer just came along: Duke McCaa of Gulf Breeze Firearms had a Dakota Model 10 in his booth at a show, with color-case-hardened receiver and scope rings, quarter rib on a 25-inch barrel, roll-marked .275 Rigby. Good wood was Don Allen's specialty, and this rifle wears awesome walnut. And it shoots! So far, I've taken it on a couple of European hunts, and it's a joy to carry and shoot. This rifle is, well, *fancier* than any No. 1 I've ever had, but I've never had a No. 1 that was upgraded beyond the Ruger factory. The action is slimmer and trimmer, but I can't say I like it *better.* It is a non-ejecting extractor gun, and after long being spoiled by Ruger's powerful ejector, I'm still learning how to best snatch a fired case from the chamber.

No matter how much you practice, *nobody* is fast enough with any single-shot to reliably reload for a second shot as quickly as can be done with any repeating action. This is part of the deal with a single-shot: You know going in that you can only count on the one shot. That knowledge makes you more careful, and that's not a bad thing. Obviously, I don't use single-shots all the time, but I've used them a lot for many years, and I've used No. 1s much more than all the rest put together. I don't recall a time when I've lost an animal or an opportunity because I couldn't reload fast enough.

Often, because of brush, movement, other animals, whatever, there's no chance for a second shot no matter what you're using, even if it's a double. Failing something bizarre like a misfire or mechanical failure, you can *always* count on the first shot with any rifle. Beyond that, there

I like single-shots and have not been completely loyal to the No. 1. Inexpensive and with myriad barrels, the Thompson/Center system is very useful. I took this West Texas mule deer with a T/C using a .30-06 barrel.

are no guarantees. However, because of its strong and reliable ejector and lack of an exposed hammer (which, if present, must be manually cocked), the No. 1 is the *fastest* single-shot I've ever used.

As much as I enjoy hunting with them, the single-shot is not a rifle for all reasons and all seasons. It is always either fully loaded or completely empty, with no half-measure of an empty chamber and loaded magazine in reserve. (This characteristic is shared by the double rifle.) In a lot of hunting around the world, your rifle is carried with the chamber clear and magazine loaded, ready for a chance encounter. It doesn't take much experience with a single-shot to learn how to keep a couple of cartridges very handy. Even so, in any fast-breaking situation, the single-shot requires a bit more fumbling than simply working a repeating action to get ready.

Largely, this is a matter of practice and familiarity. I'm *not* a one-gun man, but I've used No. 1s long enough that I've never forgotten that I have to load them when the time comes. I have done little mountain hunting with them and I've never taken one to Asia. I'm not really sure why this is because, otherwise, I've used my No. 1s all over the world, and for most types of game.

I have written elsewhere that the single-shot may not be the best choice for dangerous game because the larger and tougher the beast, the more likely follow-up shot(s) may be needed. Using a single-shot may retard a follow-up to the degree that a PH or companion chimes in when, with a double or magazine rifle, collaboration may not have been necessary. These points are valid. It is also just plain foolish to hunt dangerous game *alone* with a single-shot.

In 2017, I hunted buffalo in South Africa's Limpopo Province with Diekie Muller. Like many South African PHs, Muller didn't grow up hunting buffalo; until recently, they were scarce and expensive in his country, so buffalo-hunting experience was hard to come by. Thanks to intensive breeding of disease-free buffalo, today Cape buffalo are plentiful in his part of the country, and Muller does a lot of buffalo

Without question, my "best" single-shot is my Dakota Model 10 in .275 Rigby. However, like most other single-shots, the Dakota is an extractor-only rifle, so it takes additional seconds to pluck out the fired case before reloading.

In 2018 I used my Ruger No. 1 in .450 3¼-inch Nitro Express to take this buffalo in Mozambique. The .450 is pretty much the largest case diameter than can be housed in the Ruger No. 1 without opening up the bottom of the action. I have used No. 1s from .22 Hornet all the way up to the big .450.

hunting. Until the previous year, he carried a Ruger No. 1 in .375 H&H as his backup rifle. It was Robin Hurt who convinced him to take the plunge and do whatever was necessary to get a large-caliber double rifle. Good advice! I messed up my shot, and Diekie stopped our buffalo about six feet from his bootlaces with his almost-new Krieghoff .470.

However, I'm not a PH, and I do little dangerous-game hunting alone. Over the years, I've shot a number of buffalo with single-shots. Other than a couple with that Dakota .375, I've taken them mostly with No. 1s in several powerful chamberings. I don't recall that the single-shot ever caused a problem. If I did my job and placed that one shot as well as I could, when the dust cleared the bull was down. If I shot less perfectly, then there was usually plenty of time to reload and keep shooting (sometimes several times). This is not uncommon, although there have been times when we weren't certain what had happened until we took up the spoor and went into the thick stuff.

Luck of the draw being as it is, I've never faced a charge with a single-shot rifle. I'd just as soon not, but I don't mind doing a scary follow-up with a No. 1, knowing that a PH with a big rifle is at my shoulder. Alone, I'd *definitely* prefer not to! Although it wasn't a No. 1, I once shot a leopard with a single-shot .30-06. With a leopard, the likelihood of a second shot on the initial encounter is almost nil, and *anything* that makes you extra-careful with the first shot is all to the good. I have hunted no lions or big bears, and have done very little elephant hunting, with any single-shot. You *could*, but my experience with these animals is that the necessity for a quick follow-up shot is too common, so I'd prefer not to. Otherwise, an accurate single-shot in an appropriate cartridge is just fine for almost any non-dangerous game hunting anywhere. I've used my No. 1s in a lot of different places, for a wide variety of game.

The No. 1 has been chambered to probably the greatest array of cartridges of any non-switch-barrel production rifle. When the manufacturer did a run of the .405 Winchester, I thought it was pretty cool—I'm not sure why—and I bought this one. It's an awesome pig gun and, with hopped-up loads in the strong action, fully capable for buffalo.

I'm preparing to take a shot from a raised machan with the Ruger No. 1 in .300 H&H. Although there's no place single-shots can't be used, they are probably at their best in deliberate situations like this where the rifle can be safely maintained, loaded, and ready.

There's no particular reason, but I have done very little mountain hunting with a single-shot. In October 2020 I did take a No. 1 in .280 Ackley Improved to Far West Texas on an aoudad hunt, and I got a great old ram.

Other than heavy-barrel varmint rifles, this is the most accurate Ruger No. 1 that I have ever owned. It's a Medium Sporter with a 26-inch barrel in .300 H&H, and it always produces good groups. On good days when I do my part, it will group to one-third of an inch.

Among single-shot actions, the Ruger No. 1 is almost alone in having a strong and effective ejector, a tribute to Bill Ruger's genius. Upon opening the action, the ejector throws the empty case clear, making the No. 1 a very fast single-shot to reload.

Most No. 1s are at least adequate in accuracy, but only a few are genuine tack-drivers. This Medium Sporter in .280 Ackley Improved is plenty accurate enough for almost any hunting, but, like many No. 1s, it shows obvious vertical stringing as the barrel heats up.

It just occurred to me that it's been much too long since I took that No. 1 in .300 H&H to the field. Since I have to pick a favorite, that one is the most accurate of the bunch, and with that long barrel, its handling qualities are perfect. As I'm writing, it's January 2021, the beginning of a brand-new year that, hopefully, will see the retreat of the dread virus. I need to make a plan to do at least some hunting with that No. 1. Thanks for reminding me!

My Ultimate Mountain Rifle

Chapter 17

They don't want to admit it, but it's the truth: Sheep hunters are elitist. It's unavoidable, because wild sheep and goats are some of the most beautiful creatures on Earth, and opportunities to hunt them are limited and pricey. I don't like to think of myself as an elitist; I'm just a guy who loves being in the field, and who is grateful he's had so much opportunity.

I've climbed a lot of mountains and carried a lot of rifles up them (and back down). I *do not* consider mountain-dwelling game superior in any way to lowland species. They are typically less wary than any deer, and beauty is in the eye of the beholder. The difference is, first you have to get up the mountain! People who don't enjoy challenges don't join the Marines. I might hate the mountain and myself every step of the way, but once you get to the top, the view is magnificent.

So, I've made it to the top a bunch of times, and I've taken a lot of mountain game. At this writing, twenty-six varieties of wild sheep and thirty varieties of goats, plus duplicates. Some hunters have done more, but none in my line of work as a gunwriter. Because of my weird profession, not all of my rifle choices for these hunts have been entirely mine, and many have been questionable, if not wildly inappropriate.

In much of the work I do, I answer to editors, publishers, and producers, who must worry about advertisers and sponsors. So, I've taken a lot of rifles (and other gear) that didn't belong to me on a lot of hunts. Sometimes I do it as a courtesy, sometimes as an obligation. Given reasonable accuracy and suitability, I can make most anything work, even if it has a right-hand action and stock.

My first Dall sheep hunt, Alaska Range, 1982. Clear through the 1990s, I was mostly still using walnut-stocked rifles like this beautiful left-hand Remington M700 in 7mm Remington Magnum. This rifle was purchased used from a left-handed guy in the Safari Club who lost the sight of his left eye and had to switch. High mountains are no country for good walnut!

So, let's go back to some of my weirder choices. I took my first wild sheep with a .375 H&H! This cartridge is the ultimate utility infielder, but I wouldn't try to argue it's a great choice. I'm not the only hunter to ever club a ram with a cannon. L. S. Chadwick used a .404 Jeffery to take the world-record Stone sheep, considered by many the greatest North American animal ever taken, and consistently referred to as "the Chadwick ram." My old friend Jack Atcheson Jr., who *is* a one-gun man, rarely uses anything other than his .338. Plenty of gun, you bet. Too much, maybe, if there is such a thing. We could argue that the .338 isn't a perfect choice, but there are much worse, and Jack *knows* his .338.

I've had brief flings with this and that. The .270 WSM is an awesome cartridge, a bit flatter-shooting and delivering more energy than the .270 Winchester. These probably don't matter much on mountain game, but the greater energy yield makes a difference on elk, and on northern combo hunts where a grizzly or moose could be incidental to a ram or billy. I hunted mountain game with three different .270 WSM rifles, abandoning it only because of the occasional feeding issues that are almost inherent with the fireplug-shaped cartridges.

I used the 8mm Remington Magnum quite a bit, including on my first Marco Polo sheep hunt and a Transcaspian urial hunt in Turkmenistan. If I were a really serious elk hunter (like Jack Atcheson Jr.), chances are I would still be using it. But this discussion is about mountain rifles. Other than a personal commitment to be a "one-gun man," like Atcheson, which has advantages, there is simply no justification for hunting mountain game with anything larger than .30-caliber.

The 8mm magnum I used the most had three disadvantages: First, to get the velocity up, it had a 28-inch barrel. Second, the stock was a very nice piece of English walnut. Mountain hunting is hard on

I have used a lot of rifles, and even mountain hunting doesn't always (or often) require exotic or specialized choices. In 2008, I used a wood-stocked CZ in .270 Winchester to take my Arizona desert sheep. Was it the most perfect choice imaginable? No. Did it work perfectly? You bet!

I took this good Siberian ibex in Mongolia with an H-S Precision .270 WSM, a rifle I used on several mountain hunts in the early 2000s. The left-hand rifle was accurate and light and the cartridge wonderful, but, like so many rifles chambered to the short, fat WSM cartridges, there were occasional failures to feed, so I went back to longer cartridges for foolproof feeding.

wood, not just rocks and brush, but weather. Somehow, I managed to not ruin the stock on that rifle, but if I'd kept using it, I surely would have. Third, with that long barrel, dense walnut, mercury tube in the stock, and a big scope, that rifle weighs nearly twelve pounds! I did a lot of elk hunting in the 1990s and that big 8mm was awesome, but my first Marco Polo hunt in 1999 was the last time I tried to carry it up a serious mountain.

By then I had the Rifles Inc. .300 Weatherby Magnum, and its first mountain hunt was for my Wyoming bighorn in 1998. Now, exactly why I took the 8mm to Tajikistan the next year and not that .300, I just can't say. Probably I was being stubborn, or never having seen one, perhaps I had the idea that the big Asian sheep were a whole lot bigger and tougher than our North American wild sheep. The big Mongolian argalis are much heavier, and the larger-bodied Asian ibex and the turs are powerful, blocky animals. But the Marco Polo argali, despite its legendary horns, is mostly long legs and winter coat, probably not even as heavy as a mature Rocky Mountain bighorn. In any case, there's really no justification for anything bigger than a .30-caliber for any wild sheep or goat.

You can get by just fine with a 7mm, .270, or one of the faster 6.5mms. I shot my first Dall sheep and a few goats with the 7mm Remington Magnum, and today there are much faster 7mms. As I've said, experienced mountain hunters like my buddy Joe Bishop and the Klineburger brothers used 7mm Remington Magnums with perfect satisfaction. You already know how I feel about the .270s: The .270 Winchester is fine, and the .270 WSM and .270 Weatherby Magnum are slightly better. You also know how I feel about the .264 and the newer 6.5mms at similar velocities. The fastest 6.5mms (26 Nosler and 6.5-.300 Weatherby Magnum) are even better because they deliver more energy. This probably doesn't matter often, but it could be a factor on the largest-bodied Asian sheep and goats. When

I took this fine Transcaspian urial in Turkmenistan in 1997. This is my often-written-about 8mm Remington Magnum, powerful and wonderfully accurate. I carried it on several elk hunts and a few mountain hunts, but, with its 28-inch barrel, English walnut stock, and a mercury recoil reducer in the butt, I eventually decided it was just too heavy for mountain use.

My old friend Joe Bishop was consistent: On tough hunts, he almost always used his Sako 7mm Remington Magnum. The photo shows Col. Negussie Eshete and Joe with the mountain nyala Joe took in the Bale Mountains of Ethiopia with his 7mm. I used my 8mm Remington Magnum on this hunt. Joe's bull was taken just as cleanly, and his was bigger than mine.

the 26 Nosler was brand-new, I shot a monster ibex in eastern Turkey and was impressed with the performance of the cartridge. I have a 6.5-.300 Weatherby Magnum that shoots very well. I have not used it on a mountain hunt simply because it's a Mark V Accumark and the rifle weighs too much—but as far as the cartridge goes, it's plenty for any sheep or goat in the world at any sane range, especially with the new low-drag 6.5mm bullets we now have.

So, while magnum .30-caliber power isn't essential, after a lot of messing around, that's what I settled on. In the first decade of the new millennium, I did most of my mountain hunting with the Rifles Inc. .300 Weatherby Magnum. Although not light, it's a lot lighter than the 8mm, shoots well, and has stainless metal and a synthetic stock, and is a good rifle in all ways. I did not abandon it, but in 2010 I fell in love with the Blaser system. After an initial hunt with the .300 Blaser Magnum, I've done most of my mountain hunting with a .300 Weatherby Magnum barrel on the Blaser ever since.

The first time I used Blaser's .300 Weatherby Magnum barrel was on a Kuban tur hunt in southern Russia in 2011. Although often considered a sheep, the tur is really a goat, of the *Capra* genus. They're big and blocky; you have to see one up close to appreciate how large they are. When you see a big tur on the ground, you will not question the need for .30-caliber power, but more is not necessary. Joe Bishop and I did that hunt together. I'd had my heart attack six months earlier, and if there are steeper, more abrupt mountains than the Russian Caucasus I've never seen them. I figured if I could survive that hunt, I was good to go! I survived, shot my tur at 450 yards, and a few days later took a Caucasian chamois, an even tougher hunt.

I haven't abandoned the Blaser, either. Nobody did much traveling in 2020, but it saw use in Africa and Europe in 2019, and of course that's what I used in Mongolia in 2018. It's a great rifle, and a fine and

There are lots of great mountain rifles, and plenty of suitable cartridges. Although I have pretty much settled on my favorites, I'm not done experimenting. In 2013, when the cartridge was new, I used a 26 Nosler with a 140-grain AccuBond bullet to take this 50-inch hybrid ibex in southeastern Turkey. It's a great cartridge with plenty of power.

Turs are referred to as sheep by some, but they are, in fact, really goats. These heavy body goats offer super-tough, post-graduate mountain hunting. The Caucasus Range is steep and abrupt, and turs are often taken at long range. Of all the mountain hunts, I consider this ".30-caliber country." There are three types of tur. For the Dagestan tur (below), I used my Rifles, Inc. in .300 Weatherby. For the Kuban tur (above), I used my Blaser R8 with a .300 Weatherby Magnum barrel. In 2014 I used the latter rifle for the mid-Caucasian tur.

accurate mountain rifle. But with its walnut stock it's not light, and it's stocked in what once was good walnut. Truth is, I've just about ruined the stock. I like attractive walnut, and it's a shame to mess it up, but I don't just look at my rifles; I use them. There are places where good walnut doesn't belong. Between constant weather and rocky hillsides, mountains are among them (and so are jungles and swamps).

I talked to the Blaser folks, who are good friends, to see if the walnut could be replaced with synthetic. The "Professional" version of the R8 is fantastic; if it had existed, that's what I would have gotten in 2010. Starting immediately in Nepal, I knew the Blaser would see some hard use; I just didn't know how hard. Problem is, there's no synthetic replacement for the model I have. The stock can be refurbished, but it's still heavier than it needs to be, and it's gonna get messed up again if I keep climbing mountains with it.

Somewhere around 2015, my old friend Kenny Jarrett wanted to make me a rifle. Years ago, he built me a wonderfully accurate .30-06 that I used a lot, but that was before I was doing a lot of mountain hunting. I love the .30-06, but I prefer something a bit flatter-shooting for sheep and goats. It's just a confidence thing. Jarrett is among few gunmakers who makes his own barrels. Whether that's cost-effective or not isn't my business, but the reject rate is costly because Jarrett's standards are high. Now he was also making his own receivers (his preferred word, never "action"), and he had a left-hand version.

So we talked about it, I think at an SCI convention. I wanted one of his hand-laid synthetic stocks with checkered grip and fore-end, American classic butt, medium contour barrel. Then came the part that I knew would be sticky. Kenny wanted to make the rifle in his wildcat/proprietary .300 Jarrett, a great cartridge based on the H&H case blown out. It's accurate, but Jarrett rifles are *always* accurate. Considering the great barrel, rigid receiver, perfect bedding, and sound construction, I can't evaluate whether the .300 Jarrett is really, on average, more accurate than a .300 RUM, Winchester, or Weatherby. Other Weatherby winners use the Jarrett, including my old friend and fellow Marine Bruce Keller. I've used it and it's a great

I took this wonderful old Gobi argali in Mongolia in 2018 with the Blaser R8 with a .300 Weatherby Magnum barrel and a 200-grain bullet. After a long stalk, we caught this ram in his bed at a hundred yards. Under such circumstances many rifles and cartridges would have worked just fine (even a .25-35!). However, in the mountains, it's best to be prepared for the worst.

cartridge, but I knew that (as a gunwriter), my use of the rifle would be limited if it was chambered to a non-standard cartridge.

So I insisted that he chamber it to .300 Weatherby Magnum, my comfort zone for many years. And, by that time, Federal and Hornady, among others, were loading factory ammunition for that cartridge. Jarrett grumbled, but finally assented. Or so I thought.

A year or so passed, and then I sent Jarrett an FFL and anxiously awaited this magnificent new rifle. It finally came and was signed for, and I tore the box open. Imagine my surprise when I discovered it was not a .300 Weatherby, but a .300 Winchester Magnum! I have not had this discussion with Mr. Jarrett, so if he happens to read this, he may be surprised. I don't know if Kenny had the last laugh, or if it was a result of convention confusion!

At first, I was crushed. It took a while, but over time I realized he did me a favor. The .300 Winchester Magnum is now the world's most popular magnum cartridge, with a rich choice of loads. More importantly, with new propellants, the velocity gap between the

Winchester and Weatherby .300s has narrowed. With its 24-inch barrel, there's less than a hundred fps difference between the Jarrett rifle and my Blaser with its 24-inch .300 Weatherby Magnum barrel (which, as I've said, is shorter than optimum for a .300 Weatherby). That's definitely not enough difference to worry about, considering the longer case and the powder burned to get there.

The rifle is Jarrett's "Ridge Walker" configuration. The synthetic stock is light, classic, and fits perfectly; the barrel is medium contour. Although I haven't (and probably will not) embrace the extreme range shooting so bandied about today, I'm comfortable shooting somewhat farther than I might have considered twenty years ago because we have better optics. So, I put a Leupold VX6 3–18X on the rifle, a big scope, but not massive. It wears Leupold's CDS turret, calibrated for the 200-grain Hornady ELD-X at 2,915 fps at 5,000 feet elevation and 40 degrees Fahrenheit.

We can talk about "mountain rifles," but I also expect versatility from my rifles because I do a lot more hunting of other game besides sheep and goats. In part, this is why I've gravitated to fast .30-calibers, and also why I'm now mostly using heavy-for-caliber 200-gain bullets. I used the Jarrett rifle on this big Cape eland in South Africa's Eastern Cape. Note the vestigial third horn above the right eye.

I took this good Brooks Range Dall ram with Jordan Wallace on the seventh day of a tough backpack hunt. On the third day, we passed on this ram at 600 yards because of unreadable wind. Four days later, I took the shot at 120 yards. I used the Jarrett in .300 Winchester Magnum with a 200-grain bullet.

The velocity is what Hornady's Precision Hunter load develops in that rifle. I doubt I can beat it with handloads, but I can match it. Elevation and temperature were sort of random. My range is near sea level, and temperatures vary from 100-plus degrees in the summer to below freezing in winter. I figured 5,000 feet was a good average for the places I'm most likely to take this rifle, likewise 40 degrees. In California, Colorado, Texas, and South Africa, I can consistently ring steel to 900 yards. I will never shoot at game that far, but half that is likely, and maybe a bit more.

All in, unloaded and without sling, and with that substantial scope, the rifle weighs 8.5 pounds. Note, please, that this is considerably heavier than Donna's less-than-six-pound MGA .270! However, she is six inches shorter than I am and weighs a third less. I am not comfortable with rifles that light, finding them a bit whippy and unstable when I'm breathing hard. Also, while I am *not* an extreme-range guy, I'm comfortable and confident shooting farther than she is. I want the power projection of a fast .30-caliber. On the other hand, I don't want anything to do with a six-pound .300 magnum because, without a muzzle brake, it's too much of a good thing. The Jarrett rifle is stable and comfortable to shoot. At 8.5 pounds, I can carry it, and I can shoot it.

I happen to know I can carry it, because the first time I used it was on that abortive backpack Dall sheep hunt in 2015, where no shots were fired. I carried it again on another backpack Brooks Range hunt in 2017, with Dave Leonard and Jordan Wallace of Mountain Monarchs of Alaska. Amazingly, my creaky old knees held up, and I took a really nice ram on the seventh day. The stalk was epic, but the shot nothing: about 120 yards. That's the way it is with mountain hunting. You should be prepared for the worst, but the actual shot is often fairly routine.

This particular barrel took a while to break in, but now it's printing wonderful groups and really likes that aerodynamic 200-grain ELD-X. I like it too! That Dall ram is the only mountain animal I've taken with the Jarrett (so far), but it's been to South Africa twice, and I've used that 200-grain ELD-X to take two eland bulls.

Leupold's CDS (Custom Dial System) on the VX6 calibrated to the 200-grain ELD-X load enables me to ring steel out to 900 yards with little difficulty. I would never shoot at game at such distance, but it's a huge confidence builder to have that capability; shots at half the distance don't seem so daunting.

The Jarrett .300 Winchester Magnum was another rifle with a barrel that took quite a bit of careful shooting and cleaning to break in. That done, it's a wonder. I had to hunt and peck a bit to find a really good handload with the 200-grain ELD-X *bullet that I wanted to use. Good old IMR 4350 powder did the trick. These groups use differing charge weights, but the bottom left five-shot group, with all shots touching, looks plenty good enough.*

Regardless of the rifle, cartridge, and scope system one chooses, it's essential to practice. On a ranch in California, I am working with the Jarrett Ridge Walker, ringing steel at long range. There's a gong somewhere on the next ridge.

With a Leupold 3–18X scope, my Jarrett "Ridge Walker" in .300 Winchester Magnum weighs about 8.5 pounds all set to go. It's possible to go a lot lighter, but I find this weight range light enough to carry and still heavy enough to be stable when out of breath and shooting from imperfect positions.

With its synthetic stock, a bit less gun weight, wonderful accuracy, and the scope system dialed in, the Jarrett rifle is the rifle I will probably use for whatever mountain hunting lies ahead. How much that might be remains to be seen. I can still climb, more slowly, and I can still shoot. Goals aren't as important as they once were, but I'd like to get to thirty varieties of sheep, which is sort of a milestone for far-gone mountain hunters. Whether that happens or not depends on health, hips, knees, and finances. I haven't done any of the Siberian snow sheep, just haven't gotten around to them, so there are a few mountains I'd still like to climb. If I can make that happen, I'm pretty sure the Jarrett rifle will be with me when I reach the top.

Love My Lever-Actions!

Chapter 18

If you don't love lever-actions, then you must not like John Wayne, motherhood, or apple pie! I have a soft spot for *all* lever-action rifles, and have at least passing experience with just about every lever gun made in the last century. Almost entirely American, the lever-action was spawned in our Civil War and made legendary on our Western frontier.

I don't hunt with lever-actions all the time because most are specialized arms, limited in range and versatility by action size, which restricts cartridge length. Traditional tubular-magazine lever-actions such as Marlins and most Winchesters were further limited by the necessity to use blunt-nosed bullets with poor aerodynamics, at least until Hornady's LeveRevolution loads came along. Accuracy is also often reduced by rear-locking actions and two-piece stocks.

There are exceptions. With a rotary magazine under the bolt, the Savage 99 was always capable of using sharp-pointed bullets. Despite their rear-locking action and two-piece stock, some 99s are very accurate. I love the Savage 99, and I also love the Winchester Model 88, which used a box magazine, had a one-piece stock, and locked with a rotating bolt head. Similar in appearance was the Sako Finnwolf, a rare *European* lever gun. I have no experience with the Finnwolf, but it was legendary for accuracy. The Savage 99, Winchester 88, and Finnwolf are all restricted to .308 Winchester-length cartridges.

Browning's BLR, in production for more than fifty years, is the lever-action that breaks all the rules. It has a geared lever with a ridiculously short throw and is offered in both short and long

I took this nice black bear with Manitoba outfitter "Trapper Don" McRae using a Browning BLR in .358 Winchester. The BLR is available in short and long action lengths. It is the last production rifle chambered to the underrated .358 Winchester and is the only production lever-action ever chambered to magnum cartridges.

actions, the only production lever-action ever chambered to belted magnum and short-magnum cartridges. Like the Winchester 88 and Finnwolf, it has a forward-locking bolt and box magazine. It does have a two-piece stock, but this is not the kiss of death for accuracy. So does the Blaser system and other rifles known for accuracy. I've used several BLRs; they are light, fast, and handy, and in my experience consistently shoot straight.

I like the BLR, and should have kept one I had in .358 Winchester. Actually, I really should get another, since it's the last factory rifle chambered to .358, a mild-mannered and effective cartridge that should be more popular than it ever became. I've never pressed the trigger on a Sako Finnwolf, but I've had several Winchester 88s. Probably should have kept them, too.

Every now and then I check the web for Model 88s. After Models 94, 92, and 73, the Model 88 was Winchester's fourth most popular lever-action. There are plenty of them out there and prices aren't high. The problem is, factory 88s have horrible, mushy triggers. I have only known two gunsmiths who "broke the code" and figured out how to fix Winchester 88 triggers. One was Joe Balickie, long retired, who made John Wootters' famous Model 88 .308 (and my .270 on a Carl Gustav action). The other was our local Paso Robles gunsmith, Norm Bridge. A Navy Seabee veteran of Guadalcanal, Norm passed away in 2019 at the age of 94, still working in his shop daily until a few weeks before his death. He built the Model 88s in both .308 and .358 that I've written about, with crisp, clean triggers.

So, I admire the Winchester 88 (except for the factory trigger), and I'd probably like the Sako Finnwolf, which I hear has a good trigger. I'm totally good with the BLR, which is chambered to the greatest range of cartridges of any lever-action. Brad Fitzpatrick, one of our better young gunwriters, recently described the BLR in a *Guns & Ammo* article as "the best lever action ever."

Because of action length, the historic tubular-magazine requirement for blunt-nose bullets, and the fact that most are used with rimmed cartridges, traditional lever-action rifles are different. Since extreme range is almost unattainable in lever-actions, my tastes run to short, stubby, and powerful. Some of my longtime favorite lever-action cartridges are, left to right: .338 Marlin Express (with Hornady FTX bullet); .348 Winchester; .358 Winchester; .45-70; .475 Turnbull.

The rotating-bolt Winchester Model 88 was Winchester's fourth-most-popular lever-action (after the 94, 92, and 73.) A fore-end screw into the barrel and a mushy trigger reduced accuracy, but it was an awesome rifle, essentially chambered to the .308 Winchester family of cartridges. Few gunsmiths took the time to fix its problems. One who did was my friend Norm Bridge, who built this awesome M88 in .358. I never owned one of his M88 rifles, but I borrowed a couple, including this .358 that I used for my Wyoming Shiras moose when I drew a permit in 1998.

I am not prepared to argue. As with any rifle chambered to a fast .30-caliber, there's almost nothing you couldn't do with a BLR in .300 Winchester Magnum. And, since it will handle the .300, if you wanted more power, a long-action BLR could probably be rebarreled to .338 or, why not, .416 Taylor or .458 Winchester Magnum. I've never heard of such a conversion, but I'd be surprised if it hasn't been done.

I love my lever-actions, but despite the capabilities of "modern" designs, I tend to consider lever guns best for closer range, fast-breaking situations. I have trouble picturing myself taking a lever-action on a sheep hunt, although it's been done. Remember desert bighorn hunter Charlie Ren and his Savage .25-35? Much more recently, the Grand Slam/Ovis organization recognized a modern "grand slam" of the four North American wild sheep taken with a lever-action .30-30 by George Lawrence III. In 1915, the .250-3000 in the lever-action Savage was the fastest and flattest-shooting cartridge out there. In 1920, the stubby .300 Savage cartridge came "as close as dammit" to .30-06 ballistics of the day. Both the .250 and .300 Savage were used by a fair number of mountain hunters back in the day.

Despite its hundred-year run and nearly a million rifles made, the Savage 99 was complex to manufacture and became too expensive. It's a shame it isn't still with us, but I've had a long procession of Savage 99s. I mentioned that .358 that was stolen, but in the 1980s, I also had a 99 in .308 that I took to Africa. Since then, I've had several older Savage lever-actions. As is sometimes the case with vintage rifles, not all of them shot well. Others, well, somebody else wanted them more than I did.

Right now, I have two 99s, one in .250-3000, the other in .300 Savage. The .300 is an honest rifle that's seen a lot of use. I was looking for a .300 Savage because I had ammo and dies, but I'd sold the last .300 I had. I saw it at Capital Sports in Helena, Montana. The price was good, and they gave me a military discount. The vintage 2.5X scope that came on the rifle was toast, but I put an old Leupold 3–9X compact on it. It shoots well, maybe 1.5-inch groups with handloads.

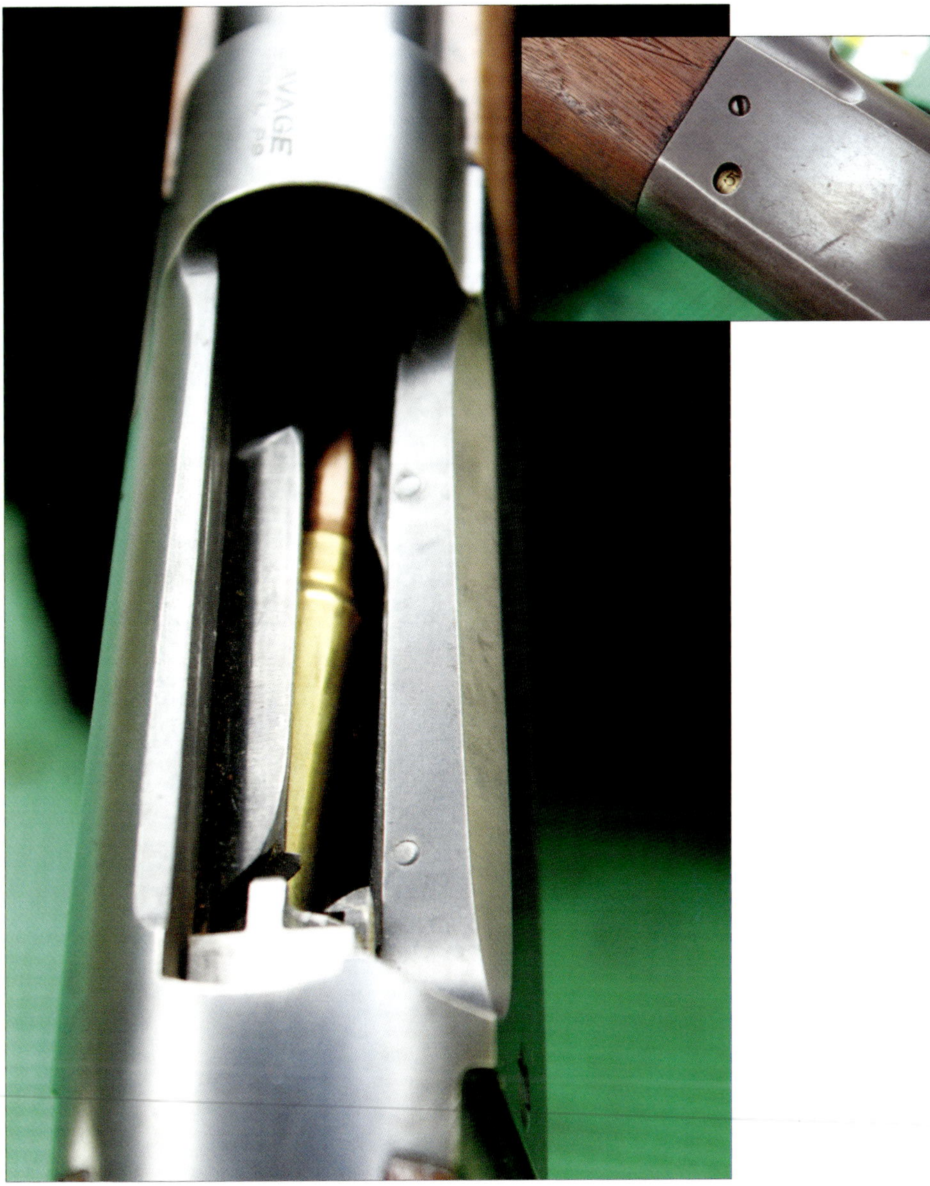

The Savage 1899 is another of my pets. Manufactured for a century to nearly a million total, the 99 has unique features, including a rotary magazine that allowed the use of sharp-pointed, aerodynamic bullets, and a "cartridge counter." Unlike the top-eject Winchesters, all Savage lever-actions can easily be scoped. Although sales never matched Winchester's tubular-magazine lever-actions, back in the day, Savage was serious competition to Winchester. I consider the Savage a superior design.

I shot my Kansas buck with it in 2019 (*fun*), and in January 2020 I carried it on an Alabama whitetail hunt. I'm not yet certain it's a "keeper" but, as Savage 99s go, it has an exceptional trigger.

The .250 is kind of a special rifle. It's an 1899 (not 99) ".250-3000 Rifle," a takedown with pop-up tang receiver sight, from my buddy Joe Bishop's collection. Early .250 Savage rifles had a 1:14 twist, to stabilize the initial 87-grain load (which enabled the .250 Savage to become the first factory cartridge to break 3,000 fps). This barrel will stabilize *some* 100-grain lead-core bullets, but longer homogenous-alloy bullets—and any bullets over 100 grains—tumble and hit the target sideways. Combining iron sights with my current vision and adding limited bullet selection, the rifle isn't versatile, but it's in wonderful shape and shoots extremely well. It's a "keeper," and not just because it was one of Joe's rifles. I've hunted hogs with it, and it's taken whitetail does on the Kansas farm.

Although I love my lever-actions, I generally use them for "less serious" hunting. Hogs and meat deer, you bet. Black bear hunting over bait or with hounds, for sure. But I'm probably not going to use a lever-action if I'm in search of the buck of a lifetime, and I'm not likely to carry one up a sheep mountain. That doesn't mean I love them less, only that I tend to limit their application. There have been exceptions. I used a Norm Bridge-modified Winchester 88 in .358 when I drew a Shiras moose permit in Wyoming. And, when the cartridge was brand-new, I took a .338 Marlin Express on a Colorado elk hunt. It's a shame that cartridge didn't take off; it's probably the most versatile cartridge ever designed for lever-action rifles. Timing is everything: when it came out, lever-action sales were at their nadir, and Marlin was in trouble. Maybe now that Ruger has acquired Marlin, that cartridge can have a second chance.

Despite my experience with Savage 99s, Winchester 88s, and BLRs, most of my experience has been with traditional tubular-magazine lever-actions. I wish I'd bought that .338 Marlin Express; they're scarce today. I have two other Marlins, an 1895 .45-70 that belonged to Chub Eastman, and an 1894 in .44 Magnum. That little rifle, in stainless and

In 2020, I used a vintage Savage 99 in .300 Savage to take this Kansas whitetail. In 1920, the .300 Savage approached .30-06 loads of the day. Today, it lags a bit behind the .308 Winchester but is still an extremely effective hunting cartridge.

laminate, is the slickest lever-action I've ever owned, and one of the most accurate. If the Ruger folks figure out how to make lever-actions as good as that rifle, then we'll have Marlins for many years to come.

As a lefty, I'm drawn to lever-actions like a moth to flame because of the ambidextrous operation, even though lever guns are only "almost ambidextrous" since most eject on the right side. Even so, I can't resist them. I also have a Big Horn Armory Model 89 "Spike Driver," made on the Winchester pattern, but midway in size between the big 1886 action and the small 1892 action. In the .500 S&W handgun cartridge, it's an awesome rifle, but it's a hard-luck gun so far; despite several attempts, I have yet to get a shot at game with it.

So, that's an eclectic (and partial) litany of my long addiction to lever-action rifles. Mostly, though, I'm drawn to vintage Winchesters. Models before 1886 sort of pre-date my interest zone (although I don't know why). I've had a couple of 1892s, and have little experience with the 1895. I have plenty of history with the Winchester 1894, now around 8 million produced. Dad had one—who doesn't have a Dad, grandfather, or uncle who didn't have a 94? I still have Dad's .30-30, and others. One is a freaky-accurate short-barreled Trapper .30-30, another is a 1906 saddle-ring carbine in .25-35. In addition, I have a Mossberg 464 in .30-30, a rifle that cribs on the John Browning design, but with some major improvements. I've hunted with all of them and probably will again.

But to narrow it down, the lever-action I have the longest and most consistent experience with is the Winchester Model 71. I love them all, but the 71 is my favorite. Announced in 1935, the M71 was the last iteration of the Winchester Model 1886. Mechanical changes were few: coil vice leaf springs, which reduced hammer cocking tension and improved the trigger. The 1886 was Winchester's "big action." John Marlin's 1881 lever-action was the first repeater that could house the .45-70 Government cartridge, but the John Browning-designed Winchester 1886 went several steps further. Introduced in .40-82, .45-70, and .45-90, it would later be chambered to the massive .50-110 and, with nickel-steel barrels, was strong enough to make the transition to smokeless powder.

In 1903, the smokeless .33 Winchester cartridge was added to the blackpowder chamberings. Ultimately, it would be the most popular of the 160,000 1886s manufactured. As is the case with the .270 Winchester's .277-inch bullet and John Rigby's .416, no one knows exactly why Winchester's engineers settled on a unique .348-inch bullet for the final cartridge for the Model 1886 action. The several blackpowder cartridges had long since been dropped, but obviously they wanted a new cartridge that was more powerful and would replace not only the .33 Winchester, but also the .35 Winchester that was still chambered in the Model 1895. The .348 Winchester is based on the massive .50-110 case necked down, thus pretty much maxing out the big action.

The 1886/71 has a tubular magazine, so until Hornady developed the FTX bullet, aerodynamics weren't part of the equation. Even so, the .348 Winchester was the fastest cartridge ever housed in a

Although my tastes run to classic lever-actions, I'm all in favor of new technology. Hornady introduced its LeveRevolution bullet technology, first in 2008 with the .308 and then in 2009 with the .338 Marlin Express. Here, Tom Arthur and I pose with the nice Colorado bull that I took in 2009 with a Marlin XTR in .338 Marlin Express, my choice for the most versatile lever-action cartridge ever. It's a shame this lever-action didn't take off better than it did.

tubular-magazine lever-action. When the .348 was brand-new, Elmer Keith immediately lamented the lack of a 250-grain load. Apparently, the first load available was a 200-grain bullet at 2,530 fps. Keith got his wish; a 250-grain load at 2,350 fps came along soon, and there was also a 150-grain load at a zippy 2,890 fps. The 150-grain bullet, though fast, was too light for caliber and didn't last long. The 250-grain bullet, with good sectional density, was the powerhouse, adequate for anything/everything in North America, but deer hunters didn't need it, and only 200-grain bullets have survived in factory loads.

The problem with the .348 was (and is) that it's a one-horse race. Other than a small run in the 1885 High-Wall single-shot, the .348 has never been chambered to any other factory rifle. The original M71 endured until 1958 with some 47,000 produced, but was never chambered to any other cartridge. Add the oddball .348-inch diameter, and bullet selection is limited. When I started reloading for the .348, there were still a few light bullets and some 250-grain bullets available, but today it's pretty much a 200-grain game, except among smaller, specialty bullet makers. Recently, I wanted to load up some .348 ammo to hunt California hogs, where unleaded bullets are mandated. Kyler Hamman, one of our local outfitters, suggested Hammer Bullets in Montana, who make a 162-grain flat-point hollowpoint in .348-inch. Problem solved, but you won't find these bullets unless you look hard.

Although I'd read about it and knew what it was, I don't recall that I was looking for a Model 71 when I got my first one. It was the mid-1970s, and I was in Kansas City, home on leave from the Marines. My trap-shooting buddy Dave Bledsoe called and said a friend had a Model 71 Deluxe. He brought it over and I bought it; I can't remember the price but, since I was a lieutenant, it couldn't

One of my few "good guns" is this Savage 1899 ".250-3000 rifle" from my friend Joe Bishop's collection. With the pre-1920 1:14 twist, it's very limited in the modern bullets it can stabilize, but it's a gorgeous old rifle with a factory pop-up aperture on the tang. I used a 100-grain Hornady Interlock bullet to drop this big New Mexico feral hog in its tracks at forty yards.

After a major production break and before its acquisition by Ruger, Marlin was producing some of the finest lever-actions in its long history. This Marlin 1892 in .44 Remington Magnum is one of the smoothest and most accurate tubular-magazine, lever-action rifles I have experience with. I used it to take this Nebraska 10-point whitetail in 2019.

have been much! Although there were options, variations in these rifles were limited: The rifles had 24-inch barrels, the carbines had 20-inch barrels, and all had a short magazine. The deluxe models had factory aperture sights and checkered fore-end and pistol grip; the standard came with buckhorn rear sight and uncheckered wood.

Some years passed before I actually hunted with that rifle, but I had it for a long time. I like aperture sights, and until fairly recently I could shoot them pretty well. I recall one hog I shot with it at nearly 250 yards, but even before my eyes started to go, that was pushing it!

Before 1940, when the M71 and its .348 cartridge were new, Jack O'Connor used it to take one of his desert rams in Sonora. Unfortunately, there are no details and no photos are known to exist, just one offhand comment in one of his books. Maybe the hunt and shot went well, maybe not so well, but my assumption is that he knew the .348 wasn't an ideal choice for a desert bighorn hunt, and wrote almost nothing about it.

I've never hunted any sheep with the M71 or any other lever-action, but I've shot wild hogs and some black bears. The .348 is a wonderfully hard-hitting cartridge, and the M71s I've owned have been smooth and accurate, but it is a heavy rifle. I never hunted any of the big bears with a .348, but I had (and still have) a yen to hunt elk with one.

In my early sixties I developed an astigmatism that was causing me to distinctly see *two* front sights with all iron sights. Always blessed with exceptional vision, I got frustrated and mad at myself. I cleaned house and sold several iron-sighted rifles, including my .348. I should have gone to the eye doctor first! An ophthalmologist who was a pistol shooter fixed me up with a prescription that mostly fixed the problem. I'll never again shoot iron sights like I did in my twenties and thirties, but it's good enough.

I started shopping, and after losing several Gunbroker bids, I bought another M71 in .348. This one was *cool*, the deluxe model,

In lever-actions, my preferences (and favorites) run to larger calibers, but that's not meant to denigrate the rest. I have a .25-35 and multiple .30-30 lever guns. On a fine day in South Texas in 1991, I took this excellent whitetail with well-remembered friends. I'm flanked on my right by Gary Sitton and on my left by John Wootters.

I took this nilgai along the Texas Gulf Coast with a Winchester M71 Deluxe in .348 Winchester. This rifle has a factory receiver-mounted Lyman aperture sight. I owned this rifle from the 1980s but sold it in a hissy fit over my inability to resolve the sights. Once glasses corrected my vision, I started shopping for another M71, as I felt it to be an essential part of my battery.

made in the first year of production. It has a long tang with the original aperture sight mounted on the bolt, not on the receiver. The rifle shot really well; I shot some hogs with it and took it on a black bear hunt in Idaho, and I intended to keep it. Then, a reader contacted me. He had an M71 with Pachmayr tip-off scope mount. I tried to resist, but it was too interesting. On the one hand, the guy wanted too much for the rifle, but he agreed to include seventeen boxes of original ammo, a mix of 200 and 250 grain. The ammo made it a bargain, and I can resist almost anything except temptation!

With a vintage Weaver three-quarter-inch 2.5X scope on the unique tip-off mount, the rifle shoots extremely well, certainly better than I can shoot with an aperture, even with my new glasses. Well, I'm not a collector, and I didn't need two. My son-in-law, Brad Jannenga, also likes lever-actions, so he took my awesome first-year-production rifle and I'm keeping the one with the scope. Regrettably, my new rifle is a standard model, but that ancient scope is surprisingly clear, and the adjustments track perfectly. I'm OK with the deal, and we have plenty of ammo.

With some difficulty, I worked up loads for the new scoped M71 with the 162-grain Hammer unleaded bullets, quickly discovering there is no *current* data for light bullets for the .348. I found some old recipes and cut back a bit and went to the range. The primers were only slightly flattened, but velocity was almost 3,000 fps. That scared me, so I cut back a bit more. The Hammer bullets grouped well. Time for pigs!

I took it out to my friend Tony Lombardo's ranch north of town. We caught one of those days when nothing was moving and we couldn't even buy a pig. Late in the afternoon we finally found a sounder and a big hog went streaking off to the right. I swung the rifle ahead of it and got the shot off.

The big, strong, sturdy, and smooth Winchester Model 1886 action is easily my favorite. Bottom, a first-year production (1936–1937) Winchester Model 71 Deluxe, with bolt-mounted aperture sight. The M71 was Winchester's final iteration of the 1886, but it hasn't died. Top, a Browning reissue 1886, this one rebuilt by Doug Turnbull in his powerful .475 Turnbull cartridge.

Although the .35 caliber has never been popular in the United States, Winchester has a rich history of .35-caliber cartridges, and I like the .35. Winchester .35-caliber cartridges to date have included: .35, .348, .358, .356 Winchester, and the new .350 Legend. All except the Legend were designed for lever-action rifles.

In a tip of the hat to "maturing" eyes, my current M71 .348—a Standard (not Deluxe) version and also a "long tang," first-year-of-production model—is adapted with a Pachmayr swing-off side mount. The vintage scope tracks well, and it beats the heck out of iron sights.

Incredulous that I'd hit the pig and dropped it, Tony said something unprintable. I should have blown smoke from the barrel and said, "Of course." But it wasn't a shot I could have made with iron sights. Nor, until the hog went down, was I certain I'd hit it. I kept my mouth shut and figured I'd probably made the right choice in which M71 to keep!

Since the 1980s, working with longtime partner Miroku in Japan, both Browning and Winchester have marketed limited runs of both Winchester Model 71s and 86s, the former in .348, the latter in .45-70. The reproductions are faithful, so Winchester's "big action" has gotten quite a new lease on life, with expanded opportunity. The .348 is powerful, and the .45-70 with modern loads (and bullets) in modern actions, can do amazing things, but neither approaches the full limit of the action.

Back in the 1950s, Harold Johnson of Coopers Landing, Alaska, wildcatted the ".450 Alaskan," necking up the .348 case to take a .458-

Among several, this is the best Winchester M71 I have ever owned. It is from the first year of the Deluxe production, it has a bolt-mounted aperture, and it shoots very well. I used it to take several wild hogs in Texas, but I gave it to my son-in-law who wanted it more than I did.

I took this great Mozambique swamp buffalo with PH Willem van Dyk Jr. using the Turnbull reproduction Winchester M1886 in .475 Turnbull. Although the traditional iron sights made the shot more difficult, the power was impressive and there was no problem.

inch bullet. The conversion was fairly common. In the late 1980s, the Pony Express gun shop that I traded at in the San Fernando Valley got in a Model 71 converted to Parker Ackley's .450 Alaskan Ackley Improved. Unable to resist, I bought it. Problem was, with the original stock with its thin, sharp butt, and a barrel that was all hole and little steel, the thing was a beast. One of my big mistakes is that I don't have any photos of the rifle, which speaks to the short time I kept it. Recoil was so severe that it was impossible to keep the lever closed during firing. I loaded 400-grain bullets to well over 2,000 fps with ease; with those loads, power was much the same as the .450/.400. That rifle got passed along quickly.

So the action obviously has potential beyond the .348 or the .45-70. Remembering my painful experience with the .450 Alaskan, I was skeptical when Doug Turnbull started working up his .475 Turnbull, necking up the .50-110 case to take a .475-inch bullet. Although not exactly factory, Turnbull jumped through the hoops to make his .475 Turnbull a SAAMI-standard cartridge. With a recoil pad and heavier octagon barrel, mine, on a new Browning 1886 action, isn't that bad to shoot. It pushes a 400-grain bullet at about 2,100 fps, so it is also much the same as the .450/.400, with less sectional density but more frontal area. I've only shot one Cape buffalo with it, but it sure was fun! The 1886 in .475 Turnbull is another rifle I need to spend more time afield with, but now that I have a scoped M71 .348, other rifles need to wait their turns.

One Last English Double

Chapter 19

The double-barrel or "two-pipe" is the most specialized of all sporting rifles. It is limited in accuracy and range because, regardless of chambering, it is impossible to bring the barrels perfectly together so that bullets from each barrel travel exactly parallel to each other. At some point the bullet paths will cross, and then drift ever farther apart. Or they start out more or less parallel, but eventually must drift apart. Effective range of any double depends on the cartridge, the sighting equipment, and the skill of the regulator.

The majority of magazine rifles are readily adaptable to a wide variety of sights, from iron to aperture to red-dot (reflex) to magnifying scopes. Some doubles can easily be topped with range-enhancing optical sights, but absent extensive gunsmithing, many cannot. In the case of older doubles, such modifications may enhance the rifle's versatility and utility, but may also reduce value. With his eyesight deteriorating (something we all must face sooner or later), my friend Joe Greenfield put a red-dot sight on his Holland & Holland Royal, allowing him to use it on a couple more safaris. The very thought of making such a modification to a rifle like that makes me cringe. (Or, as Jack O'Connor might have said, "gives me the vapors.")

Of course, nobody really *needs* a double rifle. Magazine rifles are more accurate, stronger, and chambered to a wider range of cartridges. Top-end production bolt-actions and full-up custom bolt-guns and single shots are more expensive than some double rifles

Tracking buffalo from one palm island to another in Botswana's Okavango. The rifle is a boxlock .470 by C. W. Andrews, plain but well-made. Of course, I wish I'd kept it! It saw a lot of use in the 1980s and 1990s; it would be another quarter-century before I owned another English double.

built today. However, when you compare apples to apples, doubles are the most expensive sporting rifles.

Precise modern manufacturing reduces, but cannot eliminate, hand work and fitting. And, since no two rifle barrels are *exactly* alike, regulating the two barrels to shoot (more or less) together remains a trial-and-error process, not much different than it was in 1900. Smaller shops (and some large firms) have *thought* they could bring double rifles to market at significantly lower prices, but few succeeded. During the period when Rigby was in our little town of Paso Robles, I spent a lot of time on the range watching the regulation process, occasionally doing some of the shooting. With the big Nitro Express cartridges, it wasn't unusual to go through a thousand bucks worth of ammo!

Butch Searcy, out in California's Mojave Desert, figured out how to make (relatively) affordable doubles. Searcy probably made as many doubles as anybody. Most Searcy rifles are plain, but very serviceable. His slogan was "the dream of a double." He fulfilled that dream for a lot of people, and many of his rifles are still in use. Some Continental doubles made today are also very reasonable, and the ones I've used are good guns, dependable and well-regulated. In 2017 I bought a basic boxlock Sabatti in 9.3x74R. Prices have gone up (they always do!), but at the time, the retail price was about $2,500. Many not-so-fancy bolt-actions are in that price range.

Although not ornate, the Sabatti is a nicely made, good-handling rifle. I managed to get a left-hand buttstock for it, and fitting it was one of the last jobs Norm Bridge did for me. Using the Italian Contessa mount, I mounted a Leupold VXR 1–4X scope. With Hornady's 250-grain GMX load, it prints two shots from each barrel as tight as 1.5 inches at 100 yards. It's a legitimate 200-yard gun. You can't ask for more from any double.

Bill Jones and I are on the range with Ernest Hemingway's .577 Westley Richards. In Jones's collection are several rifles owned by famous hunters, including famous East African PH John A. Hunter's last .500.

Krieghoff's .500/.416 was fairly new when I used one in northern Australia in 1999. This rifle was the first scoped double I had ever used, and I took this banteng at 125 yards. The regulation was perfect, and the .500/.416 is a wonderfully versatile double-rifle cartridge. The only catch: With higher velocity, it produces about the same energy as the ".450-plus" Nitro Express cartridges, so recoil is also about the same.

The double may be the most expensive of all rifles, but it's also the fastest and most foolproof for a second shot that may save lives. Nobody has to have a two-pipe, but the folks who need one the most are those who can afford them the least: young professional hunters, who tend to be brash and are still acquiring the experience that will, over time, temper their aggression with caution.

Thirty or forty years ago, doubles were rare in Africa, but today many older PHs carry them. An increasing number of younger PHs have also ponied up and acquired doubles, or will as soon as they can afford one. That said, the double isn't for everyone. My old friend and longtime Tanzanian PH, Michel Mantheakis, tried a double but just couldn't get used to it; he carries a big .450 Dakota. Jumbo Moore, who hunts in several countries, also tried doubles, but settled on a bolt-action .500 Jeffery. Harry Selby started out with a double, but when a lorry backed over it, he ran down to Kenya Bunduki and bought a .416 Rigby that he used for the rest of his career.

I am *not* an exclusive double rifle guy, but I'm also not a PH! As I've said before, as a visiting hunter or "client," year in and year out, I will take more and bigger buffalo with a scoped magazine rifle than with a double. So, for sure, I don't *need* a double rifle, but I've been fascinated by them since I was a teenager.

This is a result of reading and dreaming. Although he hated its heavy triggers, Hemingway had a double .470 on the *Green Hills of Africa* safari. Ruark had a Westley Richards .470 on his *Horn of the Hunter* safari. It didn't sound like much fun when it started doubling and knocked him tail over teakettle, but he loved his .470 and used it frequently, not only in Africa, but also for tigers in India and brown bears in Alaska. J. A. Hunter's books were in our junior high library, and I devoured his adventures with his double .500. I *wanted* a big-bore double rifle!

I don't know where Hemingway's or Ruark's .470s wound up, although I hope *somebody* has them and knows who they belonged

I took this fine Caprivi buffalo with my Krieghoff in .500 3-inch Nitro Express. After the .470, the .500 3-inch is probably the second-most-popular chambering in new doubles. With heavier bullet and greater frontal area, I believe the .500 gives a bit more performance than the .450-to-.475 group, but without noticeable increase in recoil.

With a scope, my Sabatti 9.3x74R prints both barrels withi two inches at 100 yards, making it a viable 200-yard doub rifle. One cannot ask for more!

to. Collector Bill Jones has Hemingway's .577. I was with him in Botswana when he bought it on auction via satellite phone (never mind the price). I could have had J. A. Hunter's last .500. David Ommanney, who guided my uncle's 1956 safari and mentored Michel Mantheakis, had it at a convention in the 1980s, with provenance. George Hoffman and I looked at it together. Asking price was $10,000; even then, .500s commanded higher prices than .450 to .475 doubles. Hunter's rifle was worn but sound, the price only slightly premium for a famous hunter's documented rifle.

Bill Jones looked at it, too. Why he didn't buy it, I can't say. I didn't because I didn't have ten large! I probably could have scraped it up, but I had a baby daughter and I was being responsible. I've kicked myself ever since!

Postscript: At the 2019 SCI convention, Bill Jones dropped by my booth. That Hunter .500 had come back on the market, and this time Bill did buy it. He has an amazing collection that includes several documented rifles: A Selous 6.5x53R, Jim Corbett's .450/.400, Hemingway's .577, Fletcher Jamieson's .500 Jeffery, a couple of Elmer Keith rifles . . . and now J. A. Hunter's last .500. I have no idea what he paid for it; when I asked, he commented, "Well, more than we could have bought it for when we should have!"

Speaking of Elmer Keith, it was old Elmer who had much to do with keeping double rifles alive in those dark days when ammo was unavailable. In the mid-1950s and on into the early 1960s, as Britain's colonial empire truncated, Kynoch began discontinuing big Nitro Express cartridges, the less common ones first, but soon there were none. All over Africa and India, hunters had to give up on their doubles for lack of ammo. Many made their way to the States where they could be picked up for a song. Elmer had several doubles, using them in Africa with Truman Fowler and, later, Bob Petersen and Tom Siatos. Feeding them was difficult and, absent ammo, the value of these guns was low. This was the second time in his long career that Elmer Keith was in a good spot. As a young man, he acquired several original Sharps rifles for the same reason: scarcity of ammo.

In Europe, doubles in 9.3x74R are popular for driven boar shooting. These are generally the least costly of all double rifles. They are not quite as powerful as the .375 H&H, but they are absolutely "buffalo-capable."

The ammo problem wasn't insurmountable: Fred Huntington made dies and Fred Barnes made bullets. Remaining Kynoch cases, bullets, and loaded ammo were carefully hoarded. Through the 1960s, Keith probably did the most writing on double rifles of anyone. Hunting in Africa was still unusual. Safari costs were laughable by today's standards, but the inexpensive plains game safari didn't exist; hunting in Africa took *time*, so it was more restricted to the wealthy. Those were the days for bargains in classic English double rifles. Jack O'Connor had a nice .450/.400, but I'm fairly sure he never hunted with it and so he added little to the lore and legend of the double. Keith added a bunch, including scarce loading data.

By the late 1970s, the .470 was emerging as the primary choice. I'm not convinced it was really the most popular, but a lot of British makers chambered to .470. I bought my first double in 1980, trading a really good trap gun and God knows what else for it at a gun shop in L.A. It was a Wilkes boxlock non-ejector .470. I shot a buffalo with it on the Bubye River in Zimbabwe in 1981, and then it was stolen. By then Jim Bell of Brass Extrusions Laboratories Ltd. (BELL) was making Boxer-primed cases. Bullets were mostly Barnes. Interest in double rifles was perking up.

I think Heym was first to step up to the plate with a new and affordable double. Absent a double of my own, I borrowed a Heym .470 for my rhino hunt in 1986, and used another in .500 for a 1989 elephant hunt in Mozambique. They were great guns, and in 2007 I bought their first modern .450/.400 3-inch double. Merkel and Krieghoff followed Heym in sating a growing hunger for large-caliber doubles. I have little experience with the Merkel, but friends and PHs love them. The Krieghoff is also a fine rifle, and the added safety of their cocking lever (similar in operation to the Blaser's) cannot be denied.

I borrowed one with a scope in their then-new .500/.416 for a buffalo/banteng hunt in Australia in 1999. I liked the rifle, and eventually bought one in .500 3-inch. It's actually the most left-handed double I've ever owned; others have left-handed stocks, but the Krieghoff has reversed triggers, with the forward trigger

Double rifles are fun, but visiting hunters do just fine, and in many cases better, with scoped bolt-actions. It's really African professional hunters who need *doubles. Diekie Muller was standing exactly as depicted in the photo when he stopped my wounded buffalo in full charge with his Krieghoff double .470.*

firing the left barrel and the rear trigger the right barrel. There is an advantage: When a lefty uses a two-trigger double in the right-barrel-first arrangement, the rear trigger is on the left and more exposed, and you are more likely to hit it by mistake during recoil.

On a double, it is better to fire the front trigger first. Less hand/finger movement is then required to reach the rear trigger, so the second shot is milliseconds faster. Some shooters have trouble staying away from the rear trigger during recoil, however. I call this a "physical double" as opposed to a "mechanical double" or malfunction. Whichever, it's painful when both barrels go off almost simultaneously. I've seen this a lot: If it's happening and you suspect you're hitting the second trigger, the best cure is to reverse the order, training yourself to fire the rear trigger first, then reaching your finger forward to the front trigger. This is slower and "improper" for double rifle use, but it beats getting the stuffing knocked out of you. The reverse (or left-handed) trigger arrangement on my Krieghoff makes it less likely to hit the second trigger during recoil. A good double-rifle mechanic can usually reverse the triggers, but since I don't have the problem, I leave them as is.

Now, a *true* lefty double would open by pushing the lever right-to-left instead of the standard left-to-right. Some British doubles have been made this way, but I wouldn't want one because it would confuse me, rendering my other double rifles (and shotguns) virtually useless.

I like our Heym (which is really Donna's), and I love the Krieghoff. I've also been really happy with the Sabatti 9.3x74R, so much that I bought another Sabatti in .450 3¼-inch, also a great rifle, especially for the money.

With apologies to my friends who make them, I've never thought that most of the Continental doubles fully capture the lines and "feel" of the classic British guns. In many ways, new guns are better, with modern metallurgy and machining, and new barrels. Several British firms are again in the double-rifle business, but prices for new British guns are out of my league.

I took my nice Tanzanian tusker with an American-made Rigby .450 that I had for several years. Given a choice, the .450 3¼-inch is my favorite double-rifle cartridge between .450 and .475; it uses common .458-inch bullets, and the straight case allows a slightly trimmer action. However, with older guns, condition and fit are far more important than cartridge.

Almost all older British double rifles were made before World War II. So, in the 1980s, a serviceable British double was forty-some years old. At this writing it's 2021; the "newest" vintage English doubles are eighty years old. Some older doubles have been used up and relegated to wall-hanging status, so they're scarcer today. Prices come and go. I mentioned that Thomas Turner .450/.400 3-inch I had back in the 1980s. At the same time, I had a wonderful .470 by C. W. Andrews, one of many small and nearly unknown makers. The Andrews rifle wasn't special; it was a plain boxlock extractor gun. But the barrels were sound. That's critical, because rebarreling, although possible, is expensive. Equally important, it fit me perfectly and shot like a dream. I hunted with it a lot and didn't want to sell it, but Brittany's mom and I were divorcing, and community property is what it is! I sold both the Turner .450/.400 and the Andrews .470 about the same time. Prices were low when I bought them, and I lost nothing in the sales. The Turner was the better of the two rifles; I didn't mind losing it because I'd never hunted with it, but I really hated selling the Andrews.

That was twenty-five years ago. Ever since, I've promised myself I'd have one more English double. I've had several double rifles since: the European rifles I've mentioned, also an American Rigby in .450 3¼-inch, a nice rifle that shot well. But it wasn't an English gun, and neither are the European guns. Nothing wrong with any of them, but we all have our preferences.

I kept my eyes open for a long time. Ideally, I'd like most to have an original John Rigby .450 3¼-inch. I like the lines, and the straight-cased .450 is my favorite of the large-caliber Nitro Express group. However, you can't be picky with century-old rifles, especially at my pay grade. Consider the barrel condition first; overall condition second; third,

Often, it's the sighting equipment that limits the double rifle's range and versatility. Most new doubles can be readily adapted to optical sights, while many older doubles cannot without altering their value. I put an Aimpoint on my Sabatti .450 3¼-inch double and significantly extended its effective range.

My William Evans .470 was made for Col. Richard Bright of the Uganda Rifles regiment in 1906, shipped to him via Mombasa on 28 December 1906. As a young officer, Bright was on several mapping and exploratory expeditions into Abyssinia (Ethiopia) and Sudan. The Bright gazelle is named for him.

stock fit. Caliber matters not at all. Ammo can be bought (or loaded) for all the cartridges between the three .450s, the .465, the three .475s, and the .476 Westley Richards, and all are equal in performance on game. The .500 carries a premium and, because of ammo availability, so does the .470.

I walked away from several nice rifles, was often tempted, and managed to pass. Over time, prices soared to where I wasn't sure I could justify that dream of "one last English double." Even with rifles from little-known makers, prices were five times what I paid for the Andrews, more for "name" guns. Supplies were nil, double rifles were hot, and especially once Botswana reopened elephant hunting, I wasn't the only person who wanted an English double for a special safari.

Officially, I'd quit looking, although, when it comes to rifles, I'm *always* looking. In the mid-teens I spoke to the St. Louis Gateway SCI chapter, hosted by my friend Tom Jokerst, African hunter and avid Marlin collector. Tom had a *very* nice William Evans .470, in great shape, and completely redone by New England Custom Guns. I didn't really covet a .470, but a William Evans rifle is always worth a look. Evans guns are up there with the best, and all their guns were built to order. The rifle had a right-hand cheekpiece, which means nothing; stock fit and weight were right.

I asked Tom what he might want for it *if* he ever wanted to sell it. He named a figure out of my reach. Truth is, he wasn't ready to sell. I asked him, if and when he was really ready to pass it along, to please keep me in mind. Such things are frequently said, so I figured that was the last I'd hear of it.

Botswana elephant hunting closed for several years, and ivory importation from other countries became problematic. An interesting side effect of this was that prices for used doubles went down significantly. Tom Jokerst came to my booth at the 2020 SCI convention. He told me his vision was deteriorating badly and he probably wouldn't use his .470. Unsolicited, he said, "That rifle isn't

These are just seven of eleven Nitro Express cartridges between .450 and .500. Although some are more difficult to feed than others, fresh ammunition can he had—or made—for all of them. Performance is similar enough that chambering is a minor concern when shopping for vintage doubles. Left to right: .450 3¼-inch; .500/.450; .500/.465; .470; .476 Westley Richards; .475 No. 2; .500 3-inch.

Handloading for double rifles isn't a big mystery. Often, it's a matter of matching the regulation velocity (which isn't always known). Doubles aren't strong, so it's critical to watch pressure. Colonel Bright's .470 responded quickly to 500-grain Hornady GMX loaded to 2,150 fps.

worth what it was a few years ago." Instead of "X," how about "Y?" I looked at Donna, got an eye roll and a shrug, and picked up the rifle in March.

Aside from being beautiful, it's an interesting rifle. My friend Tom is a bit more OCD than I am, so it came with a briefcase full of paperwork. The rifle was commissioned in early 1906 by Col. Richard Bright of the Uganda Rifles regiment. As a young officer, he did several mapping and exploratory expeditions in Abyssinia (Ethiopia) and Sudan. Two of his diaries accompanied the rifle, and it turns out the Bright gazelle of southern Sudan is named after him. He retired to England in 1910, was recalled for World War I, and apparently died around 1920.

The rifle was shipped to him in Uganda via Mombasa, departing William Evans on December 28, 1906. That's the story, except there's a mystery: The rifle was ordered as a .450, but the barrels are original, and the bores and proof marks are .470.

No notation in the William Evans order book explains the switch, but the timing probably does. In 1906 the .450s were dominant, but due to separate uprisings in India and Sudan, and to keep .577/.450 Martini Henry ammo away from insurgents, all .450s were banned in both colonies. The British gun trade scrambled, and in a matter of months there were alternatives: Holland and Holland's .500/.465, .470, three .475s, and the .476 Westley Richards. Joseph Lang apparently developed the .470, and it was probably the first of these similar cartridges.

According to my old friend Paul Roberts, former proprietor of Rigby in London, proofed .470 barrels first became available in October 1906. Joseph Lang owned an interest in William Evans.

Once owned by my friend Joe Bishop, this Holland and Holland double in .303 was regulated with hard-to-find 215-grain bullets. After much trial and error, shots came together with IMR 4350 propellant and 174-grain, .312-inch Hornady Interlock bullets at 2,200 fps. Once the barrels were shooting together, the pop-up tang receiver sight was lowered to bring the strikes into zero.

A beautiful Nile buffalo, taken in Uganda's Karamoja District with the William Evans .470, using handloaded 500-grain Hornady DGX bullets. This rifle was in Uganda with Colonel Bright from early 1907 until he retired to England. As far as is known, this was the first time the rifle has been back to Africa since 1910.

Per Paul, William Evans, Lang, and Rigby immediately adopted the .470, and that included changing orders in progress. Paul didn't find it surprising that no notation was made in the order book, but it's still a mystery that can't be completely solved. Meantime, it's a lovely rifle that handles well, shoots well with Federal ammo, even better with Hornady, and has easily responded to handloads.

We know the rifle went home to England in 1910, and at some point, emigrated to the States. Jokerst got it in South Carolina in the 1990s. Although he did several safaris while he owned it, for various reasons he didn't take it with him. I like to believe it never saw Africa after 1910. My mission was obvious: I needed to take at least one buffalo with it.

South African PH Mike Birch and I had a 2020 plan to hunt Timbavati, an awesome property adjoining Kruger, with spectacular buffalo genetics. It could have been an opportunity to take the biggest buffalo of my life, and of course I was going to take Colonel

Bright's rifle. The pandemic intervened and, like a lot of other plans, that one went out the window.

In early 2021, Uganda outfitter Christian Weth contacted me. Thanks to COVID, he had unallocated buffalo on quota, and I could take advantage of this if I got there quickly. There's little record of Bright's later life, but he served as a staff officer in England during World War I, and never returned to Africa. It's not known if he took his rifle to Karamoja, or to Sudan or Congo, but we know his rifle was with him in Uganda from early 1907 until 1910. Perfect. I could take the rifle on a visit to its first home!

Christian was busy with other clients, so Donna and I hunted with his partner, Jumbo Moore. I've known him for years, but never hunted with him. Turns out he's a consummate professional hunter, one of the best I've been with, and *fun*. Uganda is gorgeous, and Karamoja is amazing, plains of acacia forest surrounded by rugged mountains, Sudan just to the north and Kenya just to the east.

Jumbo Moore and I are in Uganda's Karamoja in March 2021. Although many modern PHs prefer doubles, Moore prefers bolt-actions. His personal backup rifle is a .500 Jeffery, giving him firepower and foot-pounds over the fast second shot.

Although no longer common, doubles in lighter cartridges are relatively inexpensive because everybody wants a big bore. I consider my .303 double as "the ultimate pig gun." With original 215-grain loads, it was pressed into service on this Texas hog.

Weth's area is just south of Kidepo National Park, with perhaps 10,000 buffalo. In March the grass is short and there's more water in the hunting area than in the park, so it's full of buffalo. I've never seen such a density of bachelor bulls.

Using her Blaser with .375 H&H barrel, Donna shot a fine bull the first morning. Though almost certainly a mix of local, Kenya, and Sudan genetics, Karamoja buffalo are classed as Nile, but they grow good horns. Donna's bull was big enough that I didn't expect to find a bigger one, but it didn't matter; there were plenty of buffalo to look at. We stalked several, big enough but not old enough, and a couple gave us the slip, but I knew this probably wouldn't take too long.

It didn't. Still early in the hunt, right out of camp at dawn, we drove past a lovely old bull coming from water and headed toward the park boundary. Jumbo drove on past, we unlimbered quickly, and stalked back. Karamoja buffalo aren't stupid, but there must be almost no poaching in that area; they are the most stalkable buffalo I've ever hunted, making it a great place to hunt with open sights.

We set up at seventy yards, and then the bull turned away, put his head down, and started to feed. Jumbo picked up the sticks and we advanced to about forty yards. I had a slight quartering-to shot, the on-shoulder black and huge. Honest, I never even looked at the horns; Jumbo said he was wide and heavy, and he was old and nearly hairless.

The first shot hit hard, but he ran to the right and I hit him with the left barrel. He almost went down, but gathered for another lunge. Now I was running forward, breaking the rifle while the bull scrambled up a little bank. I managed to get one shell in the right barrel and spined him just as he went over the bank. And that was that! Colonel Bright's rifle had come home.

As I wrote in another book a long time ago, when I arrived in his camp in Botswana thirty-five years ago, I had my Andrews double and old Ian MacFarlane greeted me, carrying his .475 No. 2 double, huge cartridges bristling from his belt. I looked at his double and he looked at mine, and he said, "It just makes you feel good to hunt with rifles like these." Oh, yes, it really does!

My old friend Joe Bishop left us at the start of 2019. Joe had an amazing gun collection, including some spectacular doubles: A Woodward .22 Hornet and a half-dozen Holland & Hollands from .240 Flanged Magnum to 8-bore. Two were Royals in .375 Flanged Magnum, including a marvelous "maharaja" rifle, cased and documented. I made Sara Bishop a fair offer for a Holland & Holland in .303 British. Although a Royal in excellent shape, it's an extractor gun and the caliber is undesirable, except to me. The rifle has a tang-mounted pop-up aperture sight, and it shoots well with the original heavy 215-grain bullet. After some trial and error, I found a handload with current 174-grain .312-inch Hornady bullets that regulates extremely well. I'll probably take it to Africa, and I've already done some pig hunting with it. It's a joy to shoot.

So far, I haven't been able to source who it was made for, but it's an 1895 rifle, very early since the .303 didn't go smokeless until

Maj. Richard Bright, on right, and his companion, Maj. H. Austin, in Sobat, Sudan, in 1899 during a hunting expedition. This photo was made "after shooting our Xmas dinner." Bright, who spent most of his active service in Africa, ordered his William Evans double in 1906 when he held the rank of colonel.

1892. I've often thought a double in a light caliber would be fun, but they're uncommon today because of a dearth of proper rimmed cartridges. So, although I always wanted *one* last English double, I suddenly have two. Donna tapped her foot a bit when I bought Joe's .303, especially in a crazy pandemic year. I don't blame her, but I have several rifles that belonged to lost friends and I wanted a good rifle that belonged to Joe. They say bad news comes in threes, so I hope I don't soon encounter a third English double I can't resist. Donna would have me committed, and she'd be right!